Economic and Social Transformation in Rural Kenya

Publications from the Centre for Development Research, Copenhagen

Economic and Social Transformation in Rural Kenya

John Carlsen

Published by
Scandinavian Institute of African Studies, Uppsala 1980

Publications from the Centre for Development Research, Copenhagen

No. 1. Bukh, Jette, *The Village Woman in Ghana.* 118 pp. Uppsala: Scandinavian Institute of African Studies 1979.

No. 2. Boesen, Jannik & Mohele, A.T., *The "Success Story" of Peasant Tobacco Production in Tanzania.* 169 pp. Uppsala: Scandinavian Institute of African Studies 1979.

No. 3. Kongstad, Per & Mönsted, Mette, *Family, Labour and Trade in Western Kenya.* 186 pp. Uppsala: Scandinavian Institute of African Studies 1980.

No. 4. Carlsen, John, Economic and Social Transformation in Rural Kenya. 230 pp. Uppsala: Scandinavian Institute of African Studies 1980.

This series contains books written by researchers at the Centre for Development Research, Copenhagen. It is published by the Scandinavian Institute of African Studies, Uppsala, in co-operation with the Centre for Development Research with support from the Danish International Development Agency (Danida).

Cover photograph: Jesper Kirknæs

ISBN 91-7106-170-3
ISSN 0348-5676

Printed in Sweden by
Offsetcenter ab, Uppsala 1980

Contents

Preface

This book presents some of the results of a wider study on the relationship between Population Pressure on Access to Land, Agricultural Productivity and Rural Employment.

The research was carried out jointly by two research staffs at the Institute of Development Studies at the University of Nairobi and two research fellows attached to the Centre for Development Research in Copenhagen, Denmark.

The four researchers specialised according to the various aspects of the study in the following way: Agricultural Production (Tony Moody, agricultural economist), Rural Migration (Shem Migot Adholla, sociologist), Land Tenure (H.W.O. Okoth-Ogendo, land lawyer) and Rural Non-farming Activities and Rural Employment (John Carlsen, economist).

The subject of the study was proposed by the World Employment Programme of the ILO and should be understood as one of the outcomes of the ILO employment mission to Kenya in 1971. The report of the mission emphasized policies and programmes that could increase productive employment in the rural areas and pointed at the increasing population pressure on access to land as one of the major constraints. The mission report finally stressed that more research into these problems was needed.[1]

The study focussed on the historical development of rural employment possibilities within peasant agriculture and non-agricultural activities such as trade, craft and small scale industries.

Population pressure was analysed as one of several causal variables that influenced rural employment potentials. Therefore four districts, characterised by their differences in population density, their resource endowment and their degree of integration in the colonial economic system were selected for the study.

The following districts were selected: Kisumu and Kisii in Nyanza Province and Taita Hills and Kwale in Coast Province.

A combination of various research methods and techniques was employed. District agricultural reports and other secondary sources were used to analyse the historical development of the rural employment

[1] I.L.O., *Employment, incomes and equality – a strategy for increasing productive employment in Kenya,* Geneva, 1972.

situation in the four districts and in addition questionnaire surveys were used to analyse the present rural employment situation. For each of the four areas an approx. 10 per cent sample of rural households was selected and in addition a questionnaire survey covering all small-scale industries and randomly selected trade and service establishments was undertaken.

The conclusions of this research are given in research papers from the Center for Development Research, Copenhagen.[2]

In this book the data collected for the above mentioned study have been analysed within the context of broader development issues.

The related issues of increasing peasant production and thereby the standard of living of the rural population and increasing the accumulation of capital available for local productive investment in order to restructure underdeveloped economies and break colonial and neo-colonial dependency have been the focus of development theories in recent years.

Marxist scholars have discussed the persistence of pre-capitalist forms of production and social relations and their articulation with modern capitalism in an era of rapidly increasing internationalisation of capital characterised by increasing world wide control over productive resources by multinational corporations.

In some cases this discussion might have been carried too far into abstractions and seems rather futile. However, the discussion focusses upon the possibilities for and limitations to the development of the productive forces in the rural areas and is therefore most useful for an understanding of the conditions for economic and social transformation in the Third World.

Recent work by Kay[3], Warren[4], and directly related to the Kenyan situation, by Zwanenberg[5] and Swainson[6] challenge the widespread marxist view, developed in the 1960's and early 1970's, that the countries in the Third World cannot develop within the sphere of the international capitalist system. In the works of Frank[7] and Amin[8] and, more related to Kenya, the

[2] See Carlsen, J and Moody, T, "Population Pressure, and Rural Employment in Kenya", *CDR Project Papers,* A 76, 13. Copenhagen, December 1976, and Carlsen, John, "Population Pressure and Non-Farming Activities in Rural Areas in Kenya – A Historical Review and Analysis of Prevailing Development Trends", *CDR Project Papers,* D. 76, 2, Copenhagen 1976.

[3] Kay, G., *Development and Underdevelopment. A Marxist Analysis,* London 1975.

[4] Warren, B., "Imperialism and Capitalist Industrialization", in *New Left Review,* No 27, Sept.–Oct. 1973.

[5] Zwanenberg, R., "Neocolonialism and the origin of the National Bourgeoisie in Kenya between 1940 and 1973", in *Journal of Eastern African Research and Development,* vol. 4, No 2, 1974.

[6] Swainson, N., "The Rise of a National Bourgeoisie in Kenya", in *Review of African Political Economy,* No 8, January-April 1977.

[7] Frank, A.G., "Capitalism and Underdevelopment in Latin America", *Monthly Review Press,* New York, 1969.

[8] Amin, S., "Accumulation on a World Scale", *Monthly Review Press,* New York 1974.

works of Leys[9] and Godfrey and Langdon[10] it was argued that although economic growth might take place, it would not lead to structural changes of the economy and furthermore that a local independant class of capitalists that could promote the necessary process of locally based accumulation of capital was unlikely to emerge. Therefore, in the opinion of these works, growth within the frames of the international capitalist system will only lead to "perverted", "underdeveloped", or "blocked" development and more dependency.

The critique of what has been called the dependency school has made a number of its supporters reconsider their positions and to look more closely into the historical process of capital accumulation and class formation in Third World countries. The advantages of such a more detailed and more empirically oriented analysis is clearly demonstrated in the most recent works on Kenya, e.g., by Colin Leys[11].

Among non-marxist development economists and social scientists the 1970's have witnessed increasing concern that even very rapid economic growth rarely benefitted the big majorities of rural poor in the developing countries. More attention has consequently been given to questions like income distribution, policies to increase productive employment in the rural areas and fulfilment of the basic needs of the masses of the Third World. More equitable, "reformative" policies were seen as a necessity not only in order to obtain a more just society, but also as a means to more rapid economic development.

The work of this school of "concerned liberals" has greatly influenced the discussion of a New International World Order and the discussions of development strategies of bilateral as well as multilateral aid organizations like the World Bank and ILO[12].

Thus development economists of various observations seem to have one thing in common: an understanding of the significance of productive employment and accumulation of capital in the rural areas for the overall economic and social transformation of the Third World countries.

In this book we will use the data on rural production and rural employment collected for the above mentioned study together with the

[9] Leys, C., *Underdevelopment in Kenya,* London, Heinemann 1975.

[10] Godfred, M. and Langdon, S., "Partners in Underdevelopment? The Transnational Thesis in a Kenyan Context", in *Journal of Commonwealth and Comparative Politics,* Vol 14, No 17, March 1976.

[11] Leys, C., *Capital Accumulation, Class Formation and Dependency – the Significance of the Kenyan Case,* in *Socialist Register,* 1978, p. 261 and Leys, C., Development strategy in Kenya since 1971, *Canadian Journal of African Studies,* Vol 13, Nos. 1–2, 1979.

[12] See e.g.: Chenery et al., *Redistribution with Growth:* IBRD and Oxford U.P., Oxford 1974., and I.L.O., *op.cit.*

impressive mass of material published on various aspects of rural development in Kenya during the latest years in an effort to analyse this process of capital accumulation and the consequent economic and social transformation in Kenya.

During the work on this book a great number of people have assisted and inspired me and have contributed to my understanding of these issues.

I am in a particular debt of gratitude to my colleague, Tony Moody, at the then Institute for Development Research in Copenhagen and to our two research assistants, Fannuel Majango Odero and Joshua Ambogo. Their assistance and participation in our joint collection and interpretation of information has been invaluable to me.

Other colleagues at the Centre for Development Research in Copenhagen have made useful comments to the ideas expressed in this book in various seminars and as comments to earlier working papers.

While many people have contributed I am of course the only one responsible for the final outcome as presented in this book.

The Scandinavian Institute of African Studies, which has undertaken to publish this book, and the Development Research Council of Danida which has been financing the research work as well as the publication cost, cannot, of course be held responsible for its contents.

CHAPTER I

Introduction

In the generally depressive picture of development experiences among the developing countries in Africa south of Sahara, Kenya stands out as one of the more successful exceptions.

The annual economic growth in Kenya between 1960–1977 of 6.2 per cent[1] has certainly been quite impressive taking into account that the country has had no oil or other mineral resources which could be exploited for an "easy" export oriented growth.

The backbone of the Kenyan economy is agriculture and it has been agriculture and more specifically the expansion of smallholder production that has been the dynamic element in the Kenyan growth process since the mid-fifties. From 1954 to 1977 the value of smallholder marketed output increased from K£ 5.2 mill. to K£ 210.6 mill., an annual increase of 17.4 per cent. Consequently, the share of smallholdings in total marketed output increased from 18.0 per cent in 1954 to 50.7 per cent in 1977.

In this growth process the economic and social structures of the rural areas have been transformed radically.

Based upon research on smallholder production in Central Kenya it has been argued that this growth process has had an equalising effect in the rural areas and that as a result a non-accumulating class has emerged. These researchers argue that the rapid growth in agricultural production has not contributed to local capital accumulation, that the benefits have been reaped by international finance capital and that consequently the development of a Kenyan national bourgeoisie, on which a future capitalist development could be based, has been blocked[2].

But other studies show that the growth process has led to increased differentiation among the peasantry and that a fraction of the peasantry has developed into capitalist farmers who increasingly invest their accumulated capital in non-agricultural activities[3].

[1] World Bank, *World Development Report, 1979.* Washington, D.C., August 1979.

[2] See e.g. Cowen, M. and Kinyanjui, K., *Some Problems of Income Distribution in Kenya,* Institute for Development Studies, University of Nairobi, 1977. Mimeo.

[3] See e.g. Hunt, D., *An Examination of the Distribution of Economic Status and Opportunity in Mbere, Eastern Kenya,* Occasional Paper, No 11, 1975. Institute for Development Studies, University of Nairobi.

Map 1. *Administrative boundaries and location of sample areas.*

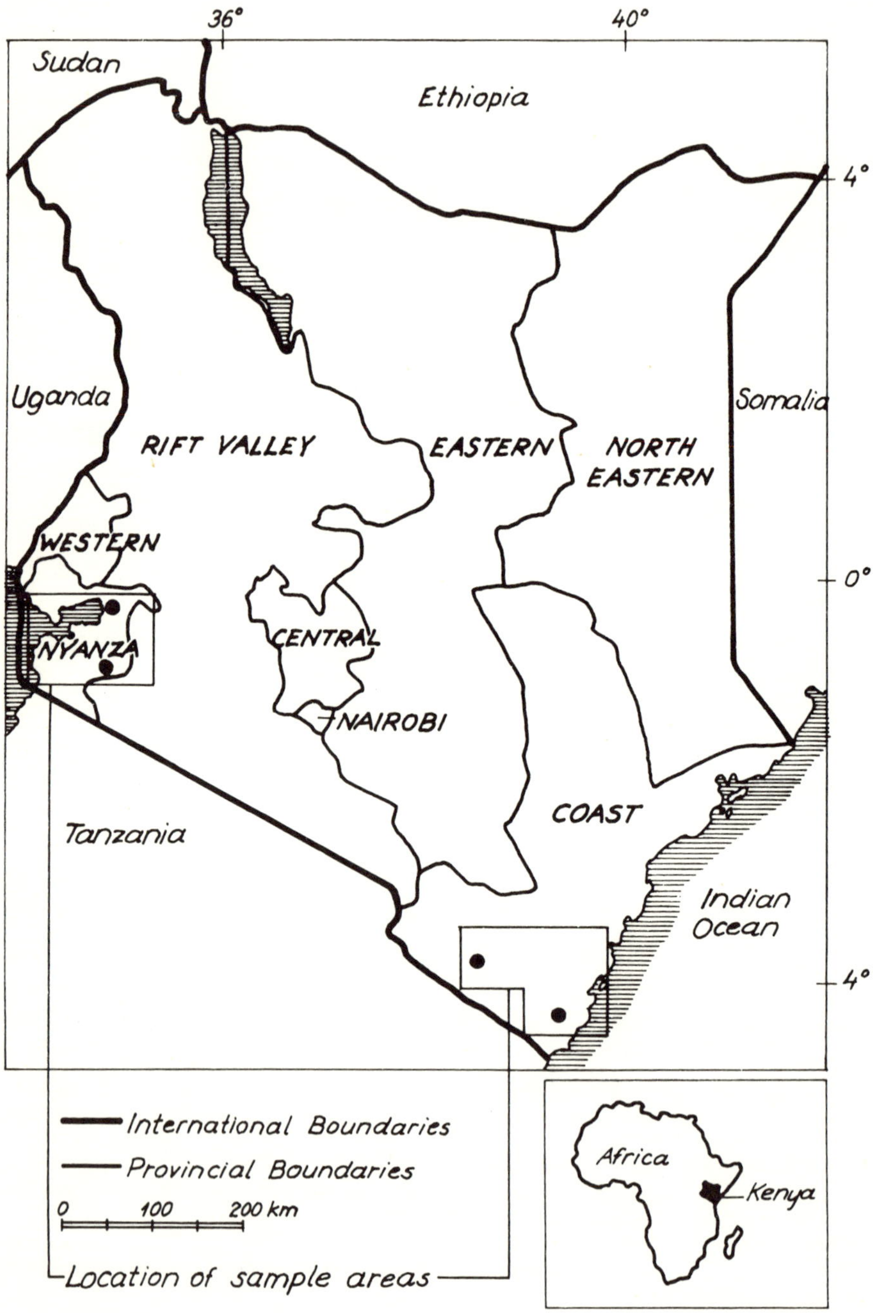

In this book the process of growth and accumulation in the rural areas of Kenya will be examined based upon field work in Kisumu, Kisii, Taita Hills and Kwale District.

These districts cannot be claimed to be representative of rural development in Kenya although they do represent big differences in ecological and demographical characteristics. The lack of comparable data from Central Province alone makes generalizations a hazardous task. The conclusions of this book should be taken with these reservations.

The dramatic increase in agricultural production in the recent past can best be understood by going back a little historically. In order to provide a framework for a better understanding of the present process of accumulation in Kenya a brief outline of Kenya's general economic history is therefore given below.[4]

Pre-colonial accumulation

The establishment of British rule in Kenya in 1895 and the subsequent policies for the economic development of the region dramatically interfered with and changed the indigenous economic, social and political systems.

But this does not mean that economic life in the region at the time was static and stagnant. On the contrary, the area had in the previous centuries witnessed rapid change due to population movements and the consequent changes in production systems and trading patterns. Many of the former pastoralist people had by the end of the last century settled as agriculturalists. A specialization in production had taken place within and between tribes and constituted a basis for local, regional and long distance trade. Land, which was not yet scarce, was communally owned and controlled by the elders of the clan but cultivated by family labour mostly in bush fallow rotation systems.[5]

According to recent research[6] a class of accumulators of the principle means of production – land and livestock – had developed before the colonial time, particularly in what is now Central Province – the most densely populated, productive and economically strategic area of Kenya – through migration to new land, cattle raiding and long-distance trade. The

[4] For a broader historical account of agricultural development see e.g. Brett, E.A., *Colonialism and Underdevelopment in East Africa, The Politics of Economic Change 1919–1939,* Heinemann, Nairobi 1973.

[5] See for example Ogot, B.A. and Kieran, J.A. (eds.), Zamani – *A Survey of East African History,* Nairobi 1968 and Gray, R. and Birmingham, D. (eds.), *Pre-colonial African Trade – Essays on Trade in Central and Eastern Africa before 1900.* Nairobi 1970.

[6] See for example the work of Cowen, M., *Differentiation in a Kenyan Location,* East African Universities Social Science Council, 8th Annual Conference, Nairobi 1972 and later works by the same author.

tendency of this accumulation was to concentrate the means of production more and more in a few hands, and to force the families excluded from this primitive accumulation to migrate.

Generally, this process of accumulation was not based upon the employment of foreign labour. Some of the tribes, however, used slave labour (prisoners of war) in agricultural production and they produced a surplus of food which was exchanged for "luxury consumer goods" imported mostly by Arabian caravan traders.

Also the development of economic specialization in the form of various non-farming activities differed among tribes. But up to the period of colonialization small-scale textile, iron and pot manufacturing could be found in large numbers of villages and homesteads throughout Eastern Africa.[7]

Some of the products produced in this way seem to have played a very important role in the structuring of trade, the accumulation of wealth and in the emerging social differentiation of society.

One example of such a product is the iron-hoe which made it possible to increase agricultural productivity. The production of iron tools seems to be known to many of the tribes that settled in Kenya[8], but in particular the skill of the Samia blacksmith from Western Kenya and of the Wakamba blacksmith had a widespread reputation.

The Samia blacksmith, who has been called the outstanding blacksmith of Kenya and Uganda[9], produced iron-hoes that were traded all over Western and Nyanza Province in Kenya and Eastern Uganda. There were by 1900 approximately 80 Samia blacksmiths, each employing a couple of assistants. If one takes into account the considerable backward linkages in mining and in charcoal burning plus the very important linkages to trade and farming it becomes quite clear that blacksmithing was a key sector of the regional economy by this time[10].

The Wakamba blacksmith had specialized in making ornamental iron chains and other decorations that, by even the coastal Swahili, was

[7] Zwanenberg, R.M.A., "Aspects of Kenya's Industrial History", in *Kenya Historical Review,* No. 1 Vol 1. 1973.

[8] There are early signs of iron working in Engaruka in the Rift Valley of northern Tanzania, See Sutton, J.E.G., "The Settlement of East Africa", in Ogot, B.A. and Kieran, J.A. (eds.) *op.cit.* pp. 89 and at the coast near Launi, Mahindi and Mombasa. See Chittick, N., The Coast before the Arrival of the Portuguese by Ogot, B.A. and Kieran *op.cit.* pp. 109.

[9] Shinnie, P.L. (ed.), *The African Iron Age,* Clarendon Press Oxford, 1971, pp. 140:183.

[10] For a detailed discussion of the importance of the Samia iron industry see Were, P.O., *The Origin and Growth of the Iron Industry and Trade in Samia (Kenya),* Dissertation, University of Nairobi, Dept. of History, Nairobi 1972.

considered superior to the iron that they got from India[11]. These iron products and in particular the production of arrow-poison, formed the basis for the establishment of Wakamba trade with the neighbouring tribes as well as their dominance over the long distance trade between the coast and the interior.

The historical evidence of the development of primitive accumulation and of the significance of non-farming activities in pre-colonial Kenya is scattered, although an increasing number of historical studies have been conducted in recent years. Thus the following brief description of farming and non-farming activities in the four study areas before colonial rule is far from complete.

Kisumu District and Kisii District

The Gusii people (who are now living in Kisii District) had first settled in Nyanza Province in the 16th century[12] but by 1800 they had been mostly pushed out of the Kano plains and Kavirondo Gulf shore by the successive immigrations of the Luo – who settled these areas at the end of their migration from the Sudan[13]. So just 100 years before the imposition of colonial power the Gusii had settled the highlands of Eastern Nyanza, whilst the Luo had largely occupied Siaya and Kisumu districts and the lake-shore of South Nyanza. The Gusii – apparently traditionally mixed agriculturalists/pastoralists – had thereby arrived at the border of Kipsigis land – the Kipsigis were then purely pastoralist and during the 19th century successive confrontations pushed the Gusii into the small land-area corresponding to the Kisii district of today. The Luo were still expanding their territory as late as 1900, and when the first Europeans observed Nyanza in 1890, the Kano plains were still the frontier zone of Luo settlement. Siaya, the Kavirondo Gulf and the lake-shore of South Nyanza were then the major areas of settlement.

Although the Luo are often described as a pastoral people, they had, by 1900, adopted a degree of settled agriculture in contrast to other pastoral tribes of East Africa. Each clan had communal rights to different land areas and land-use was divided between pastoral areas and cultivated areas. Cultivated land was mainly planted with millets (sorghum) and mixed with some maize. Supplementary food crops were leguminous: beans, sesame

[11] Lamphear, J. The Kamba and the Northern Mrima Coast, in Gray, R. and Birmingham, D. (eds.), *op.cit.* p. 85.

[12] Cohen, D.W., "The River-Lake Nilotes from the Fifteenth to the Nineteenth Century", in Ogot and Kiernan, *op.cit.*

[13] Mikamba et. al., "The Kisii-Kipsigis Wars of the late 19th Century", in *Kenya Historical Review,* Vol. 2, No. 2, 1974.

and cow-peas. Small amounts of surplus grains were traded locally for cattle and iron implements, but the agricultural economy was largely subsistence-based.

The Gusii in the highlands also practised a mixed pastoral/agricultural land-use. Their system differed in division of land-use. Whereas the Luo clans mixed land-use in the same area between grazing and cultivation: the Gusii grazing land, also communal, was at some distance from the settled areas where land-use was dominantly the cultivation of finger millet. The pastoral areas were exclusively pastoral, and for every family hamlet of homesteads found in the cultivated areas, there was a corresponding "cattle" village.

The most important non-farming activity of the Luo was fishing in Lake Victoria which now seems to be overfished but in those days seemed to be rich in fish. The inhabitants of the lakeside locations were fishing for subsistence and for barter. This trade developed out of the need for these people to supplement their low production of food-crops – due to nearly marginal conditions – with grain exchanged for fish[14]. The fish was sun-dried as a means of preservation and sold in local markets within an area of about seven to ten miles from the lake, but it was also one of the items traded with the Gusii tribe of Kisii District[15].

With regard to the construction of houses, and the making of bedding and garments, no specialization seems to have existed. "There was a time in the year when houses were mainly built, usually in July after the millet harvest. This was an opportunity for getting kinsfolk together to come and help build your house, because with granaries full it was possible for the owner of the homestead to brew beer and cook thick mush and gruel to reward the people who came to help him."[16] Bedding and garments were made out of cow and goat skins by most people themselves although the making of cloaks for elders and some repairs were undertaken by specialists among the Luyia tribe.

As for domestic utensils, pottery was made for cooking and for carrying water in some areas of the district and in other areas baskets for carrying fish and agricultural produce, nets and traps for catching fish and mats for drying fish and grain (as part of the beer brewing process) were made. There was some local trade in these items but more significant was the trade in livestock. In all the Nyanza tribes, whether pastoral or agricultural, the symbol of wealth was the possession of cattle and other livestock. Livestock therefore played an important role in local trade as well as in trade with the

[14] Fearn, H., *An African Economy – A Study of the Economic Development of Nyanza Province of Kenya, 1903–1953.* London, 1961, p. 31.

[15] Maxon, R. *British Rule in Gusiiland 1907–1963,* unpublished thesis, Syracuse, 1972.

[16] Fearn, H., *op.cit.,* p. 30.

other tribes. By selling livestock the Luo obtained agricultural implements from the Samia blacksmiths[17] and by selling pottery, fish, salt and cattle the Luo obtained grain from the more fertile Gusii inhabited highlands in the south.

Specialization and non-farming activities seem to have been much less developed among the Gusii in Kisii. This is probably due to much higher and stable rainfall in the Kisii highlands south of the Kano plains.

As with the Luo, no specialization had taken place in construction of housing and in production of garments and bedding.

Agricultural implements were produced by Gusii blacksmiths[18]. Most utensils for cooking and carrying water were homemade but some were exchanged for grain with the Luo.

Surplus agricultural products formed the most important basis for exchange in pre-colonial Gusii society. Grain, cattle and beer were used as exchange. Locally beer was exchanged for work, and beer, grain and cattle was used as payment for iron-hoes and specialized services.[19]

The Gusii traded mostly with the Luo as described above, whereas trade with other neighbouring tribes like the Kuria, the Kipsigis and the Masai seems to have been less important.

Taita Hills

The Taita tribe that now occupies the Taita Hills belongs to the group of Eastern Bantu people.[20] They were agriculturalists with a knowledge of how to make iron-tools that permitted them to clear forest and cultivate the land. But unlike the Luo and Gusii people, the Taita were involved in the trade between the coast and the interior of East Africa.

> "By 1800 a considerable inter-tribal and long distance trade network existed amongst the Eastern Bantu peoples. The Kikuyu peoples, for example, augmented their livestock by supplying food to the Masai, and iron implements to the Embu and Kamba. The Pokomo, likewise, as purveyors of agricultural produce, obtained ivory from the Galla, oxes and hoes from the Swahili, and bows and arrows from the Boni hunters. Intertribal markets could be either open or "discrete". In the latter case, usually between mutually hostile peoples, the exchange of goods was made in such a fashion that the groups involved never actually came face-to-face. Of the open markets Rabai Kaya near Mombasa was probably the largest and most famous. Here,

[17] Were, P.O., *op.cit.,* pp. 42–46.

[18] Mature and Kreya, Kisii Iron Industry before the Coming of the Europeans. Bishop Otunga High School. *African Historical and Culture Quarterly Report,* April 1970.

[19] R. A. le Vine, "Wealth and Power in Gusii-Land" in Bohannam, P. and Dalton G. (eds), *Markets in Africa,* Evanston, 1962, p. 524–525.

[20] See McIntosh, B.G., *The Eastern Bantu Peoples,* in Ogot, B.A. and Kieran, J.A. (eds.) *op.cit.* p. 198–215.

food-stuffs, livestock, hoes, baskets and cottage goods were bought and sold, and caravans of Kamba, Taita, Swahili, Dalralo and Langulu (Sanye people), Nyika and even Galla, were frequent visitors."[21].

In the long-distance trade, the chief carriers and middlemen between the interior and the coast were the Kamba. They operated as ivory hunters as far north as Samburu, and sold their ivory to Arab and Swahili merchants at the coast, either directly, or through Daruma or Digo agents. But the Taita people had commercial agreements with the Kamba ensuring safe passage and provisions to and from the coast. By the 1880's when the Kamba trading route had been taken over by the Arabs[22] and later by the Imperial British East Africa Company the Taita participated in the caravans as porters.[23]

From these lengthy quotations from historical references we can thus conclude that the Taita people by the beginning of colonial rule were already involved in exchange with the Western economy to a considerable extent. They sold surplus agricultural produce and labour in exchange for imported goods such as salt, cloth, iron-hoes and other coastal trading goods. However, the important economic tasks such as house construction, making cloth and bedding from hides and many utensils were still undertaken by family members themselves.

Kwale District

Today Kwale District is inhabited by 3 different tribes that all belong to the group of Eastern Bantu people. They are the Digo, the Duruma and the Wakamba. Some Kamba seem to have settled in the area in pre-colonial time and in the beginning of the 1950's there are reports on migrations of Wakamba from Kitui and Machakos into Duruma country. These migrations have continued with the establishment of Shimba Hills Settlement Scheme but still the Wakamba make up only a small percentage of the total population.

The pre-colonial economic system of the Digo and the Duruma was, like the other Eastern Bantu people, mainly dominated by agriculture, but due to the nearness of the coastal towns they were involved in intensive trade. They exchanged their agricultural surpluses – food and livestock, ivory and gum copal for salt, iron, cloth and other goods. Unlike the Taita the Digo and the Duruma were active participants in the long distance trade where they

[21] *ibid.*, p. 213.

[22] Alpers, A.E., "The Nineteenth Century: Prelude to Colonialism" in Ogot, B.A. and Kieran, J.A. *op.cit.*, p. 247.

[23] Clayton, A. and Savage, D.C., *Government and Labour in Kenya 1895–1963,* London 1974, p. 9.

acted as middlemen between the Kamba ivory hunters and the Arab Swahili merchants at the coast.

But besides trade another important non-farming activity by these people was fishing. Important fishing centres were Vanga, Aleni, Funzi, and Gazi. Most of the fish caught was dried and sold at markets all over the districts.

There seems to have been no specialization in construction of houses, but unlike the people of the other 3 districts studied, clothing seems to be mainly imported. However, there seem to have been people specialized in canoe building as well as in making of maize and coconut grinders.

It is probably true that the process of formation of an accumulating class based upon crop production and livestock was most advanced in Central Province of Kenya, but the same tendencies existed in other densely populated areas.

As can be seen from the various bits of information about economic activities in the four districts selected for this study, some specialization within districts as well as between districts had taken place in pre-colonial time.

Although most needs were still taken care of by family members themselves (housing, clothing, processing of food) the households mostly relied upon outside skills for agricultural implements and for some utensils. Further, there was active exchange of produce of both agricultural products and non-agricultural products between districts (tribes).

Land, cattle, important skills (like blacksmithing) and trading were the basic means of accumulating wealth, usually in the form of land, livestock or wives. Possession of wealth in these forms was associated with high social values and gave political influence.

In the coastal towns and in the plantation economies of Pemba and Zanzibar, the division of labour had gone much further and exploitation of slave labour formed an additional source of accumulation of wealth[24], but traditionally none of the coastal tribes have been slave owners[25] and there seems to have been no significant development of wage labour in the four study areas in pre-colonial time.

However, at a crucial time in the late 1980's, when decisions which were to affect the long-term future of indigenous agriculture were being taken by the colonial authorities, the economic and social systems of some of the

[24] Chittick, N., "The Coast before the Arrival of the Portuguese", in Ogot, B.A. and Kieran, J.A. *op.cit.,* p. 116.

[25] However, the most successful Wakamba and Nyika slave traders seem to have started employing slaves for their domestic and agricultural business by 1850. See Lamphear, J., "The Kamba and the Northern Mrima Coast", in Gray, R. and Birmingham, D. (eds.) *op.cit.,* p. 91.

major tribes – the Kikuyu, Kamba and Masai – were badly influenced by a series of famines, epidemics and cattle diseases.

According to various studies[26] there is little evidence to suggest that European settler farming was initially visualised when Britain actively intervened in East Africa in the 1870's. The main aims seem to have been to open trade routes with Uganda for raw material exports and British manufactured imports, and to protect this trade from foreign competition. For these purposes a concession was granted to the Imperial British East Africa Company in 1888. But as the trade generated by the company was insufficient to cover the administrative costs, the British government took direct responsibility for administering the territory in 1893.

This led to a search for ways of both generating sufficient tax revenue and stimulating additional trade to make the territory self financing, a situation made more urgent by the decision to construct a railway from the coast to Kisumu on Lake Victoria.

Thus the bad economic situation in the Kikuyu, Kamba and Masai territories at the end of the century influenced the choice of policy means adopted by the colonial government to obtain this financial self-sufficiency of the area.

A decision was taken to impose direct rule with tax collections organised through officially appointed local chiefs. And it was decided that in Kenya – as opposed to Uganda – indigenous agriculture could not be relied on as a main-spring for increased trade and output. It was at this point in time that plantation and settler agriculture began to be viewed as a serious proposition. It was the beginning of the underdevelopment of Kenya.

Development of Underdevelopment

Roughly speaking the colonial period can be divided in two fundamentally distinctive periods as far as the objective and impact of the colonial policy on the development of the local productive forces are concerned.

The aim of the policy in the first phase was to support the development of a strong economically viable settler economy. This had a totally damaging effect on the development of the productive forces in the African peasant economy. The major problem for the colonial government was to secure a stable supply of cheap African labour for the settler farms, the plantations and for the building up of the necessary infra-structure. The well-known

[26] See for example Smith, L.D., "An Overview of Agricultural Development Policy", in Heyer, J. et al., *Agricultural Development in Kenya – An Economic Assessment,* Oxford University Press, 1976.

policy of land seizure, compulsory labour, taxation, and prohibitions against African production of cash crops was used for this purpose.

The European settler farming lobby used their influence to secure a policy in this period which meant that development of the African areas could only proceed provided it did not seriously hamper the supply of labour to European farms and provided that it relied on products that did not compete for markets with those produced by Europeans.

The prevailing labour supply theory among the white settlers was that of "the backward sloping supply curve". The Africans generally resisted imperial rule by rejecting working for the administration and the settlers, who interpreted this as laziness. They therefore forced the Africans to sell their labour by introducing taxation and by limiting their ability to pay taxes from sales of agricultural produce or livestock. In order to secure that the workers stayed in the labour market for as long as possible their policy was to keep wages low and taxes high. In addition they used compulsory labour in periods when these indirect means did not create a sufficient supply.[27]

This labour market policy is considered the most significant disincentive to the development of African agriculture[28]. It is estimated that the percentages of the working male population absent from the different districts were extremely high, reaching between 50 per cent and 62 per cent in Kiambu, and over 30 per cent for many districts.[29] It is clear that this must have had an important negative influence on agricultural activity in the African areas. The absence of large numbers of young working men must have reduced agricultural output both because it decreased the amount of labour available for agriculture and because the most pressing cash needs could be provided for out of labour earnings.

The early development of the African areas was based on food crop and livestock production for subsistance, and on a few cash crops that did not seriously threaten to reduce the European farm labour supply. Some efforts were made to improve the varieties of food crops grown, to improve cultivation practices and to introduce more drought resistant crops that could serve as famine reserves in times of bad weather conditions.

Cotton and later wattle were the first African cash crops to be introduced but also hides and skins and live animals were important sources of cash incomes of the African peasants in this period.

Agricultural production techniques hardly changed in this period except

[27] For an excellent discussion of this co-ordination of real wage policy and tax policy and use of compulsory labour see Clayton, A. and Savage, D.C., *op.cit.*

[28] Heyer, J. "The origins of inequalities in smallholder agriculture in Kenya, 1920–73" in *Eastern African Journal of Rural Development,* Vol 8, Nos 1 and 2 (1975) p. 142–181.

[29] *Ibid,* p. 148.

for the Kikuyu districts and a few areas of Nyanza Province where increasing population densities forced the peasants from their traditional shifting cultivation into more continuous cultivation.

The use of agricultural implements did not change much either. In Central Province agricultural implements were made of wood and metal but in other areas like Ukambani and parts of Embu and Meru, wooden hoes and digging sticks were more common. In Nyanza there were increasing numbers of oxploughs in use but the absolute number was still very small when one considers the area involved.

In the non-farming sector there were some positive developments due to a first start in the processing of agricultural produce like hand and mechanically operated maize mills and the use of separators for the production of ghee. Also a few cotton ginneries were started in this period.

However, these sectors were totally in the hands of Europeans or Asians who also through their expansion in trade with African agricultural surplus production as well as in imported consumer goods like textiles and kitchen utensils benefitted from the shift in consumer patterns away from home-made and locally produced items towards imported items at the cost of African traders and artisans.[30]

In this way the transformation of the class of primitive accumulators of the pre-colonial days into a class of agrarian capitalists was thwarted by the settler farmers' monopoly over most of the available African surplus labour, over most of the fertile land, and over the production of most of the agricultural commodities or marketing of products on which capitalist agriculture could be based.[31]

The major consequences of this policy was to distort and delay the development in the productive forces in the African peasant economy. The African economy was *under*-developed during this period.

During this process of under-development the route of entry to the "accumulator" class, and the basis of further accumulation of the individual African within it had shifted from agricultural production to wage income, increasingly based upon education and jobs in the civil service such as, e.g., local chiefs, who in addition to their salary could exploit their position as tax collectors and the recruitment of "communal" forced labour as new means of accumulation of wealth.

[30] The colonial administration encouraged the introduction of western type consumer goods in various ways, see Fearn, H., *op.cit.* p. 111 and Maxon, R., *op.cit.*, p. 85.

[31] See Leys, C., "Capital accumulation. . .", *op.cit.*, p. 13.

The emergence of African capital accumulation

During the international economic crises in the thirties and the period of relative economic isolation and self-sufficiency of the colony during the Second World War it became increasingly clear that the policy of building the economic development of the area upon the settler farmers alone had been a total failure. While, in this period, the white settlers could only survive economically because of the heavy subsidies they received in different ways, African peasant agriculture and local trade and small-scale industries were flourishing in many of the more fertile parts of the country. Asians and Europeans had started the first industrial boom in the country, based primarily upon the processing of agricultural products for the local market, and the first import substitution industrialization – cigarettes, beverages, cement and paint had taken place during the war.

While the 1920's was a period of stagnation for African agriculture, the situation changed in the 1930's. This period was dominated by the economic depression with its strong repercussions for European agriculture and the consequent gradual building up of a protected position for the European farming sector. The demand for labour on European farms decreased and the strength of the arguments of the white settlers against increasing African production was reduced by the weakness of their economic position.

The wages of African labour in the White Highlands were even more depressed than the prices that African producers could obtain for their products and it is therefore argued that the comparative advantage of production in African areas was strengthened during this period.[32]

This led to increased African production of foodcrops, particularly maize, and as export prices obtained by European growers fell below the domestic price they realized the significance of African production for the internal market. Their response was to attempt to control African maize marketing and to force more African produced maize onto the export market, thus allowing European crops to participate in the higher priced domestic market. As observed by a number of scholars, the object of the marketing system established in the mid-1930's was to allow European grown produce to receive the best prices.[33]

But it was also in the 1930's that the colonial government, against the interest of the European farmers, granted permission for limited experiments in African coffee growing. The districts selected for these

[32] See Zwanenberg, R. Van, "The Development of Peasant Commodity Production in Kenya, 1920–40", in *The Economic History Review,* 2nd Series, XXVII, No 3, August 1974.

[33] See Zwanenberg, R. Van, *Primitive Colonial Accumulation in Kenya, 1919–1939,* Ph. D. disserttion, Sussex, 1971.

experiments were Kisii, Embu, and Meru on the grounds that these were isolated districts badly in need of high-value cash crops where coffee would do well.[34]

During the Second World War, African agriculture experienced more fundamental changes. The need to increase the production of food and essential commodities became the first priority of agricultural policies. The result was a very substantial increase in marketed food production and radical changes in the balance of production in various African areas as a result. Many more African smallholders started marketing some of their output, and there was substantially increased pressure on land in African areas.

In this process Nyanza Province (at that time including the now Western Province) had emerged as a major maize producing area mainly due to increased maize production in North Nyanza, Kericho and Kisii. Previously, in the lower areas of Central Nyanza and South Nyanza, growing cotton had been the centre of attention, but this was changed by the war. After maize other products like hides and skins and to a smaller extent cotton, ghee, millets, eggs, groundnuts and rice still played a role in exports from the African areas.

The production patterns of Central Province were also changed. Maize, which had dominated exports in the 30's, vitually ceased to be in surplus and instead wattle, fruit and vegetables, potatoes, eggs, poultry and pulses became important. There was a shift in favour of the producers near Nairobi who could supply the war-time markets for food – particularly the more perishable vegetables. Embu and Meru started producing their first noticeable exports of pulses at this time and Embu, Fort Hall and Kitui benefitted from a considerable production of tobacco. Only a few areas like Nyeri that used to produce a substantial surplus of maize seem to have suffered actual setbacks during the war.[35]

In the Coast Province, the most important development took place in Taita Hills which at the end of the war was exporting as much as K£ 60,000 worth of vegetables for the Mombasa market.[36]

The Europeans and the Asians were still totally dominating in the non-agricultural sectors. A few individuals of the settler group became involved in non-agricultural capital formation like property, real estate and to a lesser extent processing of primary products.[37] Also Asian merchant

[34] Heyer, J. (1975), *op.cit.,* p. 150.

[35] Cowen, M. (1972), *op.cit.*

[36] Heyer, J. (1975), *op.cit.,* p. 152.

[37] Swainson, N., "Company formation in Kenya before 1945 with particular reference to the role of foreign capital" in Kaplinsky, R., (ed.), *Readings on the Multinational Corporation in Kenya,* Oxford University Press, 1978, pp. 22–95.

capital started moving into small-scale manufacturing and the capital accumulated through trade and commerce and small-scale primary processing before the war provided the basis for their more profound move into large-scale industrial operations after the war. Thus the foundations of the Asian industrial empires such as the Madhvanis, Chandarias, and Manjis were laid down before and during the war.[38]

However, an increasing number of Africans participated in the local trade in foodcrops and vegetables and in the trade in imported items in the increasing number of markets in the rural areas. It is not known exactly how many such African markets existed at the time, but there was probably at least one in each location.

These markets were first under the control of chiefs and elders, but in the mid-thirties the control was transferred by the government to the African District Councils. In the 1930's and 1940's the number of these markets and of licensed African traders and plot holders increased sharply. This is quite noticeable since the growth in African participation in trade was contrary to the general policy of the colonial government. The government introduced regulations that made it difficult for Africans to obtain loans and they recommended a policy of restrictions on the number of trade licenses to be issued to Africans. Further, they restricted the successful development of African trade by interfering in the planning of the market sites and the number of plots. In order to be allocated a plot in a market place, the applicant would be requested to build a duka of stone and wattle with a corrugated-iron roof, in accordance with Health Department specifications within 3 years of obtaining his licence. Such a building was quite costly and in many cases, having spent this money (approximately 10,000 Shs. in 1954) the traders had no money left as working capital for the shop.[39]

In addition to trade, a number of services and new crafts were taken up by Africans in the A.D.C-markets as a substitute for the more traditional crafts that had stagnated due to the competition from imported commodities.

These activities developed with the introduction of European consumer patterns and the rise of rural incomes. They included tailoring, carpentry and a number of repair and service activities such a bicycle repair, bars, hotels, and tea shops.

The development in the 1930's and the 1940's did not in itself increase the

[38] *Ibid.* p. 40. See also Murray R., "The Chandarias: The development of a Kenya Multinational" in Kaplinsky, R., *op.cit.* pp. 284–308, and Zarwan, J.I., *Indian Businessmen in Kenya during the Twentieth Century: A case study.* Ph.D. dissertation, Yale University, 1977.

[39] Fearn, H. *op.cit.* p. 175.

African participation and control over capital accumulation in Kenya. But it had two important indirect effects.

Firstly, the relative economic success of the new African elite, especially during the war, created a political self-confidence that initiated the nationalist movement and finally resulted in independence in 1963. The new group of African "accumulators" which had based its economic position on education and employment in the civil service found its expansion into other economic sectors blocked by various regulations imposed by the colonial government and by the competition from Asian traders. In order to put pressure on the colonial government to widen the scope for their accumulation they formed semi-political pressure groups such as the Kikuyu Central Association and the Kavirondo Taxpayers Welfare Association. By the end of World War II a direct challenge to the limitations and restrictions on expansion of African business activities was finally articulated by the more militant wing of the Kenya African Union, leading finally in 1952 to the declaration of emergency.

Secondly, the expansion of agricultural production and the consequent increase in purchasing power in the African areas attracted British firms to invest in Kenya – especially after the war.

Only a few British firms had established subsidiaries in Kenya before 1939. They produced items like beer, cigarettes, soap, cement, canned fruit and vegetables. Up to 1940 the Imperial Policy was against the development of industries in the colonies, but after 1945 this policy was changed. One of the possible reasons for this change was that during the war settler and Asian capital had moved into import substitution due to the shortage of consumer goods previously imported.

After the war many British and also U.S. multinational corporations found it worthwhile and necessary to invest in import subsitution in order to regain and defend their former markets. After this the British firms and the British government – who needed increased production in the colonies as a contribution to the solution of the dollar shortage after the war – had an interest in the development of the African areas of Kenya. Consequently, the white settler privileges could no longer be maintained and the colonial state slowly began to dismantle the barriers to indigenous capital accumulation.[40]

In 1954 three major reports from Commissions set up by the British government demonstrated the change in policy. The first was *The East African Royal Commission* which called for a free market in land. The second was *The Swynnerton Plan* which advocated the consolidation of all African holdings and the rapid introduction of all suitable cash crops. The third was

[40] Leys, C. *op.cit.* p. 15.

The Carpenter Report which argued the case for a rapid rise in cash wages to a family minimum level.[41]

Of these Commission reports, the Swynnerton plan had the greatest impact. The plan advocated what at the time seemed to be a revolution in African land tenure and the introduction of all cash crops to African farmers and involved the consolidation and registration of all African land which meant the creation of private peasant landed property. The plan was quite explicit in stating its goal – the creation of a landed African middle class for whom near-landless labourers would provide a work force.[42] It was first introduced in Central Province as an anti-guerilla tactic in order to reward the "loyalists" and to punish the "freedom fighters" who in their absence could not claim their rights to inherited tribal land.

The implementation of the ideas in the Swynnerton Plan, which was initiated in the fifties but continued and even speeded up after Independence, finally destroyed the elements in the earlier colonial policy which had thwarted the development of the productive forces in the rural areas of Kenya. As a result Kenya has experienced an exceptionally rapid growth in agricultural production since the end of the fifties.

The growth process has been based upon the introduction of cash crops like coffee, tea and pyrethrum. But also the production of hybrid maize and vegetables as well as dairy production has increased substantially.

Such an agricultural policy has, however, had much more to offer to the high potential agricultural areas of Kenya which receive plentiful rain, and among these the areas with good infrastructure and access to markets have benefitted the most.

In the next chapter the agricultural development of the four selected districts Kisumu, Kisii, Taita Hills, and Kwale will be discussed within the framework of the general expansion of smallholders' production since the mid-fifties.

41 See *Report on the East African Royal Commission 1954–1955,* cmd 9475, HMSO, 1955. R.J.M. Swynnerton, *A Plan to Intensify the Development of African Agriculture in Kenya.,* Nairobi, 1954. Report of the Committee on African Wages, Nairobi, 1955.

42 Zwanenberg, R. Van, "Neocolonialism and the origin of the National Bourgeoisie in Kenya between 1940 and 1973" in *Journal of Eastern African Research and Development,* Vol. 4 No 2, 1974.

CHAPTER II

Agricultural Development in Kisumu, Kisii, Taita Hills and Kwale Districts

According to recent estimates 10.3 mill. people or 87 per cent of the total Kenyan population of 13.4 mill. were living on small holdings in the rural areas in 1975. The sector is made up of nearly one and a half mill. smallholdings[1], the majority less than 2 hectares, and very few more than 5 hectares in size (see Table II.1).

The sector is extremely heterogeneous as far as natural conditions for agriculture and population densities are concerned and therefore there have been drastic differences in the development experiences of various regions over the past 20 years.

Agricultural potential and population

The natural environments in the rural areas of Kenya vary from cold, wet, highland forest, through warmer highland areas with plenty of rain, down to warm lowlands with less rain that can nevertheless support agriculture quite well, and then hot, semi-arid areas in which agricultural conditions are marginal. These contrasts can be found over short distances, and there are several districts in which the full range of natural conditions is represented[2]. Therefore the differences between the highland areas, for which the Swynnerton Plan had a great deal to offer, and the lowland areas for which there was much less, do not stand out clearly in the district comparisons, because so many districts include both highland and lowland areas[3].

[1] Republic of Kenya, *Integrated Rural Survey, 1974–75. Basic Report.* March 1977.

The small farm areas include (i) the former African areas (non-scheduled areas) with more than one million smallholdings and fifty thousand pastoral holdings, (ii) the settlement schemes with approx. thirty-five thousand holdings. (iii) the irrigation schemes on which there are about three thousand five hundred tenants, and (iv) the areas of illegal settlement in which it is estimated that as many as three hundred thousand small farmers live.

The size of the smallholdings is between 0.2 and 12 hectares though there are some outside this range.

[2] Heyer, J. and Waweru, J.K., "The Development of Small Farm Areas" in Heyer, J. et al., *op.cit.* p. 187.

[3] Heyer, J. "The origins. . .", *op.cit.,* p. 170.

Table II.1. *Percentage distribution of holding by holding size group and province*[1].

	Central	Coast	Eastern	Nyanza	Rift Valley	Western	Percent Total
Below 0.5 hectares	6.74	20.37	9.55	15.72	22.99	21.53	13.91
0.5–0.9 hectares	10.50	18.46	17.35	26.18	12.11	17.67	17.92
1.0–1.9 hectares	36.96	22.52	33.39	22.03	17.59	17.27	26.99
2.0–2.9 hectares	16.47	11.42	14.82	15.23	14.78	14.68	15.11
3.0–3.9 hectares	11.86	7.68	8.57	6.79	10.11	8.60	8.89
4.0–4.9 hectares	5.92	8.15	9.68	8.13	5.78	4.36	7.22
5.0–7.9 hectares	7.63	5.87	5.43	4.09	6.87	10.22	6.50
8.0 ha. and over	3.92	5.53	1.22	1.83	9.83	5.68	3.47
Total	100.00	100.00	100.00	100.00	100.00	100.00	100.00
No. of holdings	329,530	69,861	353,159	386,431	89,823	254,618	1,483,422
Percent of holdings	22.2	4.7	23.8	26.0	6.1	17.2	100.0

[1] Excludes pastoral and large farm areas

Source: Republic of Kenya, Integrated Rural Survey 1974–75. Basic Report, Table 7.1. p. 44.

In order to get a picture of the relative agricultural potential in various districts agricultural land has been classified according to annual rainfall into three broad categories of high potential, medium potential and low potential land.

The results are given in Table II.2. As can be seen from this table only 13 per cent of agricultural land in Kenya is classified as high potential, whereas as much as 81 per cent is low potential land. The differences between provinces and districts are outstanding. In Kisumu and Kisii Districts almost all land is classified as high potential. Kwale District in Coast Province has more high potential and medium potential land than the national average, whereas Taita Hills have below average potential.

Also population densities vary widely between districts from over 300 per km^2 in the most densely populated district, Kisii, to under 25 per km^2 in other agricultural districts like, e.g., Kwale District and Taita Hills (see Table II.3).

It should be emphasized, however, that local population densities vary considerably and that, e.g., the densities in the selected sublocations' sample areas of Kisii and Kisumu Districts are as high as 557 and 331, respectively.

Generally, population densities are highest in the areas with a high agricultural potential, but there are also high potential areas in which population densities are relatively low.

In order to get a more realistic picture of the population pressure on land than the one presented by mere population densities, the availability of high

Map 2. *Mean annual rainfall in Nyanza Province.*

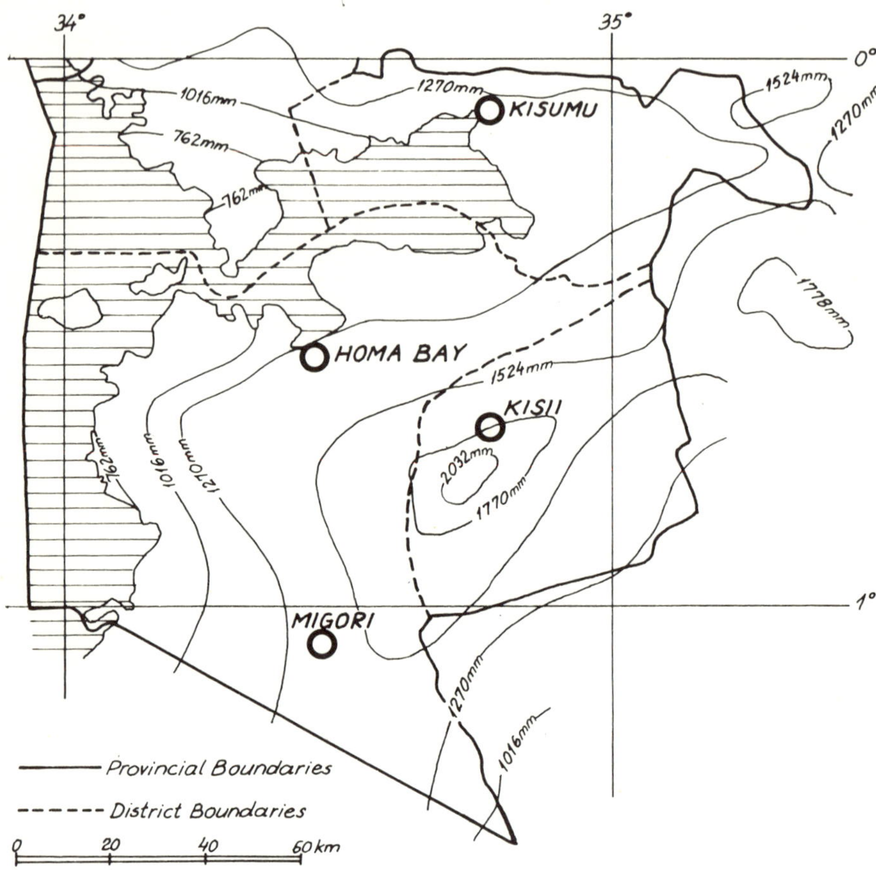

potential land equivalents are shown in Table II.4. It should be stressed that this computation of high potential equivalents involves a high element of uncertainty.

In addition, Table II.4 shows the average size of small holdings in the various provinces in 1975.

From Tables II.2, 3, and 4 the following picture of the comparative agricultural potential in the selected 4 districts emerges.

Kisumu district consists of the Kano plains between the Nandi escarpment and the South Nyanza highlands – and a small part of these highlands. The Kano plains are a distinctive feature of Kisumu district. Ranging from 3700 feet to 4000 feet in altitude the area is characterized by soils that are very fertile but difficult to drain and work. Moreover, the area, particularly the east Kano Plain, is susceptible to flooding from the Nyando escarpment.

Map 3. *Mean annual rainfall in Coast Province.*

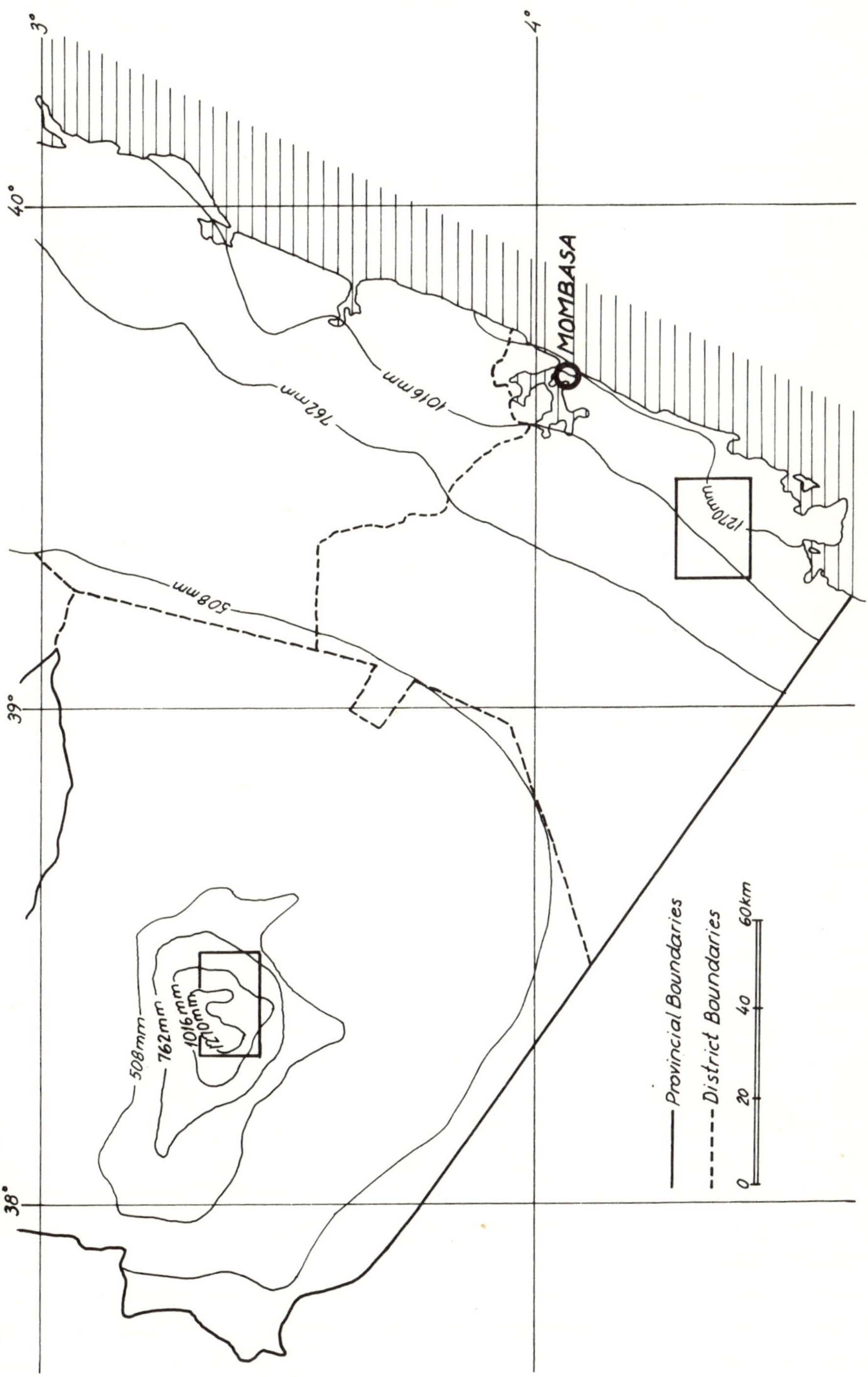

Table II.2. *Categories of agricultural land.*

	Total land '000 hectares	High potential (%)	Medium potential (%)	Low potential (%)
Central Province	*965*	*94.2*	*1.6*	*4.3*
Coast Province	*6,832*	*5.5*	*11.6*	*82.9*
of which Kwale	796	15.8	20.3	63.8
Taita	642	6.5	1.6	91.9
Eastern Province	*14,145*	*3.6*	*15.5*	*81.0*
North Eastern Pr.	*12,690*	*0.0*	*0.0*	*100.0*
Nyanza Province	*1,252*	*97.3*	*2.7*	*0.0*
of which Kisumu & Siaya	461	93.7	6.3	0.0
Kisii	220	100.0	0.0	0.0
Rift Valley Prov.	*15,368*	*19.7*	*0.8*	*79.5*
Western Province	*741*	*00.0*	*0.0*	*0.0*
Total Kenya	52.047	13.0	6.1	80.9

Source: Statistical Abstract 1977. Table 81 p. 104.

Most of the cultivated land in Kisumu and Siaya District is classified as high potential, but since this classification is based upon annual yearly rainfall the main characteristic of Kisumu District – the unusually unreliable rainfall in the Kano plains – is not taken into account. Moreover, in evaluating the agricultural land base available for smallholder farming it should be taken into account that the best watered parts of the Kano plains, at the foot of the Nyando Escarpment, are alienated lands devoted to sugarcane plantations, (approx. 10 per cent of the land in Kisumu District).

For these reasons the figures given in the tables for population densities and of high potential land equivalents for Kisumu and Siaya District overestimate the availability of agricultural land for smallholder production in Kisumu District. A more realistic figure would be in the range of 0.9 to 1.1 acre per person.

The unreliable rainfall in Kano plains is a very important feature, which partly explains land use patterns, cropping patterns and the relatively poor agricultural performance of smallholders in the District. It has encouraged development strategies based on intensive irrigation schemes which are now changing the face of land use in parts of the District.

Kisii District is the highest part of the South Nyanza highlands, which are rich in red laterized volcanic soils. It consists of rounded, steepsided hills intersected by narrow valleys. They normally receive sufficient rainfall, and

Table II.3. *Population and population densities 1969.*

	Population (100)	Pop. per sq. km.
WESTERN	1,328	161
Kakamega	783	222
Bungoma	345	112
Busia	200	123
NYANZA	2,122	169
Kisumu	401	193
Siaya	383	151
S. Nyanza	663	116
Kisii	675	307
CENTRAL	1,676	127
Kiambu	476	194
Murang'a	445	180
Nyeri	361	110
Kirinyaga	217	181
Nyandarua	177	50
RIFT	847	82
Kericho	479	98
Nandi	209	76
Elgeyo	159	59
EASTERN	1,826	32
Embu	179	66
Meru	597	60
Machakos	707	50
Kitui	343	12
COAST	625	17
Kilifi	308	25
Kwale	206	25
Taita	111	7

Sources: Statistical Abstracts; District Agricultural Reports. Quoted from Heyer, J. "The origin of inequalities. . .", *op. cit.* p. 170.

the area is well served by the tributaries of three main rivers which flow into Lake Victoria.

Kisii District is the smallest and the most densely populated of the 4 selected districts, but all of the land is high potential and very fertile. Kisii is therefore one of the areas which have benefitted from the introduction of cash crops like coffee, tea and pyrethrum. But the future development potential is problematic due to the scarcity of land, the very high population density (the highest in Kenya) and the consequent small size of agricultural land available per person.

In a climatic sense, *Taita Hills* is like an oasis in the desert as it is situated

Table II.4. *Estimated availability of agricultural land.*

	High potential land equivalents acres/person	Average size of smallholdings in 1975 (acres)
Central Province	1.6	6.6
Coast Province	3.7	5.9
of which Kwale	2.0	
Taita	1.2	
Eastern Province	1.4	5.4
Nyanza Province	1.5	4.8
of which Kisumu+Siaya	1.5	
Kisii	0.7	
Rift Valley	4.7	7.4
Western	1.6	6.1
Total Kenya	3.0	5.8

Source: Computed from Migot-Adholla, S.E., *Migration and Rural Differentiation in Kenya,* Ph.D. Thesis, University of California, 1977, Table 3.3, p. 44. The data in second column is from Republic of Kenya, *Integrated Rural Survey.* 1974–75. Basic Report, table 7.5.

Note: The table has been calculated under the assumption that 5 hectares of medium- and 100 hectares of low potential land are equivalent to 1 ha of high potential land.

in the dry area of what is today Tsavo National Park. Since the rain mainly falls at the top of the hills, the fertility of the land in the district differs very much according to location. Only the land in the valleys at the top of the hills which make up 6.5 percent of the 642,000 hectares of agricultural land in the district is high potential agricultural land. Therefore, in years of bad rainfall the Wataita are not able to grow enough food and have to rely on other sources of income in order to subsist.

Population density *per se* is very low but when related to the availability of high potential land it becomes evident that there is a strong population pressure on the land which, although less than in Kisii, compares to the population pressure in other fertile highland parts of Kenya, like for example, some of the districts in the Central Province.

Kwale district can be divided into two broad agricultural zones. The coastal belt, which has a relatively high rainfall and fertile land, is suitable for tropical agriculture with emphasis upon tropical tree cash crops, whereas the hinterland, which is relatively dry, is suitable for drought resistant crops and cattle keeping.

Kwale district is the biggest of the 4 study areas, but the population is less than in both Kisumu and Kisii. Sixteen and twenty per cent of this land is high and medium potential respectively, and although a considerable part of the most fertile land along the coast was alienated in the colonial period it seems

Table II.5. *Estimated minimum sizes of farms in Kisii, Kisumu, Taita Hills and Kwale (hectares).*

District	Minimum farm sizes (ha.) Subsistence	Subsistence+2,000 shs.
Kisii	1	2 1/4
Kisumu & Siaya	2	4 1/2
Taita Hills	8	13
of which		
Taita Hills crop land	2	3 1/2
Kwale	7.5	14 1/4
of which		
Kwale crop lands	2 1/4	3 1/2

Source: Republic of Kenya, Coast Province and Nyanza Province, Regional Physical Development Plan.

that the population has been able to feed themselves and to pay tax from sales of treecrops like coconuts and cashewnuts rather than by participating in the migrant labour economy. Thus, most of the labour on the plantations in the district and in Mombasa town was supplied by Luo and Kikuyu workers.

Translated into high potential land equivalents (see Table II.4), it appears that Kwale is better off than the other districts as far as the availability of agricultural land is concerned. Only the districts in Rift Valley Province and the districts on the northern Coast have lower population pressure on land. Due to the relatively low population density, the colonial government as early as 1938 had plans for a settlement scheme in the district, and at the beginning of the fifties the first families of Taita and Kamba settled in the Shimba Hills Settlement Scheme, which in 1969 had a population of 7,819.[4]

To summarize: out of 31 Kenyan districts for which population pressure on land has been calculated as the availability of high potential land equivalents per person, Kisii is ranged as the district with the highest population pressure, Kisumu district ranges 7, Taita Hills 8, and Kwale district 15. It should, however, be emphasized that the annual rainfall criterion which has been used to classify land into high, medium and low potential is a very poor measurement of the fertility of the land. Thus, for example, it is quite evident that one acre of high potential land in Kisii is more productive than one acre of high potential land in any of the other 3 districts.

[4] Palmer, G.B., *The Shimba Hills Settlement Scheme: The administration of large-scale innovation in Kenya,* Ph.D. thesis, University of Minnesota, April 1971.

Table II.6. *Population 1969 (census), 1980 and maximum farm population in Kisii, Kisumu, Taita Hills and Kwale.*

District	Actual population 1969	Estimated[1] population 1980	Max. farm population under subsistence[2]	Max. farm population under subsistence+ 2000 shs.[2]
Kisii	675,000	930,000	1,320,000	588,000
Kisumu & Siaya	784,000	1,082,000	1,390,000	618,000
Taita Hills	111,000	154,000	442,500	253,000
of which Taita Hills crop land	60,000	83,000	71,000	42,000
Kwale	202,000	280,000	646,900	343,250
of which Kwale crop land	80,000	111,000	212,000	127,000

Source: Republic of Kenya, *Nyanza Province Regional Physical Development Plan,* May 1970 and Republic of Kenya, *Coast Province Regional Physical Development Plan,* May 1971.

[1] Projected population based upon 3 per cent annual growth rates.
[2] The estimates are based on Table II.5 and average family size of 6 persons.

In the regional physical development plans for Nyanza and Coast Province the following estimates of plot sizes necessary for subsistance plus a yearly cash income of 2,000 shs, respectively, are given (Table II.5).

Based upon these estimates of district agricultural officers and population growth rates a picture of the relative population pressure on land in the four districts is given in Table II.6.

When interpreting this table it should be kept in mind that the figures are only crude estimates. With these qualifications in mind it can be seen that population pressure has become a problem already in 1969 in Kisii, Kisumu and Taita Hills crop land areas, in the sense that the average size farm can no longer provide subsistence and a minimum cash income to the average size family of 6 people. According to these estimates, the average size farm would still be able to provide a subsistence to its population in the 4 districts, but it is evident that an increasing number of small farms will be subdivided (by inheritance) into plots too small to provide a living for a family and that subsequently a rural landless proletariat will emerge as it has already happened in Kenya's Central Province.

Agricultural production and regional inequalities

Agricultural production has increased impressively fast in Kenya since the beginning of the implementation of the Swynnerton Plan at the end of the fifties.

Table II.7. *Value of gross marketed output from large and small farms 1960–1978.*

	Large farms (K. £ m)	Small farms (K. £ m)	Total (K. £ m)	Share of small farms (%)
1955	32.8	5.1	37.9	13.5
1960	37.7	9.5	47.2	20.1
1961	35.7	10.4	46.1	22.5
1962	37.1	10.6	47.7	22.2
1963	40.7	11.3	52.0	21.7
1964	35.8	24.6	60.4	40.7
1965	33.3	23.8	57.2	41.6
1966	36.0	32.7	68.8	47.5
1967	32.9	34.1	66.9	51.0
1968	34.4	35.8	70.2	51.0
1969	37.9	38.3	76.2	50.3
1970	41.2	44.2	85.4	51.7
1971	42.1	44.6	86.7	51.4
1972	50.3	55.6	105.9	52.5
1973	60.0	63.3	123.3	51.3
1974	73.4	75.0	148.4	50.6
1975	71.8	90.1	162.0	55.6
1976	122.1	128.0	250.0	51.2
1977	206.0	208.5	414.6	50.3
1978[1]	143.8	183.3	327.2	56.0

Source: Republic of Kenya, Economic Survey 1970, 1975 and 1979.

[1] Provisional.

Between 1960–1978 agricultural production has grown in real terms at an average annual rate of 4.8 per cent.[5] Very few developing countries have experienced similar growth rates in their agricultural production.[6] The growth of production was most rapid in the sixties with an annual increase in real production of 5.9 per cent, whereas the situation has been less favourable in the mid-seventies due to drought. However, the most recent years, 1976, 1977, and 1978, have been extremely good years for Kenyan agriculture with real growth rates of 6.2, 11.6, and 1.4 per cent respectively.

As can be seen from Table II.7, the rapid increase in the value of gross marketed production in the sixties was largely caused by a quadrupling of the value of marketed output by small farmers. Thus, the share of small farms in total marketed production increased from 20 per cent in 1960 to 50 per cent at the end of the decade (See Table II.7.)

[5] World Bank, World Development Report, *op.cit.,* table 2 and Republic of Kenya, *Economic Survey 1978.* Table 8.2.

[6] Among the developing countries in Africa only Cameroun, Liberia and Ivory Coast have had comparable growth rates in this period. *Ibid.* Table 8.2.

Table II.8. *Percentage distribution of smallholder sales by commodity and type of buyer, 1976/77 (per cent).*

	Cooperative societies	Marketing Board or its agent	Trader	Consumer	Other	Total
Maize	8	20	59	12	1	100
Finger Millet	0	56	16	26	2	100
Sorghum	0	66	0	33	1	100
Beans	0	16	55	28	1	100
Potatoes	0	0	84	7	9	100
Cabbages	3	0	54	42	1	100
Tomatoes	0	0	96	4	0	100
Bananas	0	0	36	63	1	100
Chickens	0	0	43	47	10	100
Eggs	0	0	13	86	1	100
Milk	63	9	11	16	1	100
Sheep	0	0	56	33	11	100
Goats	0	0	71	21	8	100
Cattle	6	0	73	10	11	100

Source: Republic of Kenya, Economic Survey 1978, Table 8.9.

Since the end of the sixties marketed output has expanded at the same rate in large and small farms. It should, however, be taken into account that Table II.7 only covers that proportion of smallholder production which is marketed through the formal channels, e.g., the cooperatives and the various commodity marketing boards. For a number of reasons the statistics seem to underestimate the significance of smallholder production.

Recent information shows that more than 50 per cent of farm production on smallholdings is still retained on the holding for consumption.[7] Subsistence output has probably at least kept pace with population growth of more than 3 per cent per annum and there is nothing to suggest that marketed output has expanded at its expense.[8] More important, however, is the tendency for small farmers to sell their agricultural produce legally or illegally outside the formal system. Recent data show the comparatively insignificant role played by the cooperatives and marketing boards as an outlet for smallholder sales of many products. Cooperatives form the main outlet for milk sales only and the Maize and Produce Board purchases the major part of the sorghum and millet crops offered for sale. For maize and beans less than 20 per cent of the marketed production is sold to marketing

[7] Republic of Kenya, Economic Survey 1978, *op.cit.* p. 99.
[8] Heyer, J. and Waweru, K., *op.cit.*, p. 191.

Agricultural labourers being paid during coffee harvest. (Jesper Kirknæs)

boards and for all other products for which information is available the formal buying system plays little or no role. The major proportion of smallholder marketed production is disposed of either directly by the producer to the consumer or through the small-scale trader in the local markets (see Table II.8).

But also the illegal trade in produce between districts has been growing in the seventies. Thus Heyer notes:

> "Outside the official network of control which is very persuasive in Kenya's agricultural marketing system, there is a significant amount of smuggling and black marketeering. Products are moved in substantial quantities over long distances contrary to rules and regulations which are not being strictly enforced. Black marketeering is most widespread in maize: smuggling across borders of neighbouring territories in sugar, and black marketeering in urban areas for milk and meat. The amount of evasion of legal marketing rules appears to be increasing both because the enforcement

mechanisms are breaking down and because incentives are increasing, particularly in the lucrative markets available in Uganda and Tanzania."[9]

To the list of smuggled goods one could add coffee, the smuggling of which took a dramatic upswing in 1977 and 1978.

Taking into account that trade in locally produced food in local markets and that various forms of illegal trade have probably been increasing in the 1970's, it is most likely that the share of smallholders in total production is increasingly being underestimated in the official figures on marketed output. In 1977, the difficulty of selling maize through the marketing board and the resulting removal of Government restrictions on maize marketing so that farmers could move their stocks to any market destination in the country, has probably further raised the share of smallholders in marketed production above the level indicated in Table II.7.

Coffee, and later tea, pyrethrum and dairy products have been the major contributors to the dramatic increase in marketed output from small farms since the early sixties, but many other products, e.g., hybrid maize and vegetables have also played a role.

The relative importance of different products in marketed output from small farms is shown in Table II.9. After 1967 the official statistics no longer distinguish between large and small farms.

As can be seen from this table, the growth of the 1950's and early 1960's was based upon coffee. Thus the share of coffee in total cash revenue to small producers increased from 16.3 per cent in 1958 to 31.1 per cent in 1962 (Table II.9). Production of coffee more than doubled between 1959 and 1962 (Table II.11).

Since 1964, coffee production has grown less rapidly. Total production has increased from 41,400 tons in 1964 to 97,066 tons in 1977, an annual increase of 6.2 per cent (see Table II.10). Smallholder coffee production, however, increased more rapidly than total production with an annual rate of 8.4 per cent between 1959 and 1977 and of 7.5 per cent between 1964 and 1977. Thus, the share of smallholder production in total production increased from 15.5 per cent in 1959 to 40.4 per cent in 1964 and to 60.0 per cent in 1967. Smallholder production stagnated between 1967 and 1972 due to the quota restrictions in the International Coffee Agreement but rose again in 1973 and 1974. Since 1975 the share of smallholder coffee production has been approx. 50 per cent (see Table II.11). As many as 27 per cent of the 1,483,422 smallholdings in Kenya were growing coffee in 1974–75.[10]

[9] Heyer, J., "The marketing system", in Heyer, J. et al., *op.cit.*, p. 318.

[10] Republic of Kenya, *Integrated Rural Survey 1974–75*, Basic Report, Table 9.5.

Table II.9. *Cash revenue to producers, small farms, 1958–67 (£'000)*

	1958	1959	1960	1961	1962	1963	1964	1965	1966	1967
1. Coffee	1,266	1,830	2,241	2,816	3,295	3,022	5,808	5,388	9,335	8,409
2. Pyrethrum	89	200	545	611	533	359	422	796	1,791	2,275
3. Maize	1,118	1,006	960	1,082	1,131	1,244	1,487	820	1,416	1,346
4. Tea	–	40	66	26	54	122	366	542	754	1,081
5. Vegetables, fruits and flowers	499	435	434	354	503	566	581	603	643	828
6. Cotton	348	499	545	505	460	440	594	641	681	603
7. Sugar	–	20	16	13	24	45	209	244	109	566
8. Wheat	–	–	–	–	–	–	122	265	313	493
9. Coconuts	236	405	289	286	215	246	324	403	449	450
10. Pulses	373	294	307	312	251	282	263	308	529	438
11. Cashews	57	120	193	252	68	113	156	393	395	392
12. Oil Seeds	329	173	241	216	284	337	222	216	359	349
13. Wattle	267	193	231	147	220	268	281	218	329	344
14. Potatoes	60	96	125	199	105	132	147	66	180	190
15. Sisal	3	65	284	435	132	519	706	197	65	15
Total Crops	5,225	5,977	7,176	8,055	7,904	8,455	121,188	11,490	17,973	18,336
1. Cattle and calves for slaughter	1,876	1,848	1,955	1,760	2,120	2,184	7,091	7,271	8,738	9,169
2. Dairy products	200	178	180	246	161	260	1,630	1,450	1,950	2,440
3. Hides and skins	n.a.	n.a.	n.a.	n.a.	n.a.	n.a.	472	470	592	630
4. Sheep & lambs for slaughter	242	248	248	252	306	316	244	252	247	181
5. Poultry and eggs	64	74	57	62	82	54	85	8	80	110
6. Pigs for slaughter	153	25	8	5	9	5	21	84	62	75
7. Wool	–	–	–	–	–	–	6	24	37	63
Total Livestock	2,535	2,373	2,448	2,325	2,678	2,819	9,549	9,559	11,706	12,668
Total crops & livestock	7,760	8,350	9,624	10,380	10,582	11,304	21,737	21,049	29,679	31,004

Source: Statistical Abstract 1961, 1968. Quoted from Heyer, J., The Origins . . . . , *op. cit.* p. 165.

Table II. 10. *Marketed production of major crops ('000 metric tons) 1959–77.*

	1959	1964	1966	1968	1970	1972	1974	1975	1976	1977	Annual growth rates (%) 1964–77	1959–77
Wheat	95.2	134.7	128.4	216.3	221.5	164.4	159.5	158.1	186.8	169.8	1.6	3.1
Maize	183.8	136.2	134.3	352.6	205.7	373.0	365.4	487.8	564.8	424.0[1]	11.6[2]	6.4[2]
Rice	–	13.2	16.6	18.7	28.5	33.8	33.2	32.1	38.7	41.4	8.7	–
Pyrethrum	4.8	–	–	–	–	11.6	14.4	15.4	12.8	11.3	2.1	4.6
Sugar-Cane	–	600.9	514.6	947.2	1451.2	1062.3	1719.1	1654.6	1652.7	1888.1	8.5	–
Cotton	10.0	11.0	14.4	14.3	14.0	17.0	15.0	16.1	15.8	16.3	2.9	2.6
Coffee	23.3	41.4	56.9	39.6	58.3	62.0	70.1	66.2	80.3	97.1	6.2	7.8
Tea	12.4	20.2	21.4	29.8	41.1	53.3	53.4	56.7	62.0	86.3	10.9	10.7
Sisal	55.2	67.4	64.0	50.3	43.9	41.2	86.5	43.6	33.6	33.8	–4.8	–2.6

Source: Statistical Abstract 1976, 1977.

[1] In 1977 the Maize and Produce Board was only able to buy a limited amount of the crop harvested due to strain on the board's storage capacity. Consequently, the marketing regulations on maize were released and farmers were allowed to sell all over the country. The total crop in 1977 was equal in size to the one harvested in 1976.

[2] The annual growth rate has been calculated for the period 1964–1976 and 1959–1976.

Table II.11. *Coffee production, 1964–78 ('000 metric tons).*

Year	Estates production	Smallholdings production	Total production	Share of smallholdings
1959	19.6	3.6	23.2	15.5
1960	18.8	4.6	23.4	19.7
1961	20.4	7.3	27.7	26.4
1962	41.4	7.8	49.2	15.9
1963	29.9	10.0	39.9	25.1
1964	24.8	16.6	41.4	40.4
1965	28.1	16.2	39.3	41.2
1966	28.4	28.5	56.9	50.1
1967	19.2	28.8	48.0	60.0
1968	18.8	20.8	39.6	52.5
1969	26.8	25.6	52.4	48.9
1970	27.9	30.4	58.3	52.1
1971	31.5	28.0	59.5	47.1
1972	34.2	27.8	62.0	44.8
1973	35.1	36.1	71.2	50.7
1974	30.8	39.3	70.1	56.1
1975	31.2	35.0	66.2	52.9
1976	42.6	37.7	80.3	47.0
1977	51.5	45.6	97.1	47.0
1978[1]	36.6	47.7	84.3	56.6

Source: Economic Survey 1969, 1975, 1976, 1977 and 1978.

[1] Estimates.

Smallholder *tea production* started in a small way at the beginning of the fifties but was generally thought to be uneconomic due to significant economies of scale in the factory processing of tea. This means that the collection area serving a processing plant has to be substantial. Moreover, green leaf has to reach the factory within a few hours of picking. The cost of organizing production and transport was therefore thought to be too great to justify the production of tea on small farms. But plans to increase smallholder tea production were finally drawn up and put into effect shortly before and after independence with a fantastic growth in smallholder tea production as a result.

Total tea production increased with an annual rate of 10.9 per cent between 1964–1977 (see Table II.10) largely due to increased smallholder production. Between 1964 and 1977 the acreage of tea planted by smallholders increased by 17.9 per cent annually, the number of growers increased by 13.4 per cent annually, and smallholder tea production increased by 30.2 per cent annually. The share of smallholder tea production, thus, increased from 8.0 per cent in 1964 to 37.0 per cent of total

Teapicking in Kericho. (Jesper Kirknæs)

tea production in 1977 (see Table II.12). In 1975 11.6 per cent of the smallholdings in Kenya were growing tea.[11]

The production of *pyrethrum* was introduced in Kiambu in Central Province in the mid-fifties but by 1959 Kisii had overtaken Kiambu as the most important pyrethrum producing area. Total pyrethrum production increased with an annual rate of 4.6 per cent between 1959 and 1977. The rapid increase in production between 1959 and 1967 was led by smallholder

[11] *Ibid.*

Table II.12. *Smallholder tea production 1959–1977 ('000 metric tons).*

	Smallholder production	Total production	Share of smallholder production in total, %
1959	0.1	12.4	0.8
1960	0.1	13.6	0.7
1961	0.2	12.4	1.6
1962	0.3	16.2	1.8
1963	0.5	17.8	2.8
1964	0.9	20.2	4.5
1965	1.4	18.9	7.4
1966	1.9	21.4	8.9
1967	2.8	22.8	12.3
1968	.	29.8	.
1969	.	31.1	.
1970	7.8	41.1	19.0
1971	11.3	36.3	31.1
1972	14.6	53.3	27.4
1973	14.7	56.6	26.0
1974	16.1	53.4	30.2
1975	19.4	56.7	34.2
1976	27.7	62.0	44.6
1977	31.9	86.3	37.0

Source: Republic of Kenya, *Statistical Abstract* 1968 and Republic of Kenya, *Economic Survey,* 1975, 1976, 1977, 1978 and 1979.

production which increased at an annual rate of 32.7 per cent while large farm production decreased by 10.7 per cent in this period. Thereby, the share of smallholders in total pyrethrum production increased from 12.5 per cent in 1959 to 86.5 per cent in 1967.

Production has stagnated since 1967 but with rather big fluctuations caused by weather conditions and prices paid to farmers (see Tables II.10 and II.13). Pyrethrum production is still dominated by smallholders but production is much more concentrated regionwise than the production of coffee and tea. Only 9.0 per cent of smallholders in Kenya grew pyrethrum in 1974–75.[12]

Among the food crops the production of *maize* expanded very rapidly. The substitution of maize for sorghums and millets continued in the sixties. In 1930, sorghums and millets accounted for well over 40 per cent of the area in Nyanza and Western Provinces, and as high as 74 per cent in South Nyanza and Kisii. In Central Kenya the percentages varied from 10 per cent to 30 per cent but there was less at the Coast. By 1969/70, the role of sorghums and millets had decreased substantially in all districts, some districts

[12] *Ibid.*

Table II.13. *Smallholder pyrethrum production ('000 tons).*

	Smallholder production	Total production	Share of smallholders
1959	0.6	4.8	12.5
1960	1.8	8.5	
1961	2.8	10.3	
1962	2.7	10.0	
1963	1.8	5.7	
1964	2.2	4.3	
1965	3.3	6.2	
1966	6.8	9.3	
1967	9.6	11.1	86.5
1968			
1969			
1970			
1971			
1972			
1973	9.9	11.6	85
1974	12.5	14.4	87
1975		15.4	
1976		12.8	
1977		11.3	
1978			

Source: Republic of Kenya. *Statistical Abstract 1968* and Republic of Kenya, *Economic Survey 1973,* 1976, 1977 and 1978.

recording none, the majority less than 10 per cent, and the highest, Kisumu district, only 27 per cent of the area planted.[13]

Since 1964 the production of maize has increased substantially to a large extent due to the introduction of hybrid maize. Marketed output of maize increased at an annual rate of 1.6 per cent (see Table II.10). The share of smallholders in marketed output varied according to weather conditions and prices paid by the Board compared with local market prices (see Table II.14), but approximately 90 per cent of the total maize crop is now produced on smallholdings.[14]

The relative importance of maize as a source of cash income decreased in the fifties and early sixties (see Table II.9) but has since been increasing. According to findings from the Integrated Rural Survey 1974/75 maize provided 18.2 per cent of the sales of agricultural produce by smallholdings. (see Table II.15). Most of the maize produced by smallholdings is still consumed by the peasant family. In 1974/75, 52.4 per cent of local maize and 62.1 per cent of hybrid maize was consumed by the producers.[15]

[13] Heyer, J. "The origins. . ., *op.cit.,* p. 171.
[14] Senga, W.M., "Kenya's Agricultural sector", in Heyer et al., *op.cit.,* p. 75.
[15] Republic of Kenya, Rural Integrated Survey 1974/75, *op.cit.,* tables 9.9 and 9.10.

Table II.14. *Smallholder maize marketed ('000 metric tons) through the marketing board.*

	Smallholder marketed output ('000 tons)	Total marketed output ('000 tons)	Share of smallholders (%)
1959	79.7	183.8	43.4
1960	72.2	167.8	43.0
1961	63.0	153.2	41.1
1962	69.3	150.1	46.2
1963	96.7	199.4	48.5
1964	33.2	86.9	38.2
1965	47.9	104.5	45.8
1966	71.9	132.0	54.5
1967	75.0	235.1	31.9
1968		352.6	
1969		280.3	
1970		205.7	
1971	116.9	254.6	45.9
1972		373.0	
1973		440.8	
1974		356.4	
1975		487.8	
1976		564.8	
1977		424.0[1]	

Source: For the years 1959–1967, Republic of Kenya, *Statistical Abstract 1968;* for later years *Statistical Abstract 1975* and *1977.*

[1] See note to Table II.10 for an explanation of the low value of maize marketed through the board.

Only 20 per cent of smallholder sales of maize was marketed through the Maize Marketing Board in 1976/77 (see Table II.8) and this percentage has further decreased in 1977/78 due to lack of storage capacity with the Board.

In comparison with coffee, tea and pyrethrum the production of maize is much more equally distributed over the country. Thus, by 1974/75, 86.1 per cent of all smallholdings were growing local maize and 50.2 per cent were growing hybrid maize. Only 24.1 per cent of the smallholdings were still growing finger millet and 30.0 per cent sorghum in 1974/75.[16] These crops are more drought resistant than maize and are therefore advantageous in areas of low and unreliable rainfall like, e.g., Kisumu district, and they also have the advantage of being more nutritious.[17]

Like maize, the production of *pulses, potatoes, and vegetables* has contributed to the growth of smallholder production. The total growth of marketed production of these crops has been 69.0 per cent annually between 1964 and 1977. Of these products only beans are marketed through marketing boards

[16] *Ibid.,* tables 9.2., 9.3., 9.4., and 9.5

[17] Heyer, J., "The origins. . .", *op.cit.* p. 171.

Table II.15. *Average value per small holding of production and sales by province, 1974/75 (K. shs.).*

	Central Province	Coast Province	Eastern Province	Nyanza Province	Rift Valley Prov.	Western Province	National Average K. shs.	%
Food crops sales	369	168	421	994	475	291	528	44.3
of which Maize sales	–	–	–	–	–	–	217	18.2
Export crops sales	411	2	337	192	115	20	231	19.4
Net cattle sales	218	154	299	–161[1]	577	136	143	12.0
Net livestock sales	122	99	134	10	260	42	88	7.4
Milk sales	171	126	143	149	479	61	201	16.9
Total sales	1491	549	1334	1184	1906	550	1192	100.0
Sales as % of total production	47.5	45.0	53.6	38.2	47.2	36.2	44.8	

Source: Republic of Kenya, Economic Survey 1978, p. 99.

[1] Negative value due to extensive cattle purchases.

but it seems reasonable to assume that produce marketed by the producers themselves or by small traders has increased at least at an equal rate. Most of these products, however, are primarily consumed by the household itself. By 1974/75, 77.2 per cent of the beans and 70.2 per cent of the English potatoes were used for home consumption, but sales of these products probably accounted for almost 10 per cent of total sales from smallholdings in 1974/75. Almost 70 per cent of all smallholdings were growing beans and 32 per cent were growing English potatoes that year.[18]

Livestock and *dairy production* has expanded rapidly since the late fifties. Smallholder dairy production dates back at least to the 1920's, but the restrictions imposed by the colonial authorities prevented its emergence as a significant sector until the late fifties and early sixties. Previously, dairy production has been dominated by the estates, which also controlled the Kenya Cooperative Creameries which was the single official outlet for dairy produce.

Production of dairy products depends upon improvement of the genetic potential of the stock. Some estimates show that the average unimproved zebu cow gives between 150 and 380 litres of milk per annum, while exotic

[18] Republic of Kenya, Rural Integrated Survey, *op.cit.,* Tables 9.6. and 9.7.

and grade (mixed exotic and zebu) cattle give between 800 and as much as 3,000 litres per annum.[19]

Exotic stock on smallholdings did not obtain official support in the highland areas until 1955, but in the later 1950's and early 1960's support was still very restricted and in some districts very high standards of husbandry, fodder crops and water supplies had to be demonstrated before individuals were officially supported for grade cattle. For these reasons and due to the unwillingness of Europeans to sell stock to Africans the number of peasants keeping grade cattle was very small. Thus, in 1962, the vast majority of the estimated 330,000 grade cattle were held in the estates.[20]

But since the beginning of the 1960's the number of grade cattle on smallholdings has increased from 49,400 in 1963 to 1,525,200 in 1974, an annual rate of increase of 33.1 per cent. Due to the drought the number had fallen to 1,391, 700 in 1975.[2] Thus, by the mid-1970's, the majority of grade herds were kept by African peasants.[22]

As a consequence the production of dairy products increased rapidly. Marketed output via the formal marketing system rose at an average annual rate of 7.6 per cent between 1959 and 1977, and smallholdings increased their share in total marketed production from 3.8 per cent in 1959 to approx. 95 per cent in 1974/75.[23] Thereby, the significance of dairy products in total cash income to small farmers increased from 2.6 per cent in 1958, 7.8 per cent in 1967 (see Table II.9), and to 16.9 per cent in 1974/75 (see Table II.15). But in addition to this, dairy products produced and consumed within the peasant households make a significant contribution to the diet in the rural areas. According to the findings from the Integrated Rural Survey 1974/75 as much as 60 per cent of the milk production on smallholdings was consumed by the household itself, and made up as much as 11.6 per cent of their total consumption expenditure.[24]

Livestock was the most important source of cash revenue to producers in the late fifties. This was particularly the case for smallholdings. In 1959 livestock contributed 16.4 per cent to total cash revenue to producers, but for smallholdings the share of livestock was as high as 22.1 per cent.

The marketing of livestock products has grown at a rather high rate of 7.7

[19] Raikes, P., "The development of a middle-peasantry in Kenya. Discussion of some hypotheses and examples from the dairy and horticulture sectors", *CDR project papers A.78.3.*, Center for Development Research, Copenhagen 1978.

[20] *Ibid.*, p. 17.

[21] Republic of Kenya, *Statistical Abstract 1977,* table 124.

[22] Raikes, P., *op.cit.*, p. 17.

[23] These figures are calculated from Republic of Kenya, *Statistical Abstract* 1964 and 1977, and Republic of Kenya, *Integrated Rural Survey. Basic Report* 1974/75.

[24] Republic of Kenya, Integrated Rural Survey, *op.cit.* Tables 8.14, 8.16, and 8.24.

Grade cattle are driven to the cattledip. (Jesper Kirknæs)

per cent annually between 1959 and 1977 so that the share of livestock in total marketed output only decreased slowly until the mid-1970's. However, due to the drastic increase in the value of coffee, tea and maize in 1976 and 1977 the share of livestock products in the value of marketed output had fallen to 5.2 per cent in 1977.[25]

Only a minor proportion of the livestock slaughtered in Kenya is sold in the formal marketing system. In 1969 it was estimated that 75 per cent of the slaughterings in Kenya were undertaken by small rural butchers.[26] The role of the smallholdings in the production and sale of livestock can

[25] Republic of Kenya, Economic Survey 1978, *op.cit.,* table 8.3.
[26] Republic of Kenya, *Economic Survey 1969,* p. 75.

Table II.16. *Marketed output per head from shallholders. K. shs.*

	1948	1962	1969		1974/75[1]	
			K. shs.	rank	K. shs.	rank
Western	6	14	33.8	(6)	159.4	(5)
Nyanza	.	.	37.2	(5)	423.9	(1)
of which						
Kisumu district	.	.	14.8		145.3[2]	
Kisii district	.	.	61.6		386.3[2]	
Rift	.	28	51.2	(4)	410.9	(2)
Central	10	46	107.4	(1)	305.0	(3)
Eastern	.	.	73.2	(2)	283.5	(4)
Coast	8	30	58.4	(3)	103.0	(6)
of which						
Taita Hills	.		87.4			
Kwale district	.		38.1			
National average (unweighted)	.	29.5	60.2		298.6	

Source: Statistical Abstract and District Agricultural reports. Quoted from Heyer, J., "The origins . . ., *op. cit.,* table 7. The 1974/75 figures are calculated from the Integrated Rural Survey, *op. cit.,* table 8.4.

[1] The 1974/75 figures are net operations surpluses, i.e., the value of *all* agricultural production less total production cost.
[2] Figures calculated from the Household Budget Survey, Nyanza Province 1970/71 published in Kisumu District Plan 1975.

therefore not be deducted from official figures of marketed output. However, information collected by the Integrated Rural Survey 1974/75 shows that by 1975, 94 per cent of the smallholder cattle and 100 per cent of all other livestock was sold in the rural markets (see Table II.8). The total income from sales of livestock by smallholders that year was estimated at 17 mill. K. £ which compares to approx. 24 mill. K. £ value of sales from pastoral areas and large farms.[27]

Thus, livestock and livestock products continue to play a very important role as a source of cash income to smallholdings. In 1975 the sales of cattle and other livestock contributed 19.4 per cent of total sales from smallholdings, which was more than the income from maize sales and equal to total incomes from sales of export crops (see Table II.15).

Behind the impressive growth of the small farm sector outlined above, however, there emerges a picture of *substantial regional inequality* since the

[27] The value of marketed production from pastoral areas and large farms is estimated as 94 per cent of the total value of marketed cattle plus 100 per cent of the value of other marketed livestock in 1975. Source: Economic Survey 1978, *op.cit.,* table 8.3.

products that have led the expansion in output are all products that are only suitable in the high potential areas with plenty of rain.

The districts that have really contributed to the tremendous growth of marketed output since the later 1950's are Kisii, Nyeri, Kiambu, Muranga, Kirinyaga and Meru and to a lesser extent Embu and Kericho.

In Table II.16 the regional differences in marketed output per head in 1948, 1962 and 1969 have been estimated based upon District Agricultural Reports. It should be emphasized that these comparisons should be treated with caution since unrecorded marketed output is omitted from these statistics. There is therefore a tendency to underestimate production in areas producing mainly foodcrops and dairy products which to a large extent are marketed in the rural markets. The 1974/75 figures are calculated from the Rural Integrated Survey which included the value of produce marketed by small traders or by the producer himself. In interpreting these data it should also be kept in mind that only agricultural incomes are included in these figures. This is important as non-agricultural incomes account for as much as 43.2 per cent on average of smallholder income but with big variations between provinces, ranging from 75.1 per cent in Coast Province to 28.7 per cent in Nyanza Province.[28]

When figures of marketed output to cooperatives and marketing boards are used, the dominance of Central Province is clear. In 1969 the five districts in Central Province ranked as number 1, 4, 5, 6, and 10 as far as marketed output was concerned.[29] The districts selected for our study were ranked as follows among 21 districts: Taita Hills (8), Kisii District (11), Kwale District (16), and Kisumu District (19).

But as can be seen from the table, the dominance of Central Province has disappeared in the 1974/75 figures. This is partly because agricultural produce sold in local markets is more important in Nyanza and Rift Province than in Central Province and partly because production costs are higher in Central Province than elsewhere.[30]

Unfortunately the information from the Rural Integrated Survey 1974/75 has not been broken down into districts. But from District Agricultural Reports the development in the selected four districts from the late 1950's to 1975 can be traced.

Kisumu District is one of the districts which has benefitted the least from the expansion in smallholder production since the late fifties. As mentioned above, the district ranked as number 19 out of 21 districts in 1969 as far as the value of marketed output per capita is concerned.

[28] Republic of Kenya, Integrated Rural Survey 1974/75, *op.cit.,* table 8.8.
[29] See Heyer, J., "The origins. . . ., *op.cit.,* table 7.
[30] See Republic of Kenya, Integrated Rural Survey 1974/75, *op.cit.* table 8.24.

Typical scenery from the Kano Plains, Kisumu District. (Jesper Kirknæs)

The reason for this is that the climatic conditions in most of the smallholder areas of the district, e.g., the temperature and the rainfall, are unfavourable to the growth of the successful crops, coffee, tea, pyrethrum, and hybrid maize.

Cotton was introduced as a cash crop in the district by the British Government as early as 1901 but the peasants never showed any enthusiasm for the crop, mainly due to the lack of positive price incentives, but also due

Table II.17. *Land use on small farms in Kenyan Districts 1969/70*[1] *(%).*

	Maize	Sorghum and Millets	Roots	Pulses	Cotton	Bananas	Sugar	Coffee	Tea	Pyreth-rum	Coco nuts	Cashew nuts	Other	TOTAL	Mixed crop index[2]
Western	46	13	14	9	5	7	2	1	1	0	0	0	2	100	1.39
Nyanza	41	20	10	11	9	3	2	2	1	2	0	0	5	101	1.62
of which															
Kisumu	38	27	12	15	1	2	3	0	0	0	0	0	3	101	1.83
Kisii	48	10	5	4	0	10	2	9	4	7	0	0	2	101	1.33
Central	36	1	8	26	1	11	2	6	1	3	0	0	5	100	1.80
Rift	67	6	3	10	0	0	10	0	4	0	0	0	1	101	1.19
Eastern	32	9	7	34	3	4	2	2	0	1	0	0	5	99	1.92
Coast	28	1	14	3	1	6	1	0	0	0	18	15	13	100	2.13
of which															
Taita Hills	30	1	14	19	2	7	5	3	0	0	0	0	19	100	2.09
Kwale	30	4	19	0	0	5	1	0	0	0	13	12	16	100	2.09

Source: Statistical Abstract 1977.

[1] Crops grown in mixtures are double counted. The importance of foodcrops is therefore exaggerated in this table.
[2] Calculated as the aggregate area of crops divided by the total cultivated area.

to the fact that cotton has to be planted at the same time as food-crops and therefore competes with these for land and labour.[31] In the mid-thirties there was a major effort to increase the production of cotton in South Nyanza and Kisumu District. This accounted for most of the expansion of cotton acreage and production in Nyanza and Western Province from approx. 5,600 ha. and 170.0 tons of cotton lint in 1930 to 37,600 ha. and 2,056.2 tons of cotton lint in 1940. But during the last thirty years cotton production has stagnated, despite administrative enthusiasm and extension efforts.[32]

As can be seen from Table II.17, Nyanza Province is one of the more important cotton producing areas in Kenya but most of the cotton is produced in South Nyanza District. By 1969/70 only 800 ha. or 5 per cent of the cotton area in the Province was in Kisumu District.[33]

According to the Integrated Rural Survey, 17 per cent of the smallholdings in Nyanza Province were growing cotton in 1974/75.[34] Assuming the same distribution of cotton growing between districts as in 1969/70 and an equal average size of cotton plots in the various districts it can be estimated that only 3,250 smallholdings or 5.4 per cent of the approx. 60,000[35] small farms in Kisumu District were growing cotton in 1974/75.

Besides the introduction of cotton there have been three major changes in the cropping patterns in the districts since the 1920's. First, the local variety of yellow maize began to be superseded by European introduced white maize in the 1920's and as the latter gave higher yields it soon replaced the local variety of maize and to a lesser extent the indigenous sorghum, which has the advantage of being drought resistant and well suited to the black-cotton soils of Kisumu district. Thus, the share of maize in total cultivated land increased from 27 per cent in 1930 to 35 per cent in 1950, to 38 per cent in 1969/70 while the share of sorghum and millets decreased from 47 per cent in 1930 to 31 per cent in 1950, to 27 per cent in 1969/70.[36] Hybrid maize has been available in Kisumu district since the mid-sixties but by 1969/70 it was only cultivated on 2 per cent of all the land under maize in the district. Since hybrid maize could yield almost three times as much per hectare and approx. two and a half times as much per labour-input it would

[31] See Atwood, R.H., *Cotton-growing in Central Nyanza Province, Kenya 1901–39: An Appraisal of African Reactions to Imposed Government Policy.*, Ph.D. dissertation, Michigan State University, 1975, and Moody, T., "Peasant Agriculture, Commercial Production and Employment in Kenya", in *Africa Development,* vol 1, No 2 1976, p. 66.

[32] *Ibid.,* table 2, p. 66.

[33] Republic of Kenya, *Statistical Abstract 1977,* table 92, p. 114.

[34] Republic of Kenya, Rural Integrated Survey 1974/75, *op.cit.* table 9.8, p. 83.

[35] By 1969 there were 52,040 small farms in Kisumu District with an average size of 1.5 ha. See Republic of Kenya, Statistical Abstract 1970, table 79 (a).

[36] See Carlsen, J. and Moody, T., *op.cit.,* p. 39, table 9.

seem beneficial to speed up the adoption of hybrid maize. However, it appears that the climatic uncertainty and low levels of cash liquidity make it difficult for the small peasants in Kisumu district to benefit from hybrid maize.[37]

Secondly, sugarcane has been adopted by peasant holdings in areas immediately adjacent to the sugar-belt. This has been perhaps the only major production development in Kisumu district within the context of the Swynnerton Plan.

Cultivation of sugarcane occurs both on individual smallholdings and also upon co-operatively owned blocks. The latter consist of areas of land that have been taken from individual peasant occupation by the administration, and put under the direction of the sugar belt co-operative union, from which neighbouring smallholders can invest in a share of the block cultivation. Outside those blocks there is a localized area where individual smallholders can "manage" their farm production systems within the productive matrix of maize / sorghum / pulses as subsistence crops and sugarcane and cotton as cash crops.

The cash income possibilities of sugarcane for growers in this small area are not startling. Growers can only market their cane by private treaty with a transporter, who is hired by the cooperative union. After all the transport deductions and cooperative cesses the net income to the producer is approx. 40 K.shs per ton. Smallholder yields are in the order of 25 tons per hectare

[37] My colleague, Tony Moody, investigated this problem in detail. He concludes:

"The effect of climatic uncertainty upon yields is illustrated by the results of yield trials at the Agricultural Research Station at Kibos. For 5 consecutive years hybrid maize and local sorghum were cultivated at the same place – and presumably without lacking any care in cultivation. However, in the same years, the yields of sorghum varied far less than the yields of the hybrid maize – comparing standard deviation of yields with mean results, the coefficients of variation were 25% for sorghum yields and 67% for hybrid maize yields.

At the same time the average levels of the yields of each crop were similar: therefore when hybrid maize yields varied below average, they consisted of very low returns/hectare compared with the more resilient sorghum yields. Even in optimum growing conditions, hybrid maize only yielded more than sorghum in 2 out of 5 years.

To plant hybrid maize it is necessary to buy new seed issue every year. At 20 shg. per 10 kg. packet it costs approximately 45 shg. to purchase enough seed to plant one hectare. Normal yields would cover this cost, but the seed must be purchased when household cash-flow of agricultural incomes is at its lowest point. In Kisii district the regular monthly incomes from tea and coffee are available but in Kisumu district, as we show, cotton incomes etc. are not so regular. This must be a disincentive in embarking upon hybrid maize production. The actual situation has also been such that this factor and the uncertainty of hybrid maize yields (unpredictable rainfall) have produced an overall weak demand for the seed. This has discouraged stockists and distributors, and there is a de facto poor availability of seed.

These are probably sound enough reasons together to explain the lack of innovation in grain cultivation in Kisumu district."

Quoted from *Ibid.* p. 52.

Table II.18. *Sugarcane production from smallholders and blocks in Kisumu District, 1970–75.*

Year	1970	1971	1973	1975
Tonnage	106,000	116,000	117,000	96,000

Source: Information collected from cooperatives in the district. Quoted from Carlsen, J. and Moody, T., *op. cit.* p. 61.

for the first crop, maturing over 2 years, and less for the subsequent ratoon crops. This would give an approximate annual income of 500 K.shs per hectare, gross of the producer's own costs. It is higher than average annual income from cotton, which at 200 kg./ha. would be 380 K.shs but is also considerably more labour intensive. Thus, although expansion in small-holder sugarcane production was rapid in the decade following the Swynnerton Plan, the area now cultivated may be an effective maximum area within the district.

The smallholder sugarcane area expanded from zero in 1960 to 3,600 hectares in 1968, but fell to 1,200 hectares in 1969.[38]

Statistics for cane delivered from the smallholder societies show a levelling-off of output, which could also be interpreted as a decline of planting since 1973 (Table II.18).

Sugar prices paid to farmers have increased rapidly in recent years from 62 K.shs. per ton of sugarcane in 1974 to 127 K.shs. per ton in 1977 and as a result smallholder sugarcane production has expanded in Kenya from 427,595 tons in 1974 to 630,374 tons in 1977.

There are no figures available for sugar production by smallholders in Kisumu District since 1975, but it has probably followed the general tendency outlined above.

Finally, there has been an increase in the area cultivated by paddy rice since the 1950's. The area planted increased from 720 hectares in 1960 to approx. 4000 hectares in 1975. Of this area 1500 hectares were in the Ahero Irrigation Scheme. The remainder of the district's paddy is grown in the low-lying areas of the Nyando river below Ahero, and on the marsh land around Nyakach Bay. The production of rice has grown significantly since the 1950's and most of it now enters the local district markets. In 1976/77 another 810 hectares of irrigated rice was added to the cultivated area by the new West Kano Irrigation Scheme. When fully developed this scheme will also produce sugarcane.[39]

[38] Republic of Kenya, *Statistical Abstract 1970 and 1977,* table 79(b) and table 92, respectively.
[39] Republic of Kenya, *Economic Survey 1978,* p. 111.

Table II.19. *Estimated value of produce sales from Central Nyanza District 1949–1964 (K. £).*

	1949	1954	1958	1962	1964	1969
Maize	49,266	45,700	3,521	21,653	93,175	
Sorghum and Millets	588	11,282	894	4,000	3,002	
Rice (Paddy)	5,759	28,790	98,290	2,998	17,920	
Pulses	311	4,000	3,673	1,202	43,551	
Cassava	3,774	.	.	.	717	
Groundnuts	1,884	72	9,871	15,556	64,575	
Bananas		500	28,000	6,000	6,000	
Cotton	106,304	125,790	86,967	92,128	114,724	
Sugarcane	.	.	.	6,060	270,207	
Coffee	.	.	.	640	4,000	
Sisal	449	.	.	45,000	71,421	
Total crops	168,335	216,134	231,216	195,237	689,292	
Dairy products	.	3,148	3,244	1,393	1,600	
Livestock	.	290,000	290,000	582,500	345,600	
Total	168,335	509,282	524,460	779,130	1,046,482	579,000
Population	423,000	492,400	556,400	627,000	678,700	784,000
Marketed output per head (K. shs.)	8.0	20.7	18.9	24.9	30.8	14.8

Source: Republic of Kenya, "A Report on Economic Studies of Farming in Nyanza Province 1963", *Farm Economic Report No. 26,* Nairobi 1969, and District Annual Reports 1948–1953.

[1] The figures are calculated at the basis of assumed average size holdings of 6 persons.

The limited adoption of maize in place of sorghum and the more recent introduction of smallholder sugarcane and irrigated rice growing has had a positive impact on agricultural incomes. But these improvements have had a relatively limited effect and have been insufficient to secure rising average levels of standards of living for the population of the district.

Most of the agricultural output figures available for the 1950's and 1960's are aggregate at the Nyanza Province level and it would be a hazardous task to compute the value of agricultural production of Kisumu District based on these figures. But there is evidence that the district has imported more and more food over time and that income from sales of cash crops has remained very low. As can be seen from Table II.19 the value of marketed output per head increased between 1949 to 1964 mainly due to the introduction of paddy rice and sugarcane. But the value of marketed output decreased again between 1964 and 1969. These figures are based upon rough estimates given in Annual District Reports from Central Nyanza (Siaya District plus Kisumu District) and should be interpreted with great caution. But the development trends in these figures are confirmed by sample surveys

Table II.20. *Production of major crops (exclusive cotton) in Central Nyanza 1960/61 and Kisumu District 1970/71.*

	Value of output per household (shs)	
	1960/61[1]	1970/71
Maize	324	156
Millet/Sorghum	219	98
Pulses	79	27
Cassava[2]	88	149
Sweet potatoes	10	140
Rice	4	11
Sugarcane	0	16
Total	724	597

Source: Government of Kenya, Kenya African Agricultural Sample Census, 1960/61 and unpublished data from The Nyanza Household Budget Survey 1970/71.

[1] Yields are valued at 1959 prices as paid to producers in the district since no better figures were available.
[2] No yield figures were available. The estimate is based on an average yield of 20 bags/acre valued at 1959 prices.

undertaken for the African Agricultural Sample Surveys in 1960/61 for Central Nyanza and in 1970/71 for Kisumu District.

Based on these two surveys we have estimated the value of the produce of the major crops per household in the two years (See Table II.20). It should be noted here that the figures are not directly comparable since the 1960/61 figures include Siaya District and also the sampling methods used are not the same. Moreover, the figures are not corrected for differences in rainfall in the two years and the differences in income per household might therefore just be due to this factor.

The value of cotton production is not included in the table. Approximately 800 ha. were planted in both years in Kisumu District and assuming good yields, cotton production would probably have contributed another 30–40 K.shs. to household incomes. Another important source of income not included in this table is sale of hides and skins and sales of livestock. No reliable figures are available. The table shows the very low level of crop production in the district that makes it necessary for the households to supplement their low cash income from agriculture with income from other sources. In 1970/71 the average family was far from self-sufficient in food. Of their total consumption of cereals, pulses, roots and tubers and vegetables only approximately 80 per cent was covered by their own production.[40] In

[40] This figure is calculated from *Nyanza Province Household Budget Survey, 1970/71* (unpublished).

Table II.21. *Agricultural income per household in Kisumu District 1970/71.*

	K. shs.	%
Food production	718.7	75
Animal products	181.8	19
Industrial crops	55.4	6
Total	955.9	100

Source: Kisumu District plan 1975.

years with bad weather conditions the dependence on alternative sources of income for food purchases is even higher.

From the Nyanza Province Household Budget Survey 1970/71 the absolute level and composition of agricultural incomes in Kisumu District is given in Table II.21 below. It should be emphasized that the rural households in the district receive most of their income from various non-agricultural activities (see Chapter III).

Although it is not possible to draw any firm conclusions from the poor statistical information available it seems likely that the value of agricultural production per household in real terms (purchasing power) has decreased over the years. Agricultural incomes per household in the area have probably gone down due to the increase in population and the consequent growing shortage of land and possibly also due to a decrease in the fertility of the soil, although we have no scientific proof that such a decrease in the fertility of the soil has actually taken place.

Kisii District on the other hand is one of the districts that have benefitted most from the introduction of various cash crops since the fifties. Thus in 1969, Kisii District ranked first of all Kenyan Districts as far as tea and pyrethrum production was concerned and the district ranked sixth in terms of coffee production. Despite the high population density in the district it has therefore been possible to obtain relatively high per capita incomes from sales of marketed output. In 1969 Kisii District ranked 11 in the value of marketed output per head (see Table II.16).

The expansion in the production of coffee, tea, pyrethrum and hybrid maize is summarised in Table II.22.

As can be seen from this table *coffee* was the first crop to spread through the district. Coffee had been introduced as a cash crop in the district as early as 1933 but due to white settler fear of competition the government imposed severe restrictions on the acreage of coffee that could be planted by Africans. Between 1933–41 there was a 100 acres maximum and between 1941–51

Table II.22. *Increase in smallholder cash crop cultivation in Kisii District 1956–74.*

	Coffee		Tea		Pyrethrum		Maize		
Year	ha.	% of Kenya total	ha.	% of Kenya total	ha.	% of Kenya total	Hybrid Maize (ha.)	Other varieties (ha.)	Total (ha.)
1956	876	18.0	–	.	64	5.9	.	.	.
1959	1537	14.0	50	3.8	2000	62.5	.	.	.
1964	5204	10.2	656	12.8	.	.	.	.	.
1968	7160	12.7	1726	12.9	5100	29.7	7350	13300	20650
1970	6904	11.1	2496	12.2	4800	31.4	11800	11000	22800
1971	6500	10.4	3229	15.8	9260	39.2	27300	14000	41300
1973	6700	7.3	5615	16.3	8900	32.8	32000	10000	42000

Source: Co-operative society reports, Kisii district, Heyer, J. "The origins . ." *op. cit.* Appendix tables 3 and 4. Republic of Kenya, *Statistical Abstract 1977* and District Agricultural Reports.

a 200 acres maximum on coffee planting in the district.[41] But coffee had become rather popular as a cash crop in the district and as soon as the area restrictions were lifted at the beginning of the fifties the planting of coffee trees spread rapidly. The rapid expansion was made possible by a change from compulsory block plantations to a system of individual plantations.[42] Most of the annual acreage expansion was due to its adoption by new growers, and over time, from location to location in the district. Planting started in Central Kitutu division and over the years expanded to neighbouring subdivisions in the northern and western parts of the district.[43]

Another feature of coffee planting has been that many of the households that started by growing coffee in the densely populated areas did not adopt the subsequently introduced pyrethrum or tea to the same extent as non-coffee growers. While coffee spread from the west of the district towards the east, the opposite was the case with pyrethrum.[44] Moreover, it was the opinion of the Department of Agriculture that coffee should be the principal cash crop of the area, and that tea should be confined to the higher areas not suited for coffee.[45]

[41] See Barnes, C., *An Experiment with African Coffee Growing in Kenya: The Gusii, 1933–1950.* Ph.d dissertation, Department of History, Michigan State University, U.S.A. 1976 (unpublished).

[42] Maxon, R., *op.cit.* p. 279.

[43] Garst, R.D., *The Spatial Diffusion of Agricultural Innovations in Kisii District,* Kenya. Ph.d. dissertation. Michigan State University, Department of Geography, U.S.A., 1972 (unpublished) pp. 124–140.

[44] *Ibid.,* pp. 129–132 and pp. 145–147.

[45] Maxon, R., *op.cit.,* p. 316.

The number of coffee growers in the district has increased from 3,425 in 1956 to 36,140 in 1963.[46] Coffee planting reached a peak in 1964 and has not increased significantly since due to the imposition of quota limits under the International Coffee Agreement. Since the late sixties the number of growers has stagnated, and there has even been a decline from 55,000 growers in 1969 to 51.000 growers in the district in 1973. According to the Integrated Rural Survey 1974/75, 20.7 per cent of the 386,431 households in Nyanza Province were growing 13,800 hectares of coffee in 1974/75. Approx. 90 per cent of these households are in Kisii District which means that approx. 70,000 smallholdings or 54 per cent of all the peasants in the district were growing coffee that year.

The first few commercial *pyrethrum* plots were planted in Kitutu location in 1950, but it was not until 1956 that the adoption began to increase rapidly, moving from the eastern border of the district towards the west. Pyrethrum has proven to be particularly popular with the Kisii peasants because of its desirable characteristics such as high profitability and the ease of establishing a new plot. Moreover, it can be adopted in small areas that are amenable to the intensive Kisii farming system.[47]

Between 1956 and 1959 the acreage planted with pyrethrum increased from 64 hectares to 2000 hectares and Kisii became the dominant pyrethrum producing area of the country with 62.5 per cent of the cultivated smallholder area. By 1960 approx. 40 per cent of the Kisii smallholders were growing pyrethrum.[48] It was feared that the Kisii growers would suffer as overproduction set in and therefore the acreage planted was reduced by the introduction of a system of individual production quotas in 1962. According to this quota system the peasants would receive lower payments for over- or underproduction. After that date pyrethrum adoption continued at a reduced rate until 1968 when 5100 hectares were planted by 36000 growers.

Since then, price changes have been the biggest influence over the area planted, with the planted area increasing to 9000 hectares in 1971, after the price had risen from K.shs. 2.93 per kilo to K.shs. 4.40 per kilo. The change in area was made up of a 25 per cent increase in the number of growers, and a 70 per cent increase in the average area that each smallholder planted.[49]

According to the Integrated Rural Survey 9,900 hectares were cultivated in Kisii district in 1974/75 by approx. 71,000 growers or 71 per cent of all the peasant households in the district.

[46] *Ibid.,* p. 350.
[47] Garst, R.D., *op.cit.* p. 141.
[48] *Ibid.,* p. 141.
[49] Moody, T., *op.cit.* p. 66.

Table II.23. *Changes in land-use 1930–1974 in Kisii: estimated proportion of cultivated land under maize, millet and "cash" crops (per cent).*

	Maize	Finger Millet	Coffee, tea, pyrethrum	Other crops
1930	4	74	0	22
1950	38	41	0	20
1974	53	9	20	18

Source: Heyer, J., "The origins of regional inequalities in smallholder agriculture in Kenya, 1920–73", *op. cit.* table 1, *District Agricultural Reports* and *Statistical Abstracts.*

While the overall increase in the amount of pyrethrum grown was considerable, actual individual planted area per grower was as low as 0.14 hectare in 1974/75.

Tea was introduced later than coffee and pyrethrum and did not expand so rapidly as these crops in the first years. The first tea was introduced in 1957 in the north-east area of the district due to its proximity to the tea estates in Kericho district. It is not advisable to encourage teaproduction before the marketing organization has developed infrastructural facilities such as buying posts, feeder roads and regular collection. Thus, the adoption of tea depended upon the Special Crops Development Authority, which exercised and managed the nurseries in the district, controlled and supervised cultivation by smallholders, bought the green leaf, and arranged the manufacture and sale of tea. Only after the Independence when the Kenya Tea Development Authority took responsibility for these service facilities did the district see a wide adoptation of tea.

The acreage planted increased from 656 hectares in 1964 to 5,615 hectares in 1973 and the number of growers increased at approx. the same rate from 2,560 in 1964 to 16,200 in 1973 so that the average amount planted by smallholders has remained 0.3 hectares over the period.[50]

From the Integrated Rural Survey it can be estimated that 27,400 smallholdings in the district were cultivating 5,500 hectares of tea in 1974/75.

The expansion of coffee, pyrethrum and tea cultivation has of course to some extent been at the expense of the production of food crops. But as can be seen from Table II.23 the expansion in these crops has been at the expense of the more traditional low yielding grain, finger millet, rather than maize. The planting of high yielding hybrid maize has expanded rapidly

[50] *Ibid.*, p. 66.

since 1964 and as the individual smallholder has planted only small areas of cash crops the negative impact on food production has been limited.

The European introduced maize which was adopted in Kisumu district as early as in the 1920's did not begin to replace finger millet in Kisii until the Second World War. But by 1940–1945 the introduction of higher yielding white maize led to increased surplus production over subsistence needs in the district and maize became an important cash-earner in the district. In the years 1964–54, increasing acreages under maize, favourable weather conditions and good prices all contributed to this expanded production. The years 1950 and 1954 were especially marked by large exports of maize and even after the expansion of coffee and pyrethrum in the late fifties, maize remained the most important source of peasant cash income.

Only in 1963 did coffee surpass maize in terms of its value to the district as a cash crop and for a number of years the introduction of cash crops and the consequent decrease in food crop areas led to declining marketed surpluses of maize until the adoption of hybrid maize in the late sixties and beginning of the seventies.[51]

Hybrid maize was introduced in 1964 and the great increase in yield possible with the hybrid from about 2,500 kg./ha. with ordinary maize to over 4,000 kg./ha. from the hybrid, motivated the peasants to adopt the new seed very rapidly. In addition it appears that hybrid maize also yields higher returns to labour than local maize and finger millet.[52]

In fact, the planting of hybrid maize has expanded faster than any other crop since 1964 and here it is important to note that there has been little replacement of areas planted with other varieties of maize (see Table II.22). Much of the hybrid maize expansion has been at the expense of finger millet, the traditional food stable, and some of it must represent an intensive exploitation of the land-frontier, by cultivating previously uncultivated pasture and boundary land.

The replacement of finger millet cultivation by maize has certainly been widespread. Using the crudest levels of estimation, as available data is inadequate, it can be estimated that maize cultivation has increased by over 25,000 ha. in Kisii since the 1950's. At the same time finger millet cultivation has decreased by nearly 15,000 ha. Today almost 80 per cent of the maize planted is a hybrid variety. The fact that the yields from hybrid maize are approximately 1.6 times the yields from the earlier white maize and 2.2 times the yields of finger millet means that the adoption of hybrid maize has resulted in increased production, home consumption and sales.

[51] Maxon, R., *op.cit.* p. 317.

[52] Hubert, K. et al., *Agricultural Production in Kisii District, Kenya and Proposals for its Development,* Technische Universität, Berlin 1972.

Table II.24. *Aggregate cash incomes from the major crops in Kisii district (1959–72), mill. shs.*

	1959	1967–68 (average)	1971–72 (average)
Coffee	5.38	13.5	15.95
Pyrethrum	1.50	15.8	31.60
Tea	–	2.2	11.59
Maize	5.82	0.52	1.23
Total (million K. shs.)	12.70	32.22	60.37

Sources: R. Maxon, *op. cit.* and *District Co-operative Society Reports.*

Cattle, which in Gusii tribal agricultural economy were a major source of wealth and influence over land-use, still exert an influence. A relatively large proportion of the land is still under grazing and not cultivated.

But there has been no increase in the total amount of cattle in the district between 1960 and 1969 and although there has been quite a successful dairy scheme, with the introduction of grade cattle, it has been rather limited and most of the milk produced in the district is still consumed at home. The first grade cattle were introduced in 1961 and by 1967 the number had increased to 10,000[53] or 3.7 per cent of all cattle in the district. According to the Integrated Rural Survey the grade cattle in Nyanza Province numbered only 51,000 of which a maximum of 35,000 were estimated to be in Kisii District.

Thus, Kisii district has probably benefitted much less from dairy production than the high potential areas in Central Province.

As previously mentioned, Kisii District is one of the districts that have benefitted the most from the development process that has taken place in Kenya since the mid-fifties.

Before the introduction of coffee, pyrethrum, and tea, maize was the only source of cash-incomes in agriculture in Kisii. New cash-incomes have a much wider base. The production of these crops has shown a corresponding increase in the growth of aggregate cash incomes in Kisii. These are shown in Table II.24. It should be emphasized that the figure for maize includes only the very small proportion of the maize production which is marketed through the Maize Marketing Board (probably less than the national average of 20 per cent). The fall in officially marketed output between 1959 and 1967 is probably caused mostly by increased home consumption as population grew and cash crops expanded at the cost of food crops. But since 1967 it is likely that the expansion in hybrid maize has resulted in a much faster increase in marketed output than indicated in Table II.24 since most of the maize in Kisii district is sold in local markets rather than through the Maize

[53] Garst, R.D., *op.cit.* p. 178.

Table II.25. *Agricultural incomes in Kisii district, 1970–71 (K. shs.).*

	K. shs.	%
Food production	1,941.6	76
Animal products	365.3	14
Industrial crops	235.1	9
Total	2,542.0	99

Source: Kisumu District plan 1975.

Marketing Board. The tendency to sell in local markets has increased as the price differentials between the official maize price and the "free market" price obtainable in local markets increased at the beginning of the 1970's. The total income from sale of maize can thus be estimated at approx. 6.3 mill. K.shs. in 1971/72.[54]

Table II.24 shows that agricultural incomes from these sources have increased at an annual rate of 13.6 per cent between 1959 and 1972. Total agricultural incomes have, of course, grown less rapidly.

In 1973 total agricultural incomes have been estimated at 190 mill. shs. or equivalent to 1682 shs. per household.[55] The result of the household budget survey of Nyanza Province undertaken in 1970/71 is given in Table II.25.

The table shows that agricultural incomes in Kisii were shs. 2,542 or 2.7 times as high as in Kisumu District. Therefore, contrary to the peasants of Kisumu District who had a food deficit and had to use approximately 250 shs. to supplement their own food-production, the peasants in Kisii produced a net surplus of agricultural commodities for sale after own consumption which yielded an average income of 296 shs. per household.

Taita Hills district was ranked highest among the four districts included in this study in terms of marketed output per capita in 1969. Among 21 districts Taita Hills ranked 8th, only surpassed by the high potential areas in Central, Rift and Eastern Province (see Table II.16). But the agricultural development in the district has been based upon vegetables as a cash crop rather than coffee, pyrethrum, tea and hybrid maize as in the high potential areas. As shown above (Table II.4) Taita Hills has less high potential land equivalents per capita than the Central Province and this land had already been used for

[54] Derived as 1.23 mill. times 5 (officially marketed output equal to 20 per cent of the total marketed output).

[55] Oström, I.S. and Oström, K., *Rural Industrial Development Centers in the Kisii District and the Siaya District, Nyanza* Province, Kenya. March 1974.

high priced cash crops like vegetables and chilies for a number of years before the introduction of the Swynnerton reforms in the mid-fifties.

In the early colonial period the stable crops in Taita Hills were maize, sorghum, sugarcane, beans, potatoes and bananas. But due to scarcity and instability of rain the crops were often poor and the district was for a number of years a food deficit area which had to import food to avoid starvation and famine.

In this period the official agricultural policy of the colonial government was to substitute high priced cash crops for food crops in the district. But due to the high opportunity cost of this shift in cultivation in terms of the very high prices that the peasant households had to pay for maize transported to the hills this policy never really succeeded.

Vegetables and *chilies* were introduced during World War I as cash crops for the higher and lower areas of the district, respectively, and soon became the most important cash crops of the district.

During the Second World War vegetable growing expanded very rapidly and Taita Hills became the major source of vegetables for the fast growing Mombasa market. By the end of the war, Taita was exporting 120,000 shs. worth of vegetables, an impressive growth in a comparatively short period of time.[56] But vegetable growing continued to occupy minor portions of the cultivated land. The share of vegetables in total cultivated area only increased from 5 per cent in 1930 to 7 per cent in 1969.[57]

Coffee was introduced in 1951. The ultimate target of coffee acreage in Taita was 1,000 acres according to the Swynnerton Plan, but by 1959 only 395 acres had been planted. There were serious problems in connection with the control of coffee diseases and therefore vegetables have generally been preferred as a cash crop by the majority of the growers.

The coffee area expanded throughout the sixties and reached approx. 4,000 acres or 3 per cent of the cultivated area (inclusive mixed cropping) in 1969 (see Table II.17). According to the Integrated Rural Survey there were approx. 800 smallholders or 4.2 per cent of the total who cultivated approx 750 acres of coffee in 1974/75.

The difference between the 1969 figure and 1974/75 could be interpreted as a shift back to the traditional cash crop, vegetables, but the sample basis of the Integrated Rural Survey is probably too narrow to justify conclusions of this sort.

Neither pyrethrum nor tea are well suited to the climatic characteristics of the Taita Hills and *hybrid maize* had by 1969 been adopted by only a few

[56] Heyer, J., "The origins...", *op.cit.,* p. 152.
[57] *Ibid.,* table 1, p. 147.

Vegetables are transported to the urban areas by lorry or bus. (Jesper Kirknæs)

smallholders with less than a total of 50 ha. planted.[58] As in other parts of Kenya there has been a change from sorghum to white maize since the 1930's. Thus the area of maize increased from 24 per cent of cultivated area in 1930 to 30 per cent in 1969 while that of sorghum fell from 6 per cent to 1 per cent in the same period.

According to the Integrated Rural Survey approx. 13,300 smallholdings in Coast Province equal to 19 per cent of all the smallholdings in the Province had adopted hybrid maize in 1974/75. Thus Coast Province had the lowest rate of adoption among Kenya provinces in that year.[59] Assuming that hybrid maize has been adopted at equal rates in the various high potential areas of the province it can be estimated that approx. 1000 ha. of hybrid maize was planted in Taita Hills in 1974/75. But due to the same narrow sampling base of the Integrated Rural Survey the crude nature of this estimate should be underlined.

The Taita people are primarily agriculturalist but have traditionally kept livestock, mostly for their social and ritual importance.[60] Due to the increasing land shortage the significance of cattle has been decreasing and the general expansion in the number of grade cattle on peasant holdings has had little impact in Taita Hills. By 1967 there were only 150 head of grade cattle out of a total stock of approx. 36,000 cattle in the district. According to the Integrated Rural Survey the total number of improved stock in the whole of Coast Province was only 1,800 or 0.6 per cent of the total stock in 1975.

In summary, the changes in cropping patterns and agricultural production have been less dramatic in Taita Hills than in most other districts since the mid-fifties when cash incomes from chilies and vegetables were already relatively high. The development and composition of cash income throughout the fifties can be seen from Table II.26.

Income from cash crops expanded at an annual rate of 12 per cent between 1948 and 1959 partly due to the expansion in coffee production. Thus income from coffee increased from K. £ 1,400 in 1954 to K. £ 13,600 in 1959. However, coffee played no role in the rapid expansion from 1959 to 1969 when the value of marketed output increased at an annual rate of 24 per cent. In this period the income from coffee was very much influenced by coffee diseases and thus fluctuated from year to year. But from 1972 onwards the coffee income has increased steadily (see Table II.27).

[58] *Statistical Abstract 1977,* table 92.

[59] Integrated Rural Survey 1974/75, *op.cit.* table 9.3.

[60] Merrit, E. Hollis, *A History of the Taita of Kenya to 1900.* Ph.d. thesis, Department of History, Indiana University, August 1975.

Table II.26. *Income from cash crops. Taita Hills 1948–59 (K. £'000).*

	1948	1951	1954	1957	1959
Chilies	7.8	24.6	51.0	27.1	11.6
Vegetables	8.0	6.7	13.3	15.8	13.3
Wattle		5.5	5.3	3.5	5.7
Coffee			1.4	7.3	13.6
Cotton				1.4	3.7
Sugarcane				3.6	3.9
Castor seed				3.6	1.7
Other				2.9	1.0
Total	15.8	36.8	71.0	65.2	54.5

Source: District Agricultural Reports.

Table II.27. *Income from sales of coffee in Taita 1968–1976 (K £'000).*

1959	13.6
1968	19.6
1969	11.3
1970	17.5
1971	15.1
1972	14.5
1973	22.9
1974	31.8
1975	70.7
1976	72.5

Source: Kenya Coffee Board. Quoted from Bigsten, A. "Regional Inequality in Kenya", Working paper no. 330, Institute for Development Studies, University of Nairobi, Kenya 1977.

By 1969 income from sales of cash crops had increased to the relatively high level of K. £ 485,000 or K.shs. 87.4 per head, but on the other hand Taita Hills has become a deficit producing area. The rural households therefore have to spend some of the income they receive from sales of cash crops for buying food.

There are no figures available on the value of food crop production over the years and it is therefore not possible to estimate the development in the value of total agricultural production over the years. But it should be emphasized that the relative position of Taita Hills vis-à-vis other Kenya Districts in terms of the value of total agricultural production (e.g., inclusive the value of subsistance crops) is considerably less advantageous than indicated by Table II.16 above.

Based upon observations in the districts in 1975, we would estimate that the total value of agricultural production per household is approx. 20 per

Table II.28. *Cropping pattern, principal crops, Kwale District 1930, 1960 and 1969/70.*

	1930	1960		1969/70	
	%	'000 ha	%	'000 ha	%
Maize	23	6.4	28.7	42.9	47.4
Sorghum	5	0.6	0.0	4.0	4.4
Cassava	17	1.6	7.2	13.1	14.6
Pulses	13	0.0	0.0	0.0	0.0
Cotton	0	0.3	1.3	0.2	0.2
Sugarcane	0	0.0	0.0	1.1	1.2
Bananas	0	1.6	7.2	3.7	4.1
Paw paw	0	0.1	0.4	3.3	3.6
Fruit	0	.	.	4.0	4.4
Cashew nuts	0	2.6	11.5	8.3	9.2
Coconuts	35	9.5	42.5	9.3	10.3
Other	7	0.3	1.4	0.6	0.7
Total	100	22.3	100.2	90.5	100.1

Source: 1930 figures from Heyer, J., "The origins ..." *op. cit.* 1960 figures from District agricultural reports and 1969/70 figures from Statistical Abstract 1977.

cent higher than in Kisumu District but probably only half the value of agricultural production in Kisii District. The significance of food crops in total agricultural production in Taita is much less than in Kisumu and Kisii where foodcrops counted for approx. 75 per cent of the total value of agricultural production (see Table II.21 and Table II.25).

Kwale district was ranked 16 in marketed output per capita in 1969 among the 21 districts in Kenya. Of the four districts studied only Kisumu was ranked lower. None of the crops, coffee, pyrethrum, tea or hybrid maize, which are responsible for the rapid expansion in smallholder production since the 1950's have been suited to the climatic situation in Kwale district.

Before the colonial period cassava used to be the stable food crop of the Wadigo and was grown all over the parts of the district populated by this tribe, whereas maize was the stable food of the Duruma. Rice was grown in some areas along the coast, particularly near Shimoni and Vanga.

In the 1920's, 1930's and 1940's the smallholders produced sufficient food to feed their families and they received the cash incomes necessary to pay for imported consumer articles and to pay taxes from the sales of tree-crops of which coconuts were far the most important.

Since the 1950's there has been a diversification in the cropping pattern. Many more different cash crops are grown. Cotton was introduced in 1950 and sugarcane has spread as a cash crop among the peasants living near the sugar factory in Ramisi. But these crops have never become as popular as the new tree-crops of which cashew nuts, paw paws, mangos and citrus fruits have become the most popular. However, the most significant change in cropping pattern has been the widespread adoption of maize which has taken place all over the district in relation to the extension of the cultivated area, but in particular in the Shimba Hills. The change in cropping patterns between 1930, 1969 and 1969/70 can be seen in Table II.28.

The quadrupling of the cultivated area from 22,300 hectares in 1960 to 90,500 hectares, and the even more rapid expansion in maize cultivation, is the most characteristic comparative development in the district. During the same period the population increased by 3.9 per cent annually from 146,100 in 1960 to 205,600 in 1969 reflecting the immigration which took place in the decade mainly from Eastern Province. Many Wakamba have settled in the Shimba Hills settlement scheme and in the surrounding Trust Land areas of Kikoneni, Mwereni and Shimba South Location. According to the 1969 Population Census there was an immigration into the district of 16,616 people between 1963 and 1969. The expansion in cultivated land and the change in cropping patterns that followed can thus partly but not fully be explained by this immigration of Wakamba people. Also the local Wadigo population have expanded their cultivated areas by cultivating more maize in addition to their traditional food crop cassava. None of the maize planted in 1969 was hybrid maize, but according to the Integrated Rural Survey hybrid maize had been adopted in a small scale in the high potential areas of Coastal Province in 1974/75. But the exact importance of hybrid maize in Kwale District is uncertain.

The introduction of new tree-crops like cashew nuts, paw paws, mangos and citrus fruits has led to a rapid expansion of cash income in recent years. Most of the tree-crops are sold directly by the producers to traders who sell them in the Mombasa Market, and income figures are therefore only rough estimates. The figures available from District Agricultural Report show quite a variation in annual cash income from crop production per household (see Table II. 29).

Kwale is quite an important dairy producer. By 1968, 13 per cent of the dairy produce of cooperatives in Kenya came from Kwale District which was only surpassed by Nyeri, Nyandarua and Kiambu Districts.[61] But most of the milk in the district come from local zebu cattle. By 1967 very little grade cattle had been introduced to the district due to their greater vulnerability to livestock disease and according to the Integrated Rural Survey the number

[61] Heyer, J., "The origins. . .", *op.cit.* table 6, p. 168.

Table II.29. *Estimates of agricultural cash incomes per household Kwale District 1965–1973, K. £.*

	1965	1968	1969	1970	1971	1972	1973
Cash income from crop production per family	5	10.3	15	16.4	12.1	12.2	14

Source: District Agricultural Reports.

was still very small in 1974/75. Less than 1 per cent of the total stock in Coast Province was improved stock by that year.

The Integrated Rural Survey also shows that the share of smallholdings with cows is small and the production per cow is low in Coast Province, but on the other hand the share of the production of milk sold is higher in Coast Province than in other parts of Kenya.[62]

Having this in mind and taking into account that Kwale District has generally been able to be self-sufficient in food crops, we would estimate that the total value of agricultural production per family is at the same level as in Taita Hills.

In summary, we can conclude that of the selected four districts only Kisii has been in a position to benefit from the new cash crops, the introduction of which has been the main reason for the rapid expansion in Kenya since the mid-fifties. Taita Hills and Kwale District have been able to expand cash income from vegetable and new tree-crops respectively. But in Kisumu district only the tenants on the new irrigation schemes in Ahero and Kano West and to a lesser extent – in years of good sugarcane prices – the smallholdings near the sugar estates cultivating small plots with sugar have had a significant rise in agricultural incomes since Independence. The majority of the peasant households in Kisumu District have probably had falling real incomes from agriculture over the years.

In the next section we will discuss the factors behind the rapid development of smallholder production and its economic and social consequences in greater detail.

Development of the productive forces and the creation of a landless proletariat

Whereas there can be no doubt about the impressive growth in smallholder agricultural production in Kenya since the fifties, the nature of this growth process has been a topic for discussion among development theorists.

[62] Rural Integrated Survey 1974/75 op.cit. table 10.3.

It has been argued that the growth in agricultural production has been restricted to a small group of better-off farmers in the high potential areas of Kenya and that the growth process has not been associated with any development of the productive forces since there has been no significant accumulation of capital in smallholder agriculture.[63] Others argue that the growth process has been characterized by the emergence and expansion of a non-accumulating "middle-peasantry" with small plots not sufficient in size to make regular hiring of wage-labour common and with insufficient economic and political power to control terms of exchange and the process of production of the cash crops sold in world markets.[64] However, in the near future the "middle" peasant household production in agriculture may be approaching the limits of its expansion as land becomes increasingly scarce. In that case the momentum in the growth process can probably only be maintained if the productivity of labour is increased by trying to extend capitalist relations of production in agriculture (e.g. by policies designed to polarise the smallholder areas towards kulak and capitalist farming on the one hand, and proletarianization on the other).[65]

Most of these observations are based upon field studies in Nyeri District in Central Province, and it has been argued that the absence of a process of secular differentiation is due to specific restrictive land transfer, credit, and cash crop policies in this part of Kenya.[66]

In other areas of Kenya such as, e.g., Mbere, a marginal cultivation area to the east of Mount Kenya, and Wanga, an area affected by the outgrowers' scheme of the Mumias sugar project in Western Kenya, the development of very different processes to those found in districts of Central Province has

[63] Colin Leys argues that the development of capitalist relations of production – increased use of wage labour within the peasant mode of production – and the process of gradual polarization should not let one lose sight of the fact that in the peasant mode of production the majority of the households produced very little surplus and that the main economic importance of the peasant modes of production was a source of foreign exchange for the purchase of manufactured imports and as a source of cheap foodstuffs and of subsidies for wages in the capitalist sector. C. Leys, "Underdevelopment in Kenya", *op.cit.* pp. 191–93.

[64] This point is most forcefully developed by M. Cowen. See, e.g., Cowen, M. and K. Kinyanjui, *Some Problems of Income Distribution in Kenya,* Institute for Development Studies, University of Nairobi, March 1977.

[65] Colin Leys, "Capital Accumulation, Class Formation and Dependency – The significance of the Kenyan Case" in *Socialist Register* 1978, p. 261. See also Njonjo, *The Africanisation of the White Highlands: A study in Agrarian Class Struggles in Kenya 1950–1974,* Ph.D. Dissertation, Princeton University, 1977.

[66] See Raikes, P., *op.cit.* p. 11. Research by Geoff Lamb in Muranga District in Central Province shows that here the introduction of coffee resulted in the creation of a group of wealthly peasants using wage labour. See Lamb, G., *Peasant Politics – conflict and development in Muranga.,* London 1974.

been shown.[67] In these areas the land registration programme appears to have had almost the opposite effect to that in Central Province, because the various restrictions on land transfer contained in the Central Province registration have been omitted. As a result, local notables, government officials, and politicians have moved in and purchased much of the best land. Very often the necessary capital involved in these purchases of land origins from salaried employment or trading activities, but also agricultural incomes are an important source of capital for this process of accumulation of land.[68]

In general, it is of course true that capital formation on smallholdings in Kenya is low, but it is not by any means negligible. To soil conservation and enclosure investment can be added the investment in permanent crops, all the investments in livestock, water supplies, dips and the not inconsiderable investments in farm structures of various kinds. When one adds the considerable amounts of capital involved in the purchase by Africans of land in the former White Highlands since 1959 it is quite clear that the expansion of smallholder production since the mid-fifties has been associated with an impressive capital investment.[69] But also other factors have been important, such as:

(i) The settling of more than 50,000 families on settlement schemes between 1961 and 1970 as part of the land transfer programme. Hereby approx. 1 1/2 mill. acres; a fifth of the old White Highlands or perhaps as much as 4 per cent of the total area of the country available for agriculture was brought into smallholder cultivation providing the growers with an above-average standard of subsistence and cash sales of roughly 6 per cent of the total value of marketed output from the "small farm" sector.[70]

(ii) The increase in the share of smallholdings in total cultivated land. This has resulted in an increase in aggregate production because small farms have been shown to have a higher productivity per acre than large farms due to more intensive cultivation.[71]

(iii) The change in cropping patterns and product mix on smallholdings. As shown in the previous chapter the expansion in smallholder production has been associated with the expansion of "old" cash crops, coffee, tea,

[67] Hunt, D., *Growth versus Equity – an examination of the distribution of economic status and opportunity in Mbere, Eastern Kenya.* Occasional Paper no 11, IDS, Nairobi 1975; and Barclay, A., *The Mumias Sugar Project: A study of rural development in Western Kenya,* Ph.d. thesis, Columbia University 1977.

[68] *Ibid.,* p. 334.

[69] It is estimated that between K.£. 7 m. and K.£. 10 m. of privately owned capital, mostly from Central Province, was invested in large-farm purchase. See Leys, C. (1978), *op.cit.,* p. 249.

[70] See Leys, C. (1975), *op.cit.* p. 75.

[71] See Heyer, J. et al., *op.cit.* p. 95.

pyrethum, vegetables and dairy products on small African holdings but also the introduction of new high yielding varieties of maize.

(iv) In relation to the introduction of these "new" smallholder crops a capitalisation of agriculture has taken place. A land market has developed, an increased use of wage labour has taken place[72], and more money is being spent on new seed and seedlings, fertilizer and insecticides.[73] Since the cumulative total of government and bank lending to smallholders was very small[74] the increased cost of production has been financed primarily out of accumulated savings. This explains why the benefits from the new cash crops were concentrated in the hands of few relatively well-off families with access to capital from salaried positions in the civil service and from various trading activities developed during and after the Second World War.

(v) On the other hand, there has been very little improvement in cultivation methods. In the 1930's shifting cultivation predominated in Kenya's small farm areas, and only the more crowded areas were beginning to move towards more frequent cropping. Shifting cultivation has now disappeared almost completely and most of Kenya's smallholders are involved in systems of continuous cultivation. Mixed cropping substitutes to some extent for crop rotation but since very little manure or fertilizer is used there are problems of long-term maintenance of soil fertility.

One of the important features of the expansion in smallholder production is that it has not been associated with mechanisation. Hand labour is still predominant and only initial cultivation, a little weeding and transportation are in some areas being performed with the help of oxen or mechanical power. The only important use of mechanical power is the conventional four wheel tractor which is used to a surprising degree for initial cultivation even by small farmers hiring private or government contractors. But the degree to which tractors are used for ploughing in any area is still very small.[75]

The crucial question, however, does not seem to be to what extent the expansion in smallholder production for the market is the result of capital invested in land transfer, new crops and grade cattle or new production techniques but rather the nature of this process of production, accumulation

[72] Leys, C. (1975) *op.cit.* p. 173., and Heyer et al., *op.cit.* p. 198, and Barclay, A. *op.cit.* See also Kongstad, P. and Mönsted, M., *Family, Labour and Trade in Western Kenya.* Centre for Development Research. Publication 3. Scandinavian Institute of African Studies, Uppsala 1980, table 2.10 p. 58.

[73] Barclay, A. *op.cit.* p. 198.

[74] Leys, C. (1978) p. 249 estimates this lending smallholders at K.£. 1.7 mill. between 1955–1964.

[75] Heyer, J. et al., *op.cit.* p. 199.

and differentiation that has resulted in the rural areas of Kenya. Here the research from parts of Central Province arguing that the process has supported the development of a non-accumulating middle peasantry based upon family labour is in sharp contrast to findings from other parts of Kenya pointing at the development of a land market and individual land tenure, an expansion in capitalist relations of production, i.e., increased use of wage labour, accumulation of capital based upon agriculture, but often invested in trade and transport business and finally as a result of this process a growing differentiation among the peasantry leading on the one hand to the formation of a group of capitalist farmers and on the other hand to the formation of a landless proletariat.

Unfortunately, there is very little statistical time series available for a more detailed general dynamic analysis of the development trends in accumulation patterns and differentiation in the rural areas of Kenya over the last 20 years. Information on smallholder agriculture has been collected on a survey basis first in 1950/51 and again in 1960/61 and in 1963/64 but only with the recent Integrated Rural Survey 1974/75 has a comprehensive sample basis been established that will make comparisons over time possible.

However, a number of observations could be made from the Integrated Rural Survey and other official Kenyan Statistics.

Firstly, the increased production and income from smallholder production has indeed resulted in the creation of an investible surplus within Kenyan smallholder agriculture. Data from the Integrated Rural Survey 1974/75 shows that the average rural household is able to save approx. 6 per cent out of its annual income (see Table II.30). The total savings of the smallholder households could thus be estimated at approx. K. shs. 300 mill. in 1974/75 or equivalent to 7 per cent of the total capital formation in Kenya in 1974.[76]

At the same time, Table II.30 shows the differentiation within the rural households. The upper income group with annual incomes above 8,000 K.shs., which are made up by 179,176 households or 12 per cent of the total rural households, are saving as much as 47 per cent of their total average annual income of 12,300 K.shs. The total saving of this group of wealthy peasants thus equals 1,080 mill. K.shs. or 27 per cent of total capital formation in Kenya in 1974. On the other hand, the poor peasant holdings with annual average incomes of less than 3,000 K.shs. making up 55 per cent of the rural households are incapable of making ends meet and have to borrow money in order to exist.

[76] Statistical Abstract 1977, *op.cit.,* table 52 (a).

Table II.30. *Average value and composition of income, expenditures and savings by household income group.*

	Less than 0	0–999		1,000–1,999		2,000–2,999		3,000–3,999		4,000–5,999		6,000–7,999		8,000 K. Shs.		Total	
	K. Shs.	K. Shs.	%	K. Shs.	%	K. Shs.	%	K. Shs.	%	K. Shs	%	K. Shs.	%	and over	%	K. Shs.	%
Farm operating surplus	2,624–	128	23.2	649	43.7	1,327	53.0	1,933	55.9	2,944	61.1	4,239	60.8	7,865	63.9	2,081	57.0
Non-farm operating surplus	832–	87	15.8	170	11.5	250	9.9	409	11.8	572	11.8	421	6.1	1,390	11.3	354	9.7
Regular employment	183	46	8.4	142	9.6	128	5.1	457	13.2	449	9.3	1,290	18.6	2,331	18.9	566	15.5
Casual employment	155	116	21.1	217	14.6	350	140	222	6.4	266	5.5	439	6.3	281	2.3	252	6.9
Remittances from relatives	241	159	28.9	261	17.6	389	155	390	11.3	443	9.2	404	5.8	322	2.6	324	8.9
Other gifts	38	14	2.5	46	3.1	61	2.5	45	1.3	141	2.9	160	2.3	128	1.1	75	2.1
Total household income	2,840	551	100	1,485	100	2,505	100	3,456	100	4,815	100	6,953	100	12,317	100	3,652	100
Total outlays	3,691	1,611		2,165		2,721		3,364		3,893		5,618		6,505		3,450	
Current savings	6,530	1,060–		681–		216–		93		923		1,335		5,812		202	
Number of holdings	98,982	175,057		332,813		204,972		174,002		200,501		117,919		179,176		1,483,422	

Source: Integrated Rural Survey 1974/75 *op. cit.* table 8.5.

Table II.31. *Average value per holding of income and outlays by holding size group (K. Shs.).*

	Under 0.5 hectares	0.5–0.9 hectares	1.0–1.9 hectares	2.0–2.9 hectares	3.0–3.9 hectares	4.0–4.9 hectares	5.0–7.9 hectares	8.0 hectares & over	Total
Farm operating surplus	1,369	1,855	1,610	2,344	2,255	3,424	2,659	2,946	2,081
Non-farm operating surplus	359	278	239	130	418	318	750	1,761	354
Regular employment	614	430	649	426	641	408	944	460	566
Casual employment	214	198	286	309	184	319	290	134	252
Remittances from relatives	290	349	362	267	325	328	277	357	324
Other gifts	62	63	63	82	129	77	88	97	75
Total household income	2,908	3,173	3,209	3,558	3,952	4,874	5,008	5,755	3,652
Total outlays	2,498	2,669	3,650	3,292	4,070	4,334	4,876	4,362	3,450
Current savings	410	504	441–	266	118–	540	132	1,393	202
Number of holdings	206,366	265,816	400,371	224,072	131,916	107,031	96,386	51,464	1,483,422

Source: Integrated Rural Survey 1974/75 table 8.6.

It is equally interesting to note that although the rich peasant households are receiving considerable sums of money as income from non-agricultural enterprises and from regular employment, agriculture is still their main source of income. As a matter of fact the significance of agriculture as a source of income and accumulation of capital seems to increase with rising income (see Table II.30). On the other hand, there seems to be no simple direct relationship between the size of holding, agricultural incomes and current savings. Rather, the larger holdings are characterized by very large incomes from non-agricultural enterprises (see Table II.31). If the acreages in Table II.31 had been transformed into high potential land equivalents, however, the picture might have differed considerably.

Secondly, very little of the surplus created in the small farm sector seems to have been reinvested productively within this sector. But this is not to say that the rich peasants have not been accumulating capital. Large sums have been used for buying land in the former White Highlands. It is estimated that from 1959, when Africans became eligible to buy land in the former White Highlands, down to 1970 at least K£.7 m and perhaps as much as K £.10 m of privately owned capital, mostly from Central Province, was invested in large-farm purchase. In a strict economic sense these transactions are of course not investments since they do not add to the stock of productive capital but on the other hand they are certainly an important aspect of the accumulation pattern of the indigenous class of capital in Kenya.[77] Lately savings from agricultural production have also been invested in land purchases in other parts of Kenya.[78]

Equally, peasant households have invested large sums of capital "unproductively" in improved housing and in education of their children. The official estimates of the capital formation in the semi-monetary economy, i.e., the peasant economy, show that investment in housing by the rural population has increased at approximately the same rate as capital formation in the rest of the economy (see Table II.32). By 1974 the current value of investment in improved rural housing by coincidence has exactly the same size of 300 million K.shs. as the rural "net" saving of the small farming sector.

It was argued in Chapter I that access to education and salaried positions in the colonial administration had become the most important source of accumulation of capital in the first phase of the colonial period up to the Second World War.

[77] Leys, C. (1978), *op.cit.* p. 249.
[78] See Barclay, T., *op.cit.* p. 247.

Table II.32. *Investment in improved housing by peasant households 1964–1976 at constant (1964) prices K. £. mill. and as percentage of total capital formation in Kenya.*

	K. £mill.	%
1964	5.24	12
1968	6.69	9
1969	6.75	8
1970	6.63	7
1971	6.88	6
1972	6.73	6
1973	6.42	6
1974	5.59	8
1975	7.54	9
1976	7.84	8

Source: Republic of Kenya, Statistical Abstract.

Education was introduced in Kenya by the missionaries as early as 1846 when the first mission school was established in Rabai near Mombasa. After the building of the railway to Kisumu the missionaries extended their fields of activities to Nyanza Province. They built a few schools on their stations and gradually the Africans began to realize the potential of the school as a means of improving their material way of life and their relative status in colonial society. Thus partnerships developed in which local communities provided land, built class-rooms and eventually through paying of school-fees provided support for teachers, while the missionaries developed teaching materials for trained teachers. Throughout the colonial period, the government chose to rely largely on this partnership to provide elementary education for the African people, although various grants-in-aid were given. But African opposition to missionary and settler views on the objectives of African education led to formation of self-help schools completely outside the authority of both missions and government.[79] The opposition was strongest among the Kikuyu who, between 1922 and 1952, created nearly 400 self-help schools. But many such schools were also built by the Luo in Nyanza Province.

Throughout the period following the end of the war in 1945 and up to independence in 1963, the pressure to expand and extend first level education built up more strongly. The parents were active in building schools from local materials and although the self-help efforts somehow embarrassed the colonial government, its policy in general sought to utilize self-help effort to provide school buildings and to cover maintenance cost. But at the same time attempts were made to check the expansion of schools

[79] Anderson, J.E. *Organization and financing of self-help education in Kenya*, Unesco, Paris 1973.

in order to prevent recurrent costs (teachers' salaries, books etc.), part of which came from central government funds, from rising to a level above the budgetary allocations.

After Independence the system of self-help has continued to play a major role although the government has followed a policy of taking over as many self-help schools as possible. It is estimated that in 1968, 93 per cent of the capital cost of primary schools were self-help contributions from the people.[80] In addition the local people still contributed considerably to the financing of recurrent cost, even taking into consideration that a system of free education for the first 4 years of schooling and reduced rates of schoolfees for the following years were introduced by January 1974. Considerable amounts of money are still being spent by even poor peasant families on school uniforms and teaching material for children at all educational levels. Thus, for example, primary schools collect equipment fees and additional supplemental fees for such items as building funds, activity cost, uniforms, feeding schemes, etc., that are estimated to raise over K£. 12 million from the families of the pupils. In secondary schools very high tuition fees are levied in both Government and self-help schools. In view of the rapid expansion in school enrolment in Kenya since 1964, it seems fair to assume that considerable amounts of the income generated in the rural areas have been spent on education. Enrolment in primary schools in Kenya increased by 194 per cent between 1964 and 1977, of which 51 per cent alone was due to the increase between 1973 and 1974 when tuition fees were abolished in primary schools for standard 1 to 4. It is estimated that 86 per cent of the children in the 6 to 12 age group went in primary school in 1977. The direct private expenditure on education has been estimated at K£.37.9 million in 1976 of which probably more than half originated from rural households.[81]

However, one can no longer be sure that investment in education will yield the high returns of the past. Today education is a necessary but not sufficient condition for access to well paid jobs in the "modern" sector. One can of course argue that education will have a positive long-term impact on productivity in agriculture, but without considerable changes in the existing educational system in Kenya in the direction of an adaptation to the solution of practical problems in real live in the rural areas, this by no means seems certain.

But one should not underestimate the significance of the huge amounts of capital which have been invested productively by small peasants and

[80] *Ibid.,* p. 31.
[81] *Economic Survey 1978,* p. 171.

cooperative societies in permanent crops, processing and marketing facilities and in grade cattle and cattledips all over the country. The fact that virtually no mechanization has taken place in Kenyan smallholder agriculture – the value of farm equipment and transport equipment made up only 380 shs. on the average smallholding in 1974/75 – therefore, does not mean that no capital accumulation is taking place in this sector.[82]

The lack of investment in mechanization in agriculture is probably best explained by the relatively easier, less risky, and more profitable investment opportunities that were opened up to Africans in other sectors of the economy following the Kenyanization policies introduced after Independence.

Thirdly, rich peasants and even "middle peasants" save part of their income in the banks and other financial institutions in the rural areas. But most of the savings from the rural areas are, via the banks, channelled towards investment in the urban areas.

Commercial Banks and suppliers of various agricultural inputs, i.e., fertilizers, are the major sources of credit for the smallholders. Compared to these private credit institutions, government loan schemes are of less significance. Only a small group of wealthy farmers is considered credit-worthy and in a position to obtain loans from these institutions. It has been estimated that less than 10 per cent of the peasants have been able to obtain credit from these sources.[83]

In effect, therefore, the commercial banking system has become an instrument for transfering resources from rural to urban Kenya.[84]

Fourthly, soon after Independence the Kenyan state introduced a number of Kenyanization measures such as trade licensing, state monopolies, state financial institutions, state direction of private credit, and state capitalist enterprises that made it possible for rich peasants that had first benefitted from the introduction of cash-crops to diversify their economic activities into new very profitable areas such as retail trading, services (restaurants, hotels, bars, tea shops) and transport, which had previously been dominated by the Asian population.

But the expansion of rich peasants into non-agricultural activities has to some extent been a necessity in as far as quota restrictions on acreage of coffee and pyrethrum and restrictions on land transfer, particularly in the

[82] See Integrated Rural Survey 1974/75 *op.cit.* table 7.9, p. 48.

[83] See Heyer, J., et al., *op.cit.* p. 209.

[84] Child, F., "An Empirical Study of Small-scale Rural Industry in Kenya", University of Nairobi, University of Nairobi, *I.D.S. working paper 127,* 1973.

densely populated parts of Central Province, severely limited the possibilities for capitalist expansion in agriculture in the mid-sixties.

The exact amount of smallholder capital invested in non-agricultural enterprises is not known, but the significance of these activities as a source of income can be seen from Table II.30. The average share of income from non-agricultural enterprises in the rural households was approx. 10 per cent in 1974/75, but this share varied considerably between income groups and provinces. Apparently, income from non-agricultural activities contributed relatively more to total income for the poorest households, but in absolute terms the income from non-agricultural enterprises was more than fifteen times higher for the richest group than for the poorest group of households.

The significance of income from non-agricultural enterprises and wage income from regular and casual employment is considerable and has to be taken into consideration when the development of agricultural production and the accumulation of capital in the rural areas of Kenya is analysed. Peasant households are faced with a number of income and investment opportunities in agricultural as well as non-agricultural activities and only a total analysis of all these opportunities will therefore be meaningful. The fact that the previously mentioned studies of peasant household production in Central Province does not take income from non-agricultural sources into account, might partly explain why they reach a conclusion that incomes have become more equitably distributed over the years. If income and investment opportunities in non-agricultural activities had been taken into consideration, it is very likely that a different picture had emerged.[85] It is clearly demonstrated in other studies that the rich peasants are in the best position to exploit the most profitable opportunities in the non-agricultural sector.[86] The interaction between agricultural and non-agricultural activities and the significance of non-agricultural activities for the process of capital accumulation in the rural areas in Kenya will be discussed at greater length in Chapter III and Chapter V.

Fifthly, the surplus created in the smallholder sector is to some extent being "appropriated" partly by the State as a produce buyer and partly by the private urban sector as a supplier of consumer goods via various mechanisms of "unequal exchange".

Part of the investible surplus created in the agricultural sector is, via the public sector, transferred to other sectors of the economy. The direct

[85] Cowen, M and Kinyanjui, *op.cit.*

[86] Hunt, D., *op.cit.* and Kongstad, P. and Mönsted, M., *op.cit.,* table 4.3, p. 112 and table 4.8, p. 130.

mechanisms used are income taxes and various sales taxes on consumer goods. These taxes are still relatively minor burdens on the peasant sector compared to the burden of taxes in the colonial period. Colin Leys estimates that as much as 75 per cent of the cash wages paid to Africans per annum was paid in direct and indirect taxes in 1920–23.[87] A survey of rural household expenditures in Nyanza Province in 1970/71 found that peasant households paid 5 per cent of their incomes in income tax.[88] But the direct and sales tax burden has been increasing since Independence.[89] Thus the revenue from income tax has increased at an average annual rate of 19 per cent. Sales tax was introduced in 1972/73 and by 1977/78 accounts for as much as 19 per cent of total government revenue.[90]

However, the marketing system for agricultural produce has probably been a much more important mechanism for the government extraction of surplus from the smallholder economy than taxation.[91] Since the government fixes the bulk of agricultural prices for the products bought by government marketing boards, they are in a position to extract surplus from the peasant economy by paying low prices. Throughout the sixties and seventies prices paid by the marketing boards have been considerably below the prices that the peasants have been able to obtain in "the free market". An indication of the significance of this surplus extraction is the increase in smuggling and black marketeering mentioned previously.

In addition it has been argued that surplus is transferred from the consumers in the rural areas to the private industries and to importers of consumer goods when the peasants buy their commodities. Most of these companies, it is argued, are selling in monopolistic markets and are therefore able to obtain high prices including a monopoly rent at the cost of the consumers.[92]

It has not been possible to obtain a quantitative measurement of the agricultural surplus appropriated by the government and the private urban sector via these mechanisms. Analyses of the development in terms of trade between agriculture and industry, by comparing the prices received by peasants for their produce with the prices of the commodities they buy, are often used as indicators of the development in "unequal exchange". The changes in terms of trade are used as an approximation for the changes in

[87] Leys, C. (1975), *op.cit.* p. 32.

[88] *Kisumu District Development Plan,* August 1974.

[89] Nellis, R. John, "Who pays tax in Kenya", in *The African Revue* vol. 2, no 2, 1972.

[90] Republic of Kenya, *Economic Survey,* 1964 and 1978.

[91] See Leonard, K., David, *Bureaucracy, Class and Inequality in Kenya and Tanzania.* Paper presented at Conference on Inequality in Africa, Mt. Kisco, New York 1976 (mimeo).

[92] *Ibid.,* p. 20.

Table II.33. *Prices received and paid by farmers (1972 = 100)*

	Prices received by farmers	Prices paid by farmers	Terms of trade
1972	100	100	100
1973	111	115	96
1974	129	142	91
1975	145	165	88
1976	216	178	121
1977	310	205	152

Source: Republic of Kenya, Economic Survey 1978, p. 101.

the welfare of the rural population caused by "external" market factors. It should, however, be emphasized that there are no direct relationships between the extraction of government revenue from peasant production and a positive development in agricultural terms of trade. Thus, it is quite possible that the extraction of government revenue can increase, even in relative terms, in periods of improved terms of trade for the agricultural sector if producer prices rise less than world market prices, as might have been the case during the coffee boom of 1977.

Various sources have shown that agricultural terms of trade decreased steadily between 1964 and 1975.[93] Table II.33, based upon the official Kenya estimates, shows that the decline in agricultural terms of trade continued until 1976 when export prices of coffee and tea increased dramatically. But also producer prices of maize, sugarcane and dairy produce were increased very significantly.[94]

The decline in agricultural terms of trade between 1964 and 1975 indicates that surplus produced in the agricultural sector has been transferred to other sectors of the economy via the price mechanisms, but it is not possible to give even a rough estimate of the size of this surplus transfer or an indication of the degree to which these funds have been invested productively in other sectors of the economy.

Sixthly, the Integrated Rural Survey provides new information on the existing inequalities between regions and between rich and poor peasants in the rural areas of Kenya. The figures on inequalities between regions (see Table II.15) have been discussed above and Table II.30 provides information on the distribution of income in the smallholder sector in Kenya.

The pattern of income distribution which was shown by the Economic

[93] *Ibid.,* table 1, p. 21.

[94] See Republic of Kenya, *Economic Survey 1978,* table 8.4. p. 97.

Survey of Central Province 1963/64, with a dichotomy of a few very rich and a great number of very poor households concentrated around some medium-lower incomes, seems to be less pronounced in the 1974/75 Integrated Rural Survey.[95] There seems to have been a tendency towards a large group of relatively well-off households, a relatively large group of poor households, and relatively few households between the two.[96]

When income inequality is measured through the so-called Gini coefficient[97] inequality among the smallholders appears less pronounced than in the rest of the Kenyan economy and less than in rural areas of other developing countries for example in Asia.[98]

The Gini coefficient for smallholder agriculture has been calculated for various climatic zones and the different provinces in Kenya based upon the Integrated Rural Survey 1974/75. The results are shown in Table II.34.

But the fact that Gini coefficients in smallholder areas of Kenya are relatively low should not be taken as an indication that poverty is a minor

[95] See Kmietowicz, T. and Webley, P., "Statistical Analysis of Income Distribution in the Central Province of Kenya", in *Eastern African Economic Review.* vol. 7, no 2. December 1975.

[96] See Lijoodi and Ruthenberg, "Income Distribution in Kenya's Agriculture" in *Zeitschrift für Ausländische Landwirtschaft,* Jahrgang 17, Heft 2, April–June 1978, pp. 115–128.

[97] The inequality of income is often measured by the so-called Gini concentration ratio or coefficient which is the ratio of the area bounded by the Lorenz curve and the diagonal to the area of the triangle in an Lorenz diagramme of income distribution. High inequality means that the Gini coefficient approaches 1; low inequality means that the Gini coefficient approaches zero.

[98] Thus the distribution of income appears to be more equal among rural households in the non-monetary sector than in the monetary economy. See *Hodd, Michael,* Income Distribution in Kenya (1963–72), In *Journal of Development Studies,* vol. 12 No 3 April 1976. This author estimates Gini concentration ratios for employed and self-employed in the monetary economy based upon data compiled from the Annual Enumerations of Employees and Self-employed Persons. He finds Gini concentration ratios varying between 56.0 and 39.7 in the period 1963–72.

See also *Singer, H.W. and Reynolds,* "Aspects of the Distribution of Income and Wealth in Kenya", *IDS Discussion Paper* No 41, February 1974, University of Sussex, England.

Based upon wages of regular employees 1964 and 1967 and on income of urban households in Nairobi, Mombasa and Kisumu they estimate Gini concentration ratios of 0.58, 0.58 and 0.49 respectively.

But there are no figures for income distribution covering the whole of Kenya. The estimate made by Adelman and Morris in their international study of income distributions (Gini Ratio 0.55) is not very well founded and should not be used for comparisons.

See *Adelman and C. Toft Morris,* "An anatomy of patterns of Income Distribution in Developing Countries", USAID Development Digest, Oct. 1971, and *Paukert, F.,* "Income Distribution at Different Levels of Development: a Survey of Evidence", *International Labour Review,* 108 Nos. 2–3, Aug.-Sept. 1973.

The Gini coefficient for Kenya smallholder farming appears lower than the normal for Asian smallholder farming. Data from the Phillipines indicate a Gini coefficient of 0.60 for rice smallholdings. See Nicolas, J., "Income Distribution Among Farm Households in Selected Cropping Systems. I.R.R.I. no 7718. Los Banos 1977. Quoted from Lijoodi and Ruthenberg, *op.cit.* p. 121.

Table II.34. *Gini coefficients in Kenyan smallholder agriculture 1974/75.*

Climatic zones		Provinces	
Coffee, East of Rift	0.44	Central	0.39
Coast	0.44	Eastern	0.33
Tea, West of Rift	0.47	Rift Valley	0.51
Coffee, West of Rift	0.50	Coast	0.35
Tea, East of Rift	0.59	Western	0.43
Upper Cotton, West of Rift	0.45	Nyanza	0.39
Lower Cotton, East of Rift	0.49		
Kenya, average		0.49	

Source: Lijoodi, J.L. and Ruthenberg, H., Income Distribution in Kenya's Agriculture, *op. cit.* table 5, p. 122.

problem. Firstly, within the Kenya smallholder sector the Gini coefficient varies widely as can be seen from Table II.34. Incomes in poorer low potential areas are generally more evenly distributed than incomes in better-off high potential areas, but there are exceptions. Thus, Central Province with a high average income of K.shs. 4,241 a year has a more equitable distribution of income than Western Province with a lower average annual income of 2,494.

Secondly, there is a sizable number of households with negative incomes, i.e., households who lived on consuming assets, and a very great number of households with incomes between "0 and 1,999" K.shs. who are clearly in a rather desperate economic position. When the data on these two income groups are analysed in greater detail it appears that the poverty problem is not with the households that had a negative income. On the average, they belong to the group of rich households. They own many more assets than the average, they employ much more wage labour than others, they are in a position to buy more food and they consume more than the average. Their educational standards are relatively high (see Table II.35). There is reason to assume that many of the heads of households in this class provided wrong information to the enumerators. Most of these households do not belong to the rural poor.[99]

As can be seen from Table II.35, the situation is entirely different for the households in the "0–999" K.shs. and the "1,000–1,999" K.shs. income group.

The "0–999" K.shs. group owns very few assets, they do not employ labour, they hardly buy any inputs, they buy less food than others and their food consumption is about half of the average in spite of the fact that their

[99] Lijoodi and Ruthenberg, *op.cit.* p. 119.

Table II.35. *Characteristics of low income smallholder households.*

Income class	less than 0	0–999 K.shs.	1000–1999 K.shs.	Average of total
Number of households[1]	98 982	175 053	332 813	1 483 422
Farm operations (K.Shs.)				
Sales	790	191	586	1 192
Output used on farm	83	13	47	84
Output consumed	959	458	751	1 297
Valuation changes	−2 898	−404	−516	87
Total production	−1 066	258	869	2 660
Purchased inputs	390	50	96	241
Own produced inputs	83	13	47	84
Wages	432	40	46	160
Farm repairs	654	26	30	92
Farms operating surplus	−2 624	129	649	2 081
Non-farm enterprises (K.Shs.)				
Costs	1 439	85	n.a.	279
Receipts	607	172	n.a.	633
Surplus	−832	87	170	354
Other non-farm income (K.Shs.)	617	335	666	1 217
Mean value of assets (K.Shs.)				
Land	3 215	951	1 084	1 820
Buildings	2 120	850	887	1 796
Livestock	5 012	1 060	1 505	2 462
Other	854	289	478	827
Total	11 201	3 150	3 954	6 905
Consumption (K.Shs.)				
Food, own produced	959	458	751	1 297
Purchased food	1 498	786	956	1 297
Non-food purchases	746	256	334	547
Miscellaneous expenses	488	110	125	309
Total consumption	3 691	1 611	2 166	3 450
Educational standards				
Never attended school (per cent)	68	83	87	72

Source: Integrated Rural Survey, 1974/75.

[1] The number of households differs slightly from item to item.

households count the same number of members. They survive to a great extent as casual labourers in the rural areas, by participating in subsistence non-agricultural activities like homecraft and petty trade and by receiving remittances from relatives (see Table II.30). Most households in this income group are the very poor in the Kenya society. Their food consumption seems to be so low that malnutrition is a serious problem.

But the situation is only slightly better in the "1,000–1,999" income group. Their assets are much below the average, they employ almost no hired labour but participate at a significant scale themselves in the rural labour force. They buy very few inputs and their consumption of food and other items is also much below the average.

Together, these two income groups of very poor peasants account for more than 500,000 of the smallholdings of Kenya or more than one-third.

In addition, the Rural Integrated Survey 1974/75 has shown that the size of holdings is an unsuitable indicator for poverty. Differences in household income between households with more or less land are not very pronounced, as shown in Table II.31. The assessment of the income situation and the capacity to accumulate capital has to take three major factors into account (i) the size of holding (ii) the fertility of the land and (ii) regular non-farm income.

In summary, the recent information on smallholder production in Kenya from the Integrated Rural Survey has shown that smallholder agricultural production has indeed resulted in a very significant amount of capital accumulation among the upper income strata of the peasantry, although a high proportion of the investible surplus has been invested "unproductively" in land purchases, housing and education or has been transferred to other sectors of the economy via various financial institutions or the "unequal exchange" of the market system.

The data underline the significance of the non-agricultural sector as a source of income but also as a more profitable area of investment for the rich farmers who have benefitted from the introduction of cash-crops and used their agricultural incomes to diversify into commerce, services and transport. The interrelationship between agriculture and non-agricultural activities has been of crucial importance for the process of capital accumulation and differentiation in the rural areas of Kenya since the mid-fifties. A process which has increased inequalities in income and opportunity between a group of rich peasants engaged in a variety of remunerating economic activities and a big group of poor peasants with little or no high potential land who might be developing into a landless proletariat of agricultural labourers.

CHAPTER III

The Development in Non-Farming Activities in Kisumu, Kisii, Kwale and Taita Hills

In the previous chapter we have argued that non-farming activities have played an important role in the historical development of African capital accumulation and shown the significant role played by these activities as a source of income and as an area for profitable investment in the present situation in the rural areas of Kenya.

The significance of rural non-farm activities is now being widely recognized also among international aid agencies as indicated by the following quotation from the World Bank, annual report 1978: "Because rural non-farm activities seem to combine all those elements necessary for spreading the benefits of development to lower income groups through growth in employment and wages, they deserve close attention when development policies that emphasize the alleviation of poverty are formulated".[1]

This quotation emphasizes the significant role that rural non-farm activities, i.e., trade, craft, small-scale industries and various services have for the employment and income opportunities of the rural poor in developing countries.

Development strategies directly aimed at the eradication of poverty and the satisfaction of the basic needs of the poor have become the focus of discussion in international aid agencies since the I.L.O. World Employment Conference in 1976.[2]

Increasing productivity on small peasant holdings is an important part of such a strategy, but it is not sufficient, since the increasing number of landless labourers in the rural areas of the developing countries might be negatively affected if increased productivity on smallholdings leads to less demand for wage labour.

In order to formulate basic needs strategies for the rural landless poor, there is, therefore, a need to know more about how and to what extent the landless poor can find productive employment in the rural areas in sectors

[1] World Bank/Annual Report 1978, Washington, 30. June, 1978, p. 32.

[2] See e.g. I.L.O., *Employment, Growth and Basic Needs,* Geneva 1976.

other than agriculture in the future development of various developing countries.

We know that as much as between 20 per cent and 30 per cent of the rural labour force in developing countries has its main occupation in non-farm activities and that particularly the poorer section of the rural population received the major part of their incomes from non-agricultural activities.[3] But this information in itself does not provide the answer to the future role of the rural non-farm sector in creating productive employment for the rural poor. To answer the question a more dynamic analysis of the conditions and socio- economic and political relationships which determine the medium and long run development perspectives of the rural non-farm sector is needed.

In this chapter we will discuss some of the methodological problems involved in analysing the wide spectrum of non-farming activities and we will provide a description of the existing position of this sector in Kenya with particular emphasis on the 4 districts, Kisumu, Kisii, Taita Hills and Kwale, which have been selected as case studies for this research.

The development perspectives of the non-farm sector in the 4 study areas and in Kenya in general are discussed in Chapter V based upon an analysis of our field-work data.

Important Characteristics of the Non-Farm Sector

Until the beginning of the 1970's most development economists have analysed the development process within the conceptual framework of a "dual economy" which conceived the economies of the developing countries as consisting of two virtually different sectors the so-called "traditional" sector and the so-called "modern" sector.

The traditional sector was made up of peasants in subsistence agriculture and by non-agricultural activities like craft, home industry, petty trade etc. in the rural areas. The modern sector, on the other hand, included the large farms and the urban economy with its industries, commerce and service sector. The traditional sector was characterized by low productivity and stagnation, and development economists therefore conceived the development process as a process in which labour was transferred to the modern sector as fast as it was made possible by the formation of capital in the modern sector.

[3] A research report from the World Bank provides useful information on the significance of non-farming activities for the employment and incomes of rural populations in a number of developing countries. See *Rural Enterprise and Non-farm Employment.* A World Bank Paper, Washington, Jan., 1978.

However, it soon became obvious that the modern sector could only absorb a small fraction of the rapidly growing labour force in the developing countries. It will simply not be possible to increase capital formation in the modern sector at a rate which can prevent unemployment from increasing.

This was realized by a number of I.L.O. employment missions to various developing countries, in the beginning of the 1970's. In the reports from these employment missions a "new" sector was introduced in the economic models of the developing countries. The new sector – called "the informal sector" or often also "the intermediate sector" – was characterized by its positive properties for employment creation, for utilization of local resources and as producer of cheap everyday consumer goods, services and agricultural implements. Thus, by supporting the activities in the informal sector, it would be possible to increase employment, improve the balance of payment situation, slow down rural-urban migration and support the supply of cheap consumer goods for the poor in urban and rural areas. It is evident, therefore, that there exists a close connection between the I.L.O. inspired employment creation development strategies of the beginning of the 1970's and the basic needs strategies of the late 1970's.

The critics of these development strategies have argued that they will slow down the economic growth of the developing countries partly because the enterprises in the informal sector are less efficient in their utilization of labour, capital and other resources, partly because they believe that an employment-creation oriented investment policy will increase the rate of consumption and decrease the overall investment ratio in the economy.

However, a number of research findings have concluded that certain types of informal enterprises are more efficient than modern sector enterprises in their utilization of capital as well as their utilization of labour and raw material.[4]

Therefore, there seems to be a need to distinguish between the various kinds of activities in this sector in order to obtain a better and more detailed understanding of the development potential. As the activities in this sector

[4] See, e.g., Liedholm, C. and Chuta, E., *"The Economics of Rural and Urban Small-Scale Industries in Sierra Leone,"* African Rural Economy Paper No. 14, Department of Agricultural Economics, Michigan State University, U.S.A. 1976; Spencer, May-Parker and Rose, *Employment, Efficiency and Income in the Rice Processing Industry* of Sierra Leone, in African Rural Economy Paper No. 15, Department of Agricultural Economics, Michigan State University, U.S.A. 1976.

That these findings also apply to some small-scale industries in Kenya is pointed out by Child F.C., *Employment, Technology and Growth – the Role of the Intermediate Sector in Kenya,* Occasional Paper No. 19, IDS, University of Nairobi, 1976, and also by Kaplinsky, R. "Appropriate Technology and Political Economy: A Case Study of the Bread Industry in Kenya" in Westley, S.B. (ed.) *"The Informal Sector in Kenya".* Occasional Paper No. 25, I.D.S., University of Nairobi, January, 1978.

are "formal" as well as "informal" and since "intermediate" seems to be nothing but a new phrase we prefer simply to talk about this sector as "the rural non-farm sector". The problems and perspectives of the urban "informal" or "intermediate" sector will not be discussed here.

The rural non-farm sector is made up of a great number of very different activities. Distinctions are usually made between trade, manufacturing (artisans as well as small-scale industries), repair activities, transport and various other services. But within each of these groups there exist a broad spectrum of activities, the basis and development potential of which depends on very different circumstances. Some activities like fishing, forestry, saw-mills, and charcoal production depend on the availability of natural resources. Other activities are directly based upon agricultural production and are directly dependent on its size. That is the case of, for instance, maize mills, sugar jaggeries, tea factories and coffee factories as well as trade in agricultural produce. Finally a major part of the rural non-farm activities are directed at the rural households as consumers of simple everyday consumer goods and tools, utensils and implements. These are, for instance, artisans, small-scale industries, and retail shops in the rural market-places. They depend totally on the disposable incomes of rural households. Very few small-scale industries in Kenya produce for the urban market as is the case in developing countries in Asia.[5]

Secondly, it is important to distinguish between articles produced by members of the rural households for their own consumption such as, for instance, house building, maize milling and on the other hand articles produced by family members for sale in the rural market-place. A number of articles which were previously produced by family members for consumption within the household are now being traded as a result of the increasing specialization which is normally associated with economic development.

Thirdly, it is important to make a distinction between full-time and part-time occupation in the rural non-farm sector, and also to distinguish between all year and seasonal activities. The importance of these distinctions has been demonstrated clearly in previous studies of the rural non-farm sector.

[5] In some developing countries as, e.g. India smallscale industries in rural areas are being sub-contracted by large-scale urban industries. In some developing countries small-scale industries have even been successful in producing for the export market. However in Kenya the sale of products from rural enterprises is limited to souvenirs for the tourist industry and is of little significance in the overall pattern. Also, a small number of subcontract cases were observed between rural tailors and Asian shop-keepers in Kisumu Town during our field surveys.

In rural Western Nigeria a study indicates that 27 % of the employed males had their primary occupation in the rural non-farm sector.[6] This figure corresponds well to findings from a similar study of 4 villages in Uganda that revealed that 20 percent of employed males were primarily engaged in non-farm activities.[7] But if one includes the farmers who are engaged in non-farm activities on a part-time basis, the importance of this sector becomes even more striking. In the above mentioned study in Western Nigeria, for example, it was found that if one includes part-time engaged the number of people involved in non-farming activities increased to 41 percent. Roughly similar results have been obtained from other studies.[8]

Similarly these studies showed that there are large seasonal variations in rural non-farm activity. This is due to 3 different factors: (i) seasonal variations in demand for farm labour, (ii) seasonal variations in disposable income of rural households and (iii) seasonal variations in marketing and processing of agricultural products. Luning's study, for example, reveals that while 65 percent of the males in rural Sokoto Province were primarily engaged in non-farm activities during the dry season, only 6 percent were primarily engaged in these activities during the wet season, the period of peak demand for farm labour. Norman found that males devoted 79 percent of their time to non-farm activities in February but only 27 percent of their time to such activities in August (the time of peak demand for labour).

Our own study in Kenya reveals that small-scale industries producing for the consumers in the rural areas such as carpenters and blacksmiths have no business when school-fees have to be paid (tailors benefit from making school uniforms at that time). It further shows that certain processing industries, i.e., posho mills are busier just efter harvest because people eat more food when they have plenty in stock and that certain trading activities, i.e., the women trading in local crafts like pottery, baskets, etc. and in vegetable and poultry seem to grow in the month before harvesting as the families need cash to buy food.

Fourthly, there is a traditional differentiation of activity by sex in the rural areas of most African countries. This is the case in agricultural production as well as in non-farming activity. Thus most traditional crafts like pottery

[6] International Labour Office, "Socio-Economic Conditions in the Ifo, Otta and Ilaro Districts of the Western State of Nigeria". *Working Paper, I.L.O.* Fact-Finding Report for the Pilot Project for Rural Employment Promotion in the Western State, 1970 (mimeographed) quoted from Liedholm, C., *Research on Employment in the Rural Non-Farm Sector in Africa,* African Rural Employment Paper No. 5, Department of Agricultural Economics, Michigan State University, April 1973.

[7] *Ibid.*

[8] *Ibid.*

and basket-making, beer-brewing, and petty trade at the local markets are typical women activities while small-scale industrial activities, carpentry, blacksmithing, tailoring, shoe-making, etc., and trading in cattle are typical male activities. One of the studies mentioned above found that 88 percent of the people involved in trade were women, while 86 percent of the people involved in rural industries were men.[9]

With regard to the analysis of the factors which determine the development potential of the rural non-farm sector, the following classification of rural non-farm activities (r.n.f.a.) will be undertaken.

1. r.n.f.a. based upon natural resources
2. r.n.f.a. based upon agricultural production
3. r.n.f.a. based upon the demand of rural households

In the discussion of the conditions which determine the development of these 3 categories of r.n.f.a. it is very important to distinguish between full-time and part-time occupations.

Employment and income opportunities in r.n.f.a. for full-time occupation will be determined by (i) the availability of natural resources (ii) the size of agricultural production and its composition (iii) the size of disposable income (iv) distribution of income and (v) the competitiveness of the r.n.f.a. vis-à-vis the modern urban sector, respectively.

Part-time occupation, on the contrary, often is of a completely different nature. It is to a significant extent undertaken as a purely defensive device to protect rural families against hunger in years of bad harvest.

This kind of "subsistence part-time occupation" is characterized by the predominance of women, i.e., homecraft and petty trade and by relatively low income opportunities. The income potential in these activities decreases when incomes of rural households decrease, partly because the rural households make up the major market for the produce, partly because an increased number of women would be involved in securing incomes to buy necessities for their families. By nature people in this sector are self-employed and their jobs at low productivity levels are often termed "disguised unemployment" because of the low incomes they provide.

In Kenya this kind of part-time occupation is most widespread among poor peasant families, particularly in less fertile areas of the country.[10]

[9] *Ibid.*

[10] See Mbithi, P.M., *"Non-Farm Occupation and Farm Innovations in Marginal, Medium and High Potential Regions of Eastern Kenya and Buganda".* I.D.S. Working Paper No. 114, University of Nairobi 1971, and P.M. Mbithi and F.E. Chege, "Linkages between Agriculture and Rural Small-scale Enterprises" in Child and Kempe (ed.), *"Small-scale Enterprise,"* Occasional Paper No. 6, IDS, University of Nairobi, 1973. See also Kongstad, P. and Mönsted, M., *op.cit.,* Chapter IV, pp. 107–129.

Table III.1. *Rural Non-Farm Enterprises by Economic Activity 1969.*

	Number of enterprises
Retail trade	29.559
Restaurants etc.	4.935
Tailoring	4.386
Bicycle repair	1.575
Furniture and fixture	1.549
Maize mills	1.387
Foot-wear manufacture and repair	1.147
Fishing	809
Other handicraft	672
Saw-mills	479
Charcoal burning	336
Others	4.221
Total	51.005

Source: Ministry of Finance and Economic Planning: "Survey of non-agricultural enterprises in rural areas, 1969, quoted from Mbithi and Chege *op. cit.* p. 35.

Table III.2. *Employment and Average Annual Income in Non-agricultural Enterprises in Rural Areas 1969.*

	Employment No.	Annual income K. shs.
1. Self employed	67.900	2.600
2. Family workers	27.600	
3. Total employees	81.600	900
of which		
regular	47.500	
casual	34.100	
4. Total employment	187.100	

Source: As Table III.1 and I.L.O. "Employment, Income and Equality in Kenya", *op. cit.* table 27, p. 77.

Rural Non-Farming Activities in Kenya – with Specific Reference to Kisumu, Kisii, Taita Hills and Kwale Districts

From a statistical point of view it is necessary to make one additional distinction between various r.n.f.a. namely between activities undertaken within the organization of an enterprise and activities undertaken by individual members of rural households.

The existing information on the r.n.f.a. in Kenya has been improved significantly during the last decade, at least in the quantitative sense.

The first statistical survey of rural non-farm enterprises was conducted in

Table III.3. *Percentage distribution of rural household income by source of income and province.*

	Central	Coast	Eastern	Nyanza	Rift Valley	Western	Total
Farm operating surplus	49.99	24.90	54.82	71.31	67.42	47.55	56.98
Non-farm operating surplus	7.69	18.83	14.08	9.33	6.62	5.05	9.69
Regular employment	21.72	13.50	10.56	10.61	17.39	22.41	15.50
Casual employment	8.61	14.26	10.13	2.76	2.95	6.61	6.90
Remittance from relatives	9.27	24.93	8.61	4.55	3.56	16.32	8.87
Other gifts	2.76	3.52	1.78	1.46	2.05	2.00	2.05
Total household income	100.00	100.0	100.00	100.00	100.00	100.00	100.00
Total value of household income (K. Shs.)	4,241	3,325	3,486	3,911	4,577	2,494	3,652

Source: Integrated Rural Survey 1974/75 *op. cit.* table 8.8.

1967, but the data were never published. New surveys were conducted in 1969 and 1972, but again the results were not published. However, some of the results of the 1969 survey are available from secondary sources. Table III.1 provides information on the number of rural enterprises in 1969 and Table III.2 shows the number of people working in these enterprises and their estimated yearly incomes.

According to these tables a total of 187.100 persons were employed in 51.005 rural non-farm enterprises in 1969. This is approx. 4 per cent of the adult rural population.

Since the 1972 survey there has been no general collection of information on rural non-farm enterprises,[11] but a number of investigations of small manufacturing enterprises and small shops in various rural areas of Kenya have been undertaken.[12]

Most of the rural non-farm activities, however, are organized not in the frame of enterprises but within the framework of the rural household unit. Frank C. Child estimates that in addition to the people employed in rural enterprises as many as 250.000 people had non-farm occupations in the rural areas of Kenya in 1969.[13]

The significance of these activities for the incomes of the rural households appears from the annual Integrated Rural Surveys which were initiated in 1974/75. Only the results of the 1974/75 survey have yet been published. Table III.3 shows that the average Kenyan rural household received as much as 43 per cent of its income from non-farming activities.

Wages from regular and casual employment account for most of the non-farm incomes, and since most of the incomes from urban employment appear in the statistics as remittances from relatives living and working elsewhere, most the wage income stems from farm and non-farm employment in the rural areas.[14]

From other information in the Integrated Rural Survey it can be

[11] An annual survey of employment and income in the urban, informal sector is now being conducted. See Okoth Ogundo, "Data Collection on the Urban 'Informal' Sector" in B. Westley (ed.) *op.cit.* p. 79.

[12] The most important of these studies are Marris, P. and Somerset, A., *African Businessmen – a Study of Entrepreneurship and Development in Kenya,* London 1971; Inukai, I. and Okelo, J.A., *Rural Enterprise Survey in Nyeri District, Kenya.* A report of the consultants to DANIDA, Nairobi 1972; Okelo, J.A., *Rural Enterprise Survey in Kakamega District, Kenya.* Report of the consultant to DANIDA, Nairobi 1972; Child, F.C., *op.cit.* and Loehr, W. and Powelsen, J.P., *A Financial Study of Rural Business in Western Kenya,* Discussion Paper No. 122, Department of Economics, University of Coba. Kongstad, P. and Mönsted, M., *opcit.,* Chapter V, pp. 133–159.

[13] Child, F.C., *op.cit.,* p. 6.

[14] Due to the definition of the rural household chosen for the Integrated Rural Survey, as the people eating together, income from family members working in the urban areas of Kenya is mostly accounted for as remittances from relatives.

Table III.4. *Percentage distribution of rural population by main occupation and sex 1974/75.*

	Male	Female	Total
Work on family holding	78.81	97.51	89.07
Operate another holding	0.62	0.42	0.51
Labour on another holding	2.41	0.28	1.24
Other rural work	6.83	0.49	3.35
Teaching/Gov. employment	4.52	0.98	2.58
Urban employment	6.71	0.31	3.20
Other	0.11	0.01	0.05
Total	100.00	100.00	100.00

Source: Integrated Rural Survey 1974/75 *op. cit.* table 5.7, p. 29.

estimated that approx. 30 per cent of rural wages are earned by people working on other small holdings.[15]

Taken together, income from rural non-farm enterprises and from rural non-farm wage employment thus account for nearly 25 per cent of rural household income in 1974/75. This share, however, varies considerably between provinces and among different income groups (see Table II.30 and Table III.3).

The share of the adult population who have their main occupation outside the family holding, however, is rather low. In 1974/75 only 11 per cent of the adult smallholder population had their main occupation outside the family holding (see Table III.4). The proportion is much higher for men than for women and there are considerable differences between the various provinces. Thus in Central Province and Western Province more than 25 per cent of the male adult population worked off the family holding.[16]

Table III.4 shows that 3.35 per cent of the rural population were full-time employed in rural non-farm activities. This is equivalent to 346,430 people.

The number of people who are part-time engaged in these activities is probably more than twice this figure and likely to be much more dominated by female members of the rural households.[17]

In December 1976–January 1977 a new survey of non-farm activities in rural Kenyan households was undertaken. Here again, the household, not the enterprise, was the basic unit of the survey. This survey included all

[15] This estimate is based upon Integrated Rural Survey 1974/75 *op.cit.* table 8.4 and table 8.24.

[16] Integrated Rural Survey *op.cit.* table 5.7, p. 29.

[17] See Mbithi, P.M. and Chege, F.E. *op.cit.* table 4 and table 5, and Hunt, D., Resource Use in a medium potential area: The Mbere Rural Economy, Working Paper No. 180, I.D.S., University of Nairobi, August 1974.

Table III.5. *The prevalence of non-farm activities in rural households. Rural Household Survey 1976–77 (percentage).*

Frequency of non-farm activities per sample household	Central %	Coast %	Eastern %	Nyanza %	Rift Valley %	Western %	National level %
0	63.8	31.4	49.9	39.4	58.8	44.3	49.6
1	24.7	48.4	26.3	23.5	20.3	32.8	26.4
2	9.0	12.1	11.2	20.0	11.2	11.8	13.0
3	1.4	5.6	3.6	7.4	5.9	4.0	4.7
4	0.6	2.4	2.5	3.5	2.5	3.1	2.5
5	0.6	0.0	1.5	2.9	0.2	1.5	1.3
more than 5	0.0	0.0	5.0	3.3	1.1	2.5	2.4
Total sample	100.0	100.0	100.0	100.0	100.0	100.0	100.0

Source: Government of Kenya, Central Bureau of Statistics, *Social Perspectives* vol. 2 No. 2 June 1979, table 1.

non-farming activities that were carried out in the rural households for more than a month in the previous year (1976).

As Table III.5 shows, at least half of the sampled households in the sample recorded one or more non-farm activities, which were carried out for a period of a month or longer in the year preceding the survey. Nearly a quarter of all households carried out more than one non-farm activity, indicating a significant division of effort between farming and other income-earning activities. A considerable number of the rural households were essentially multiple-activity enterprises, recording more than five distinctly different activities. Some households recorded as many as fourteen activities, often of surprising diversity.[18]

Table III.5 also shows the inter-provincial differences in the incidence of non-farm activities in rural households. Approximately two-thirds of the sampled households in Nyanza and Coast Province were recorded undertaking non-farm activities, whereas the samples households in Central and Rift Valley provinces had considerably lower frequences of non-farm occupation per household.

A degree of similarity will be noted in the provincial rankings for non-farm activities in Table III.3 and Table III.5. For example, Coast Province ranks highest in both prevalence of non-farm activities per household and proportion of income per holding from such activities. Households in Rift Valley and Nyanza also show fairly similar rankings on the two tables. This seems at first glance to point to a direct relationship between the prevalence of an activity and the proportion of household income derived from that activity. However, the divergences in ranking of households in Central, Western and Eastern provinces point to the existence of more complex relationships, possibly involving the distinction undertaken above between on the one hand productive and subsistence activities and on the other hand part-time and full-time activities.

Also the structure of rural non-farm activities varies considerably between provinces. This is shown in Table III.6. For the national sample as a whole the most important categories are manufacture of food, beverages and tobacco, and services. The relatively minor importance of trade is due to the exclusion of irregular activities undertaken for less than one month of the year.

As might be expected the simple processing of local raw materials and the provision of a wide range of "traditional" services comprise the predominant

[18] Government of Kenya, Central Bureau of Statistics, *Social Perspectives* vol. 2, No. 2, June 1977, p. 2.

[19] *Ibid.* table 4, pp. 6–8.

Fishermen at Lake Victoria. (Jesper Kirknæs)

part of the rural non-farm sector. A closer examination of individual types of activity in these broad categories reveals that in many cases, one or a few specific activities account for the relative importance of the entire category. For example, the brewing of pombe, the local beer, is clearly the most prevalent of all non-farm activities in the rural households, and largely accounts for the dominance of the food, beverage and tobacco products sector. Similarly, charcoal making, wood cutting and small shops (duka) have a large impact on the relative importance of their respective activity categories. In general, the data attest the remarkable diversity of activities in the rural non-farm sector.

The summary percentage figures for the broad categories in the six provinces reveal a fairly consistent pattern in which Central Province, and to a certain extent Rift Valley Province, are shown to be distinctly different from Nyanza, Western and Eastern provinces. In most cases, Central Province records the lowest percentage for various activity categories, with a few exceptions, such as metal products manufacturing, where it ranks highest and manufacture of clothing and furniture which are both activities depending on high rural incomes.

Table III.6. *Share of small-holdings engaged in non-farming activities by activity and province 1976/77 (per cent).*

Activity	Central %	Coast %	Eastern %	Nyanza %	Rift Valley %	Western %	National level %
Resource extraction							
of which	*2.5*	*9.7*	*14.5*	*17.5*	*10.0*	*14.0*	*12.1*
wood cutters	1.1	0.0	3.4	4.5	5.9	4.0	3.7
fishermen	0.3	4.0	0.0	5.4	0.2	4.6	2.2
Manufacturing of food, beverages and tobacco							
of which	*5.9*	*24.2*	*18.3*	*36.5*	*20.5*	*25.1*	*22.3*
pombe brewing	3.4	2.4	5.9	26.0	15.0	17.6	13.4
Plant and animal fibre products and weaving apparel							
of which	*4.2*	*21.0*	*19.6*	*12.2*	*13.2*	*6.8*	*12.4*
mats, bags & clothing	1.9	16.6	12.1	6.6	0.2	2.4	5.7
textile and clothing	2.0	4.0	6.3	4.2	5.0	3.4	4.3
hides and skins	0.0	0.0	0.4	0.6	5.9	0.3	1.4
Wood products							
of which	*11.8*	*6.4*	*17.0*	*16.9*	*11.2*	*14.0*	*14.0*
charcoal	6.7	1.6	7.2	6.0	7.3	4.0	6.1
furniture	2.0	0.8	1.3	1.4	0.9	2.5	1.5
calabashes	0.3	0.0	3.0	5.8	1.6	2.8	2.7
saw-mills	1.7	0.0	0.2	0.8	0.4	0.3	0.6
Pottery products	*0.0*	*0.8*	*1.0*	*5.4*	*0.2*	*0.9*	*1.7*
Metal products	*1.7*	*0.8*	*1.0*	*1.6*	*0.7*	*1.2*	*1.2*
Building materials	*0.8*	*0.8*	*6.0*	*4.0*	*0.4*	*2.1*	*2.8*

Building and construction	*0.0*	*1.6*	*3.4*	*2.9*	*0.4*	*2.5*	*1.9*
Wholesale and retail trading	*7.3*	*6.4*	*8.0*	*13.7*	*5.9*	*12.1*	*9.3*
shops	3.4	0.8	4.0	3.8	3.2	5.0	3.7
butchers	1.1	0.8	1.9	2.1	2.0	2.5	1.9
petty trade	0.3	1.6	0.2	1.6	0.4	2.8	1.0
Reparing of which	*3.1*	*3.2*	*8.2*	*8.9*	*2.5*	*6.2*	*5.4*
clothing repair	1.4	0.0	1.5	2.5	0.9	0.9	1.4
bicycle repair	0.0	1.6	1.3	1.2	0.4	0.3	0.8
furniture repair	0.8	0.0	1.9	2.1	0.4	0.9	1.2
shoe repair	0.0	0.8	1.9	1.2	0.2	1.5	1.0
Services of which	*14.0*	*25.0*	*26.2*	*14.7*	*10.9*	*21.4*	*17.8*
transport	4.3	0.0	6.6	0.8	2.3	4.2	3.3
hotels, restaurants etc.	3.9	0.0	10.0	4.7	1.7	2.1	4.5

Source: As Table III.5.

Note: Since many households recorded none or more than one activity each, percentage figures for provinces do not add to 100.

Rift Valley tends to follow a pattern similar to Central Province, whereas Western, Nyanza and Eastern Provinces generally rank highest on many of the broad categories listed, mainly because of the high frequencies of traditional processing and service activities such as for example wood cutting, fishing, beer brewing, cottage industries and petty trading, which are partly of a subsistence nature (See Table III.6).

Coast Province which has the highest frequency of non-farm activities per sample household (see Table III.5) is somewhat in between. It ranks high on fishing, other drinks (than beer), some cottage industries and traditional services, but ranks low on most manufacturing activities.

These differences in the structure of non-farming activities are partly due to differences in the endowment of natural resources, partly the result of the different impact that colonial policy had on the development of non-farming activities in the various parts of Kenya.

Some general characteristics of this process were outlined in Chapter I. In the following, a more detailed description of the development of non-farming activities in Kisumu, Kisii, Taita Hills and Kwale will be given.

Kisumu District

Resource-based non-farming activities

Fishing is the most important of the *resource-based non-farming activities* in Kisumu district.

Fishing in Lake Victoria has undergone fundamental changes since the pre-colonial times. In those days most fishing was undertaken by self-employed African fishermen mostly for subsistence or for the barter of sun-dried fish within the lake district itself. But under colonial rule fishing partly became a commercial activity undertaken under a capitalist mode of production with a new, more capital intensive, technique and part of the catch was "exported" to the urban areas by Asian and European controlled wholesale companies. At the same time subsistence fishing has continued and expanded in terms of the number of people participating due to the difficulties of poor families to feed themselves from agricultural activities in the less fertile parts of the districts.

One of the serious long-term consequences of this commercialization of the fishing activities has been overfishing. According to local fishermen, species of fish which were previously plentiful have now almost disappeared. Increasing numbers of people thus have to share a smaller catch. Only river fishing seems to continue very much as in pre-colonial days, by using a line, a basket or a moveable trap.

The change in lake fishing started soon after the railway reached Kisumu. Asian traders who came to Kisumu, soon saw the potential for improving the indigenous fishing operations of the African fishermen of the Gulf and marketing the fish to the growing towns of Kenya. They opened fishing stations around the lake and introduced fishing nets and fishing boats built on the same principle as the Arab dhows, which had for centuries crossed the waters of the Indian Ocean (to the East African coast land), as a substitute for locally made canoes. But the Asians did not fish themselves. They employed crews of African fishermen (usually three) to do the hard work of fishing, unloading, repairing nets etc. at wage rates far below the minimum rates laid down for the employment of Africans in the townships.[20]

The development of the commercial fishing industry was a slow process, for not only did it involve the construction of dhows and the engagement of fishermen, it also required an extension in the demand for fish and the provision of improved communications so that fish could be railed to Nairobi, where the price which could be obtained from European and other buyers would be higher than that which the Nyanza Africans would be prepared to pay. In 1914 the Victoria Nyanza Fish Protection Rules were introduced in order to protect the fishing resources of Lake Victoria. According to these rules all non-nationals of the area engaged in fishing, whether for barter or for sale, were required to have a licence. By 1915 there were 25 licenced fishermen and in 1931 the number had grown to 69 giving employment to some three hundred Africans.[21] It is not possible to give figures of the tonnage of fish marketed through this Asian controlled fishing enterprise, but it is quite clear that before 1930 the significance was still limited compared to the fishing activity of Africans using indigenous methods of catching fish which was then consumed by the family or bartered in exchange for other subsistence needs.

The growing commercialization of the fish industry was aided by the increased demand for food, due to the Second World War. The "export" trade was increased by the demands of the troops and a Nairobi firm was contracted to supply this demand, aided by the associated activity of Asian dhow-owners. In 1952 this company was taken over by a Kisumu-based company that changed the fishing industry by using lorries and boats to collect fish at the more remote fishing stations around the Gulf. In Kisumu the company had cold storage facilities and fish were dispatched daily by rail to Nairobi, Mombasa, Kampala and other towns. More and more Africans became involved in this commercial fishing activity both as labourers and

[20] Fearn, H. *op.cit.* p. 216.
[21] *Ibid.* p. 217.

Table III.7. *Estimated tonnage and value of fish caught in Lake Victoria.*

	metric tons	value K£ '000
1933	.	20
1934	1,300	17
1935	.	45
1936	3,102	.
1937	.	66
.		
1950	.	56
1965	13,215	728
1966	15,445	851
1967	15,748	868
1968	16,357	708
1969	17,442	802
1970	16,400	774
1971	14,918	768
1972	15,989	841
1973	16,797	906
1974	17,175	1,050
1975	16,581	1,065
1976	18,680	1,203

Source: Fearn, *op. cit.* pp. 220–221 and statistical abstract 1970 and 1975.

as dhow-owners. Thus in the years 1949 to 1959 an average of 290 African owned dhows were licenced annually together with 93 dhows, owned by Asians of which, however, as much as 75 percent operated only to supply the local demands of Africans for fish, and were not engaged in the "export market". Still, however, the dhow operators were of minor importance in relation to the total number of people involved in fishing. Thus, in 1953, there were about 3,000 licensed African fishermen engaged in fishing from canoes using nets or spears for catching. They sold their fish at the beach but operating single-handed they usually had only few fish for sale either to the women buying fish at the beaches or the professional fish traders who carried the fish on bicycles to inland markets where they got a higher price. Also, the fishing for subsistence was still very important.[22]

It is obvious that because of the varied market structure and the significance of the subsistence fishing it is difficult to estimate the value of the fish caught every year. The official estimate, thus, does not support the widespread opinion among the local fishermen that the fish are disappearing due to overfishing. But the figures show that the lake fishing is stagnating (see Table III.7). The total catch of fish has varied between

[22] *Ibid.*, p. 218.

15–18.000 tons in the last ten years, but in the same time the number of fishermen has increased greatly. In many areas there are more than twice as many fishermen as compared to ten years ago.[23]

Thus the increasing number of fishermen are causing decreasing catches and income from fishing per person. On the other hand the reason for the increased number of people who take up fishing as an occupation must be understood from the lack of alternative income possibilities for the people living in the Kenya lake region. As has been demonstrated in the previous chapter, the region is among the most densely populated in Kenya. Productive land is scarce and rainfall is uncertain in most of Kisumu district. Profitable and secure employment possibilities in the towns and cities are few for the majority of the population of the district, therefore many people are forced to take up fishing as a means of subsisting. Since the fishing occupation is so inexpensive to enter and because there are no real limitations on the number of people who can participate, the fishing has become very labour intensive.

Only a small part of the fishermen are earning well enough from the fisheries to make substantial productive investments in other economic sectors but the fisheries secure the livelihood for a population who would otherwise starve or have to take up even less profitable and less attractive work than fishing.[24]

Besides the people owning the capital equipment (the boats and the nets) and the people employed as fishermen, a number of people engaged in boat building and boat repairing and net repairing as well as people trading in fish are getting an income from the fishing industry. Thus, there are important linkage effects from the lake fishing. Of the average value of the yearly catch only the money spent on buying new nets from a Japanese-owned factory in Kisumu left the rural areas.

Output-based non-farming activities

In the pre-colonial days the processing of the agricultural products undertaken by the women at home. Maize and sorghum were ground into posho every day and cooked into the traditional stable food. Hides and skins were sundried and processed into cloth and bedding.

The arrival of Asian businessmen in Kisumu changed this pattern completely. They built power-driven *posho mills* in almost every trading centre so that the women would carry a headload of maize to the nearest

[23] See Jansen, E.G., *The development of the Lake Victoria Fisheries and the Possibilities for Norwegian Participation,* DERAP PAPERS No. 75, The Chr. Michelsen Institute, Norway, September 1976.

[24] *Ibid.,* p. 6.

posho mill to have it ground there. But when the African district council markets were established in the mid-thirties enterprising Africans followed the example of the Asians and set up posho mills.

Today, all posho mills in Kisumu District are owned by Africans but there seems to be a concentration of ownership in a few hands. Thus, of the approximately 50 posho mills in operation in Kisumu District in 1975, one company was controlling 40 per cent. In terms of employment the posho mills are not important. 2–3 people are usually employed per mill so that the total employment in posho mills in 1975 was 100–150 people (see Table III.10).

But the main activity of the Asian businessmen was trade. They sold imported consumer goods and bought African surplus production for export. In Kisumu District the export of hides and skins became quite important particularly since the 1930's, when the quality of skins was improved, due to a shift from the traditional method of sun-drying to a method of shade-drying, and the licensing for this purpose in African district council markets run by Africans trained in the preparation of hides and skins. Today there is a *hide and skin banda* in almost every market place in Kisumu District. The total number is approximately 25 but like the posho mills the hides and skin bandas, giving employment to 1–2 people, are insignificant in terms of employment. The dried hides and skins are still sold to Asian traders in Kisumu and from there most of it is exported undressed.

Thus, very little employment has been created in the processing of the traditional agricultural products in Kisumu District. However, the introduction of new cash crops like sugar and cotton has given rise to some additional non-farm employment.

The first *cotton ginnery* was opened in Kisumu as early as in 1908 employing 15 Africans and 3 years later its output and employment had tripled.[25] However, the ginnery was based upon cotton from Uganda and the mill therefore had to be closed down in 1920 when the Uganda government prohibited the passing of seed cotton unginned to Kisumu. Since then the development of cotton ginning has been dependent on the slow development of cotton growing in the district. The only ginnery in the district was re-opened in Kibos near Kisumu in 1935. In 1972 and 1973 the number of people employed was 8 and 44 respectively, the figures showing the variations in employment due to variations in the cotton production.

Since Asian farmers were allowed to settle on the land under the Nandi escarpment in 1904, they have not only grown but also processed sugarcane. Before the establishment of the two sugar plantations and their sugar

[25] Fearn, H., *op.cit.* p. 68.

factories, the Victoria Nyanza Sugar Company at Miwani and the Muhoroni Sugar Company at Muhoroni, in the late twenties, there were 56 Asian families growing sugar-cane and processing the cane in *small sugar jaggeries.* Between 1909 and 1921, 1,441 tons of jaggery were exported from these small-scale sugar factories. With the establishment of the two factories the production of sugar increased. In 1929 the Miwani factory, which also purchased cane from Asian smallholders as wel as crushing its own cane, produced 6,617 tons of sugar and the Muhoroni factory 812 tons. Since 1960 African smallholders have started growing sugar in the areas near the sugar belt, and rich Nairobi Africans have been buying up some of the Asian farms. One more sugar factory has been built in Chemelil and many people are now employed in the 3 factories. In 1972, 1973, and 1974 the total number of employed was 2,234, 2,479 and 2,044 respectively, and they earned an average income of 5,380 Shs., 5,125 Shs. and 5,460 Shs. respectively.[26] Thus, the processing of sugarcane is by far the most important of the output-based non-farming activities in Kisumu District.

Demand-based manufacturing and repair activities

We know that most of the activities that existed in precolonial time like blacksmithing, pottery, basket-making, mat-making, beer-brewing and house-building have been influenced by the introduction of imported substitutes and other elements of colonial policy. But it is difficult to estimate the exact impact of the colonial rule upon employment and earnings in the non-farming sector in the rural areas.

Blacksmithing is probably the activity that was most negatively influenced by the importation of European made hoes. Thus we know that the number of people working as blacksmiths in Samia was dramatically reduced between 1900 and 1960,[27] and similar developments have probably taken place in Kisumu District. Recently, however, there has been an increase in the number of people working as blacksmiths. They are making kitchen utensils (charcoal cookers, cooking pots, buckets and knives) and agricultural implements (hoes and pangas) from scrap metal and they undertake repairs.

In the rural markets of Nyando and Winam division in Kisumu District there were 17 registered blacksmiths in 1975, but in addition a large number of people worked as blacksmiths in their homes. Thus, for example, the male adult population in the rural areas of Kibos seem to have specialized in making hoes from scrap metal bought from scrap dealers in Kisumu town.

[26] Kenya Bureau of Statistics.
[27] Were, P., *op.cit.*

In a small area there were 17 people working in their homes as blacksmiths in 1975. We estimate that as many as 50 people worked as blacksmiths in the rural areas of Kisumu District in 1975 and based upon interviews with 26 of these we estimate their average monthly income to approximately 250 Shs. In addition the blacksmiths employed approximately 50 people at an average salary of 150 Shs. a month (see Table III.10).

Pottery, basket-making, mat-making, the *making of sisal ropes,* etc. is still undertaken in the homes and carried to the rural markets for sale on market days, but other activities like beer-brewing and house-building are increasingly being undertaken within the frame of rural enterprises.

Almost every market in the district has a *beer hall* licensed to sell local beer and in each beer hall women take turns in selling their beer against paying a fee to the owner of the bar. Based on interviews with women brewing beer in Rabour, Nyangande and Ahero market we estimate that as many as 1,200 women are involved in brewing and selling beer at the licensed beer halls in Kisumu District making an average income of approximately 60 K.shs. a month. But in addition to this a number of women are engaged in illegal brewing.

More and more people in Kisumu District are having their houses built with roofs of iron sheets. Thus in 1971 approximately 10 per cent of the rural households in Kisumu District had houses with roofs of iron sheets.[28] Since the construction of these houses is more complicated than the building of grass-thatched houses, they are almost all built by local specialized house builders. Thus, we find that approximately 5,000 houses in the district have been built by *local builders* in the rural areas of Kisumu District. The majority of these houses have been built within the last 5 years. The local builders charge about 400 K.shs. for labour for an average sized house so that the 10 local builders in the rural areas of the district have had an average income of approximately 2,000 K.shs. a year. They usually employ 1–2 people to assist them at an yearly wage of approximately 1,000 K.shs. each.

In addition to the traditional non-farming activities of the pre-colonial time, a number of new activities have developed with the introduction of European consumer patterns.

The most important of these are tailoring, carpentry and a number of repair and service activities such as bicycle repair, bars, hotels and tea shops.

In the first years the demand for clothing was for a limited range, mainly dresses and khaki shorts and shirts. Most of this was imported. But with the introduction of school-uniforms, traders have been able to obtain contracts

[28] Kisumu District Development Plan 1975.

on making them. Many Asian dukas in the trading centres and in the townships had one or more sewing-machines, at which African apprentices or employees were sewing these garments. When the African traders started opening up dukas in the African District Council markets they followed the example of the Asian duka owners and bought sewing machines. They hardly ever employed any hired or paid labour. Instead they employed apprentices, learning the trade for a year. The apprentices paid a training fee, in return for which they would be kept and housed and taught a little tailoring. This system has meant that *African tailors* have been able to take on contracts for Asian firms in Kisumu town at very low rates. The Asian traders supply the material and sell the finished product in town while the African tailors supply cheap labour. No doubt tailors are the most numerous group of craft people working in the rural market-places. We estimated that there were approx. 300 people working as tailors in the rural market-places in Kisumu District in 1975 with an average monthly income of 200 Shs.

Other durable goods like furniture and bicycles came within the purchasing power of the consumers in the rural households and little by little *carpenters* and *bicycle repairers* opened up work-shops in the rural markets. The jobs performed by the cycle repairer were, and are still today, simple ones, mainly mending punctures and replacing damaged spokes. But some of the carpenters were quite enterprising in the variety of goods which they made, such as beds, tables and cupboards. However, very little has happened in terms of extension of the range and quality of goods produced, the technique and tools employed or the earning possibilities. The number of carpenters, however, has sharply increased and there is strong competition in the business. We estimate that in 1975 approximately 40 people with a monthly average income of 200 Shs. were working as bicycle repairers and that there were 30 rural carpenter workshops giving employment to about 80 people with monthly average income of 150 Shs. in the rural areas of Kisumu District.

Since the establishment of African District Council markets in the mid-thirties the councils have been trying to encourage Africans to engage in business other than petty trade with a limited range of goods. As a result *hotels* and *tea shops* were opened in most markets.

The hotels did not and still do not provide accomodation, but only food and drinks. The establishments which only provided tea and mineral water were called "tea-shops" to distinguish them from "hotels" which provided hot meals. In 1975 there were 40 registered hotels, restaurants and tea shops in the rural markets of Nyando and Winam Division. We estimate that the total number of these establishments in the rural market-places of Kisumu District was approximately 70 and that some 200 people worked there.

Trading

We have seen how the building of the Mombasa-Kisumu railway and the arrival of Asian traders and farmers influenced the development of such non-farming activities as fishing, grain-milling, sugarcane processing and blacksmithing. But first and foremost the significance of the Asians lie in their impact on the development of trade. The first Asian traders established themselves in Kisumu in 1901 selling a limited range of consumer goods and buying for export the African surplus agricultural produce of maize and hides and skins. They influenced African participation in trade partly through their negative influence with imported substitutes for locally made products, and partly by employing Africans in their business. When the regulations which were designed to prevent the non-natives from going into the reserves of Nyanza Province without a passport were abolished in 1909 the Asian traders could travel anywhere in the province provided that they did not go off the road, except for visiting an established trading centre. As roads were constructed by forced African labour, the number of trading centres increased and African agents were employed by the Asian traders to collect small quantities of produce from the peasant producers and to bring it to a collecting point, usually an Asian duka in a trading centre.

When maize and produce control was established in 1942 it instituted a system of licensing individual produce buyers and more Africans became directly involved in the profitable trade in maize. They worked on a commission basis and had to pay the declared producer price to the Africans bringing the produce for sale. Whether or not more buyers should be licensed in any one season was within the discretion exercised by a European marketing officer and he would make this decision with regard to the expected crop yields and available clearance facilities. There would always be one or more buyers in the trading centres and in the African markets. By 1955 approximately 50 per cent of the maize delivered to the inspection centre in Kisumu was marketed by African traders. A study undertaken in 1954 shows that the leading African produce buyers in Central Nyanza had an average income (trader commission) from the trade in maize, sorghum, wimbi and cassava of 1,436 Shs.[29]

The increase in the number of shops in registered townships and trading centres of Nyanza Province is shown in Table III.8, but in addition to this we must count the trading activity in markets in the rural areas where exchange of livestock and produce took place as in the pre-colonial period.

It is not known exactly how many such African markets existed previously. They were usually located where the chiefs headquarters were

[29] Computed from Fearn, *op.cit.* p. 263 table 5.

Table III.8. *Plot holders in townships and trading centres in Nyanza Province.*

	Townships and trading centres	African plot holders	Total no. of plot holders
Nyanza Province:			
1909	11		.
1917	46	.	343
1954	49	355	1,682
Central Nyanza 1954	13	176	920
South Nyanza 1954	22	64	274

Source: Fearn, *op. cit.* p. 118 and p. 163.

Table III.9. *African traders in Nyanza Province A.D.C. markets (1954).*

District	Number of markets	Number of licensed African traders	Total African population (1948)	Average number of people per trader
North Nyanza	133	1,322	633,568	479
Central Nyanza	173	2,397	462,772	193
South Nyanza	175	1,532	545,284	356
Kericho District	46	380	212,608	559
Nyanza Province	527	5,631	1,854,232	329

Source: Fearn *op. cit.* p. 175, 176.

established and there was probably at least one market in each location. The markets were first under the control of chiefs and elders, but in the mid-thirties the control of these markets was transferred by the government to the African District Councils. In Table III.9 the numbers of licensed African traders operating in these markets are shown (1954).

The growth in the participation of Africans in trade was contrary to the general policy of the colonial government which wanted the Africans to remain the labour reserve of the colony. Therefore it introduced regulations that made it difficult for Africans to obtain loans and it recommended a policy of restrictions on the number of trade licenses to be issued to Africans. Further, it restricted the successful development of African trade by interfering in the planning of the market sites and the number of plots. In order to be allocated a plot in a market-place, the applicant would be requested to build a duka of stone and wattle with a corrugated-iron roof, in accordance with health department specifications, within 3 years from

Women traders in open area markets on market day. (Jesper Kirknæs)

obtaining his licence. Such a buildings was quite costly and in many cases traders having spent this money (approximately 10,000 Shs. in 1954) had no money left as working capital for the shop. More serious for the development of trade in the district, however, has probably been the limited cash which was available for the purchase of commodities from the shops. Fearn estimates that in 1954 the average cash income, making up the demand for goods traded by the shops in Central Nyanza, was less than 1,600 Shs. per shop and that the net income of the shop owners therefore was no more than 260 Shs. a year. Although this estimate is based on rather loose assumptions it probably gives a fair assessment of the income opportunity in this business.

In 1975, out of 736 registered plots in Nyando and Winam division 439 were registered as petty traders, butcheries, ration stores, medicine shops and bakeries. Based on this we estimate that some 1,240 people were employed in 620 dukas in the rural areas of Kisumu District in 1975. Unfortunately it is not possible to compare this figure to the figure given from Central Nyanza in 1954. We interviewed a random sample of the shops in 10 market-places in the district and found that average daily sales varied between 10 Shs. and 170 Shs. A conservative estimate would be an average net income of 3,000 Shs. in 1975 per shop. We therefore find that the net income of duka owners has increased considerably since 1954.

Still, however, the trade which takes place in the open area, between the lines of dukas on four sides, is far the most important both in terms of turnover and in particular in terms of the number of people engaged. Here agricultural produce, fish and home-made craft products such as pottery, baskets, mats, and sisal ropes are traded. Some of the women trading in these markets are professional traders who travel widely over the country, but most of them are local residents who only occasionally occupy themselves with a little trade in order to get money to buy sugar, kerosine and cooking oil, and to buy maize when no more is left in the granary. But no figures are available in order to quantify the significance of this type of trade in the district.

In Table III.10 we have summarized some of the findings of the above analysis of the present significance of rural non-farm activities. The table shows that approximately 6,208 of the rural population or 3.8 per cent of the rural adult population of the district are engaged in permanent employment in non-farming activities in the district. In addition to this a number of people are employed in the public sector as school-teachers and as labourers on the construction of the new irrigation scheme.

It is important to note, however, that fishing is excluded from Table III.10. We estimate that approximately an additional 8,000 people are directly engaged in fishing and that some 4,000 are having regular incomes from related jobs such as repairing nets and boats and trading in fish.

It should also be noted that the table only includes people working on a permanent basis in *rural enterprises*. Thus the great number of people working part-time or occasionally with non-farm activities organized within the household unit are excluded from this table. Most of these occupations are dominated by women, for instance, home craft, petty trade and illegal beer brewing. The number of people engaged in these occupations are probably more than double the number engaged in rural enterprises.

It should be emphasized that the figure on total wage employment and average wage income is heavily influenced by employment in the sugar

Table III.10. *Estimate of people permanently employed and their income in non-farm rural enterprises in Kisumu District 1975.*

		Self-employed		Employed		
	Number of enter-prises	Number	Average yearly income (K. Shs.)	Number	Average yearly income (K. Shs.)	Total number in work
Maize mills	50	*	•	150	4,800	150
Hides and skins	25	25	1,200	25	900	50
Cotton ginning[1]	1	*	•	44	4,787	44
Sugar factories[2]	3	*	•	2,044	5,460	2,044
Blacksmith	50	50	3,000	50	1,800	100
Beer brewing in beer halls	40	1,200	720	80	1,200	1,280
House building	10	10	2,000	20	1,000	30
Tailors	300	300	2,400	•	•	300
Carpenters	30	30	3,000	80	1,800	110
Bicycle repairs	40	40	2,400	•		40
Hotels and tea shops	70	*	•	200	1,200	200
Shops in rural markets	620	620	3,000	1,240	1,200	1,860
Total	1,239	2,275	1,689	3,933	3,608	6,208

Source: Own estimates based upon field surveys.

* Often the owners of the enterprise do not work in the business themselves and often they do not live in the rural areas.

[1] The figure is from 1973.
[2] The figure is from 1974.

industry. This should be kept in mind when employment and income in non-farm enterprises in the four study areas are compared.

Kisii District

The development of non-farming activities in the rural areas of Kisii district has followed very much the same pattern as outlined for Kisumu above. Some activities that were formerly undertaken by family members themselves have become commercialized (grinding of maize, beer brewing, making of cloth, construction of houses), traditional crafts have met competition from modern industry (blacksmithing, pottery), new activities have grown up in the rural areas to cater for new needs (carpenters, bicycle repairers, automobile repairers, shops in rural markets etc.) and the introduction of new crops (coffee and tea) has given rise to new processing industries.

Resource based non-farming activities

Resource based non-farming activities are of less significance in Kisii than in Kisumu District. There is very little *river fishing* in the district and *wood cutting* which used to be of some significance has decreased in importance due to the high population density and the high proportion of the land cultivated.

Output-based activities

The development of maize mills and hide and skin bandas proceeded in Kisii very much as in Kisumu district. The first maize mill was opened by a European trader in Kisii town as early as 1914 and during the 1920's a start was made in the shade drying of hides and skins which had by then become one of Gusiiland's major exports. As a sign of early African capital accumulation, maize mills owned by Gusii were brought into operation already in the late 1920's. Many of them were built by the wealthy chiefs along streams utilizing the water as a source of power. The colonial administration gave encouragement to the building of mills and decided that non-natives should not be given mill concessions in the reserves.

Today there exist some 60 power-operated maize mills giving employment to some 180 people and a similar number of hide and skin bandas giving employment to approximately 60 people.

The introduction of cashcrops like coffee, tea and sugar has given rise to new processing industries in the district but the pyrethrum is being processed in Nairobi and Nakuru.

The first small *coffee factory* was built in 1937 and as production of coffee increased so did the number of small coffee factories. There were 8 factories in 1944 and by 1974 the number had increased to 62 which gave employment to some 250 people and an additional 1,000 during the peak months of July, August and September.

Tea planting had begun in the late 1950's and the first *tea factory* was built in 1962. In 1974 the two tea factories of the district together employed about 300 people. In addition there are 3 small sugar jaggeries in the district employing some 15 people altogether.

Demand-based activities

Handicraft seems to have been much less developed among the Gusii than among the Luo in pre-colonial days. Thus the Gusii exchanged agricultural produce in order to get pots for cooking and for carrying water.

There is evidence of the existence of *blacksmiths* in precolonial Gusii society,[30] but they seem to have been more vulnerable to the competition

[30] Mature and Kreya, *Kisii Industry before the Coming of the Europeans.* Bishop Otunga High School. AFR Historical and Cultural Quarterly Report. April 1970.

Shoemakers in Kisii District. (Jesper Kirknæs)

from imported commodities, like cooking utensils, hoes and iron buckets which the administration succeeded in introducing. Thus, we did not find any blacksmiths producing agricultural tools during our field work in the district in 1975. The main products of the blacksmith in Kisii district today is the jiko (charcoal cooker) and the small oil lamps made out of tins, but in addition he also often works as a bicycle repairer. We estimate that there were approximately 80 blacksmith/bicycle repairers in Kisii district in 1975 with average incomes of approximately 100 shs. monthly.

Of the traditional homecrafts the *brewing of local beer* and spirit seems to have managed quite well in the competition with imported items. From our survey of non-agricultural activities we estimate that as many as 10 percent of the rural households or approximately 12,000 women were brewing and selling beer. The average monthly income is about 100 shs.

As in Kisumu District *house-building* is increasingly being undertaken by skilled masons. In 1975 there were approximately 50 local masons who built approximately 1,000 iron-sheet roofed houses in the rural areas of the district. This gave them an average monthly income of 350 shs. each and approximately 150 shs. in monthly income to the 100 people whom they employed.

Carpentry, tailoring and *shoe-making* belong to the category of new activities that developed particularly after the Second World War, when cash incomes had grown due to large increases in cereal production, increases in sales of coffee, compulsory sale of cattle and the conscription of labour. In 1975 there were about 50 carpenter workshops employing 150–200 people, 150 tailors and some 50 shoe-makers/repairers.

Trade

The building of the administrative station in Kisii in 1907 and the beginning of collection of hut tax immediately changed the pre-colonial trading patterns. As the administration insisted that the tax be paid in money, the Gusii were forced to sell cattle, goats, and sheep in order to obtain cash to pay the tax. As a result, many Swahili and Somali cattle traders were drawn to the district and two Indian shop-keepers opened up stores in Kisii.

Kisii town became a centre of outside influence in Gusiiland. After 1909, when all government stations and trading centres in Nyanza were opened up to non-Africans, who were no longer required to have a pass for entry, the alien population of Kisii grew rapidly and by 1914 a market shed had been created and eight plots had been leased to Asian and European traders. In this way the trade in agricultural surpluses was taken over by Asian and European traders and their dominance over the trade in these items was complete until the Maize and Produce Control was established in 1942. Then for the first time Africans were licensed as produce buyers and by 1944 nearly half of the surplus grain produced in South Kavirondo was bought by African produce buyers. The number of Africans holding produce licenses increased from 20 in 1942 to 208 in 1947. In 1954 the most successful of the African produce buyers had an average turnover of 57,000 shs. which gave them a net annual income of approximately 3,000 shs.[31]

[31] Fearn *op.cit.* pp. 263–264.

A similar development took place in the trade in imported goods in small shops in the rural market. At first this trade was completely in the hands of the Asians but after the depression years in the 1930's when the Gusii agricultural cultural incomes from export of maize began to rise again, a large number of African owned shops were opened in the rural market centres. After the Second World War this trend continued when many people who had earned high incomes wanted to set up shops, hotels and bars. In 1946, over 1600 trade license applications were received by the administration of which 417 were issued. In this period the African shop owners felt the competition from Asians particularly hard and they therefore formed the Kisii Farmers and Trade Association with the aim of getting a monopoly of the distributive trade and putting Asian traders out of business. But due to lack of capital they did not succeed.[32]

Also the number of rural markets increased greatly in the period, from 6 in 1939, 24 in 1946 to 45 in 1950. But as in Kisumu District, the African traders suffered from lack of working capital partly due to the high construction cost caused by the high standard required by the health department, and partly due to the restrictions on loans to Africans.

We do not have precise information about the number of shops, bars and hotels and butcheries in the rural areas of Kisii District by 1975. But we estimate that there were approximately 750 small shops, 100 butcheries and 100 hotels, bars and tea-shops employing altogether some 2,000 people.

Table III.11 summarizes our estimates of employment and incomes in non-farm enterprises in Kisii District 1975. A total number of 4,445 people were employed on a permanent basis in rural enterprises this year. This equals 1.7 per cent of the adult population of the district.

As mentioned previously, a significant number of women are engaged in beer and alcohol brewing at home and in addition to this a large number of women are engaged in full-time and part-time trade, selling vegetables, bananas and other agricultural products. But the Gusii women are not to the same extent as the Luo engaged in the making and selling of home craft.

Taita Hills

We have very little information from secondary sources about the development of non-farming activities in the rural areas of Taita Hills. Thus most of the following is based upon our own observations during field-work in the area in 1975. From this it appears that small-scale industries have been much less developed in Taita Hills than in Kisumu and Kisii district. The

[32] Maxon *op.cit.* p. 100.

Table III.11. *Estimate of people permanently employed and their income in non-farm rural enterprises in Kisii District 1975.*

		Self-employed		Employed		
	Number of enter-prises	Number	Average yearly income (K. sh.)	Number	Average yearly income (K. shs.)	Total number in work
Maize mills	60	*		180	2.000	180
Hides and skins	60	60	1.200	60	1.200	120
Coffee factories[1]	62			500	3,000	500
Tea factories[1]	2			300	3,000	300
Sugar jaggeries	3	*		15	2,400	15
Blacksmith	80	80	1,200			80
House building	50	50	4,200	100	1,800	150
Tailors	150	150	3,600			150
Carpenters	50	50	9,600	200	1,800	250
Shoe-making/ repair	50	50	2,400			50
Butcheries	100	100	+	100	1,200	200
Hotels and tea shops	100	*	+	200	1,200	200
Small shops	750	750	2,000	1,500	1,200	2,250
Total	1,517	1,290	2,536	3,155	1,765	4,445

Source: Own estimates based upon field surveys.

* The owner does usually not work in the enterprise himself.
+ Average profit not known.
[1] The coffee and tea factories are owned by cooperative societies.

reason for this, however, does not seem to be that rural incomes have been substantially lower in Taita Hills than in the other two districts, but rather that the traditional small-scale industry products like furniture, kitchen, utensils, clothing and foot-wear could be bought cheaper and in better quality in Mombasa, where most of the cash income was earned, than within the district, mainly due to the high cost of transporting the raw materials, which could not be obtained locally, into the hills.

Resource-based non-farming activities

A number of people are engaged in *timber cutting* and *sawmilling* in the district. They are often employed directly by the people who own the carpenter workshops but there are also saw-mills in the district. We estimate that approximately 400 people are full-time or part-time engaged in this sector at average monthly incomes of 100 shs.

We also found a number of *brick-makers* forming bricks from clay and burning them. We estimate that there are 10 brick-makers employing 20 people in the district.

Output-based non-farming activities

Unlike Kisumu and Kisii the processing of maize into maize flour is still to a great extent undertaken in the homes by the women in Taita District. Moreover, Taita is a deficit maize producing area and most of the maize which is imported has already been grinded into maize flour. Therefore, there has been very little development of the *grain milling industry* in the district. In 1975 there was only 2 posho mills in Werugha location, and we estimate that there were 10 mills in the whole district employing on average 2 people at 70 shs. per month.

There are also fewer *hide and skin bandas* in Taita district than in the other districts and as the cattle are concentrated in the lowlands of the district so are the processing facilities for hides and skins.

Formerly the dried hides and skins were sold for further processing at the Plateau *Wattle Extract factory* in Konza together with the wattle produced in the district. In 1964 this factory gave employment to 86 people but according to statistics from the statistical bureau the factory has now been closed down. We estimate that by 1975 there were 10 hide and skin bandas in the district giving employment to 10 people at approximately 50 shs. per month.

In Taita Hills *beer* is brewed by the women mainly from sugarcane and bananas. From our field-work in Werugha we estimate that approximately 10 per cent of the women or approximately 3,000 are self-employed in commercial beer brewing in the district. From this, we estimate, that they get average monthly incomes of 100 shs.

Since 1910, when the first sisal estates were established, *fibre processing* has been the most important non-agricultural activity in the district. But production and employment has fluctuated according to export prices of sisal and there has been no long-term growth in the industry. In 1964, 1,106 were employed in the fibre processing industry in the district[33] but when sisal prices started rising, as a consequence of rising prices of fibres made from oil products in 1973, the production and employment in the Kenyan sisal processing industry rose sharply. In Taita District the number employed in the industry increased from 2,577 in 1972 to 3,265 in 1973 and 4,325 in 1974.[34] The average earnings of the people employed in this industry in Taita Hills were approximately 2,100 shs. per annum in 1974.

[33] Calculated from Ogendo, R.B., *Industrial Geography of Kenya,* Nairobi, 1972, table 2a p. 239.
[34] Unpublished data from Kenya Bureau of Statistics.

Of the new crops introduced in Taita District during colonial rule, only the coffee and some sugarcane is being processed locally whereas the vegetables and chilies are being exported from the district in unprocessed form. In 1974 the *coffee industry* employed 35 people at yearly wages of approximately 2,000 shs. and *the sugar jaggery* employed 2 people at yearly wages of approximately 2,300 shs.

Income-based non-farming activities

As already mentioned, it has been more difficult for the traditional income-based non-farming activities in the rural areas of Taita Hills to manage the competition from imported goods and develop into rural industries than in the other districts. From our field-work it seems that the choice for the consumers has been between either to make these products themselves at home or to buy imported goods when they were working in Mombasa, and could afford to buy these products. Therefore, there has been very little demand for products made by local craftsmen and amongst the traditional crafts only *pottery* seems to have survived as a commercial enterprise, whereas some *basket-making* is still done for individual consumption. *Blacksmithing*, however, has completely disappeared as a rural industry in Taita Hills. Only a few people are making metal products from scrap in the township of Voi and today most of the kitchen utensils and agricultural tools are imported into the district.

However, in recent years there seems to have been a rapid development in the number of *carpentry workshops* in the upper locations of the district based on timber from the forests in the hills. Equally, the number of *tailors* has been rapidly increasing, since the transportation cost of cloth has gone down due to the building of the new road between Mwatate and Wundanyi. Based upon our field-work we estimate that there are 5 bicycle repairers, 5 shoe-makers, 40 carpenters, 15 masons and 45 tailors working in the rural areas of the district.

Trading

Since Taita District has often had a shortage of foodcrops due to low rainfall there has been very little export trade of maize from the district. In the worst years famine relief has been distributed and there has been a prohibition against export of stable foodstuffs out of the district. The Asian traders who established themselves in the townships of Voi, Mwatate and Bura controlled all the import trade into the district as well as the trade in hides and skins and wattle bark which was bought by the Asian-owned wattle extract factory in Konza.

Before 1920 the African traders were mainly engaged in the local trade in agricultural produce and in homecrafts like pottery. This trade took place on a weekly market day in the 4 rural markets of the district. However, by 1920 there were already some 9 African-owned shops in the rural areas of the district but it was difficult for them to compete because they had to buy their stock from the Asian traders in Voi at retail-prices.

African participation in trade outside the local markets did not become significant until after the Second World War, when export of vegetables and chilis started to rise. A number of co-operative societies were formed to handle this trade, of which the most important was the Taita Vegetable Growers Society, but also some private companies and individual traders participated in this trade. Today, most of the trade in vegetables is controlled by the cooperative societies.

In order to receive some revenue from the collection of licence-fees the local native councils tried to regulate the internal trade by setting aside plots for shops and market areas in the barter markets that already existed in each location.

Plots were planned and set aside under the control of the health inspector of the district in 17 market-places in the district, but the traders avoided the planned markets, and for many years the greater part of trade was still undertaken in women's markets. The development of planned markets did not start until the administration decided in 1958 that traders' licences would only be issued for trade in gazetted markets.

A large number of small shops were opened in the rural areas of the district in the middle of the fifties, but as in Kisumu and Kisii many failed and had to be closed down again due to the lack of working capital, the strong competition and the limited demand from the rural population.

In 1958 there were about 400 small dukas in the district[35] and from the area we surveyed in the district, we estimate that the number has increased to some 500 by 1975. In addition, we estimate that there are 65 hotels and bars, 40 butcheries and 1 bakery in the rural areas of the district in 1975.

We can now summarize our estimates of non-farming activities in the rural areas of the district in Table III.12.

Table III.12 shows that a total of 6,780 people were permanently employed in non-farm enterprises in Taita Hills district in 1975. That is equal to 13 per cent of the adult population of the district. It should be emphasized, however, that nearly two-thirds of the total employment are people employed in the sisal factories, and that a significant proportion of these workers have come from other parts of the country.

[35] Taita District file DC/TTA/2/1.

Table III.12. *Estimate of people permanently employed and their income in non-farm rural enterprises in Taita District 1975.*

		Self-employed		Employed		
	Number of enterprises	Number	Average yearly income (K. shs.)	Number	Average yearly income (K. shs.)	Total number in work
Timber cutting	*			380	1,200	380
Saw-mills	2	2	5,000	20	1,200	22
Brick-makers	10	10	2,000	20	840	30
Posho-mills	10	8	5,000	20	840	28
Hides and skins	10	10	1,200	10	600	20
Sisal factories[1]	**			4,325	2,100	4,325
Coffee factories[2]	1			33	2,000	33
Sugar jaggeries[2]	1			2	2,800	2
House building	15	15	3,000	30	1,500	45
Bicycle repair	5	5	2,400			5
Shoe-making	5	5	2,500	5	480	10
Carpentry	40	40	6,000	120	1,080	160
Tailoring	45	45	3,600	45	720	90
Small shops in rural markets	500	500	2,400	1,000	600	1,500
Hotels and bars	65	•	•	130	600	130
Total	709	640	2,735	6,140	815	6,780

Source: Field survey undertaken in 1975.

* The timber cutters are often employed by the carpentry workshops.
** We do not have information about the number of enterprises.
[1] The figures are from 1974 (source: Kenya Bureau of Statistics).
[2] The owners of the enterprise rarely work in the business themselves.

When employment in the sisal factory is excluded the proportion of the adult population in Taita Hills District employed in non-farm enterprises can be estimated at 4.7 per cent.

Part-time activities like homecraft and petty trade are less significant as a source of income in Taita than in Kisumu and Kisii District, but also here beer brewing is an import source of non-farm income.

Kwale District

It was difficult to trace archival information about the historical development of non-farming activities in Kwale district. The following, therefore, is based upon our interviews and observations in the district in 1975.

Table III:13. *Quantity and value of fish landed in Kwale District 1967–1974*

Year	Metric tons	K £'000
1967	1119	72.1
1968	1611	103.6
1969	1530	97.7
1970	1570	107.7
1971	2206	148.0
1972	2247	152.2
1973	819	72.9
1974	736	87.9

Source: Statistical Abstract 1970 and 1975.

Generally speaking, Kwale district differs from the other 3 districts of this study, by its relatively low degree of integration into the colonial economy. In relation to the development of non-farming activities this has meant that traditional handicrafts have been less subject to competition from imports and modern workshops and industries, whereas the development in new forms of non-farming activities has been relatively slow.

Resource based non-farming activities

The most important non-farming activity in the district is *fishing* which takes place all along the coast.

The methods of fishing have not changed much over the years. Most of the fishermen are still using small wooden canoes and hook and wire and most of the fish caught are still dried and sold to markets all over the district by fish traders on bicycles.

The growth of the population of Mombasa has increased the demand for fish and it is likely that this has led to an increase in the number of people engaged in fishing and in the amount of fish caught and marketed.

The official statistics do not give figures on the number of people engaged in fishing, but from the statistics for fish landed on the south coast it appears that there are big fluctuations in incomes from this activity (see Table III. 13).

Besides fishing, a number of people are engaged in *woodcutting* and *saw-milling* in the forests of the district.

Output-based non-farming activities

As mentioned above, cassava has been the traditional food crop of the Wadigo until the mid-sixties when maize was adopted all over the district. Previously the amounts of maize produced in the Wadigo parts of the district

Bicycle repair workshop in Kikoneni, Kwale District. (Hanne Rakov)

were too small to make it possible to operate posho mills economically, and therefore the processing of maize was still undertaken at home by the women much later in Kwale district than in other parts of the country. Thus, we found that craftsmen in the district were still making *maize grinders* as well as *coconut grinders* to be used by women at home. We estimate that as many as 50 people were part-time engaged in this craft in 1975.

However, as the production of maize increased in the sixties, *maize milling* started becoming a profitable business and a number of mills were established. Based upon field surveys in the district, we estimate that by 1975 there were 33 posho mills in the district giving employment, including self-employment, to 66 people.

About half of the district is relatively dry and has been used mostly for cattle keeping. But cattle keeping has been difficult due to the prevalence of the tse-tse fly in parts of the district and therefore the number of cattle kept per family on small farms appears to be much lower than in the other 3 districts. Therefore, there are only a few *hide and skin bandas* in the district. We estimate that by 1975 there were 15 hide and skin bandas in the district employing 15 people as self-employed and a similar number as wage-employed.

Brewing and distilling is an important source of income for the women of the rural areas in most parts of Kenya, but since most of the people living at the coast are Muslims who according to their religion do not drink alcohol, *beer and liquor production* are far less significant in Kwale district than in the other 3 study-areas. A local liquor is made from coconuts, but since nobody drinks officially, it was impossible to find out how many people were engaged in the business.

Of the industrial crops only sugar is being processed in the district. This takes place at the *large-scale sugar factory* in Ramisi where in 1975, 615 people were employed. Traditionally many of the workers on the plantations in the district have been Luo and Kikuyu workers. This is still the case and it should be noted that of the 615 people employed in Ramisi sugar factory, only a minority are local people. From an employment point of view it is therefore questionable whether the sugar factory could be considered a local rural industry.

Income-based non-farming activities

The fact that the Wadigo became less integrated into the colonial economic system than the population of the 3 other study-areas has been of great significance for the development of the non-farming activities in the district. Generally, the traditional activities like *blacksmithing* have continued in much the same way as before the colonial time, whereas new activities like *carpentry, tailoring* and *bicycle repair* have developed much later in Kwale district than in other parts of Kenya. The reason for this was partly, that few people entered the colonial labour market so that money incomes were scarce, partly that it was difficult for local craftsmen to compete with workshops in Mombasa.

House-building alone seems to be an exception from the general observation that non-farming activities in Kwale district have become less commercialized than in other parts of Kenya. Thus in our sample in Kikoneni location as many as 78 per cent of the houses had been built by local craftsmen and not by the family itself. Estimates of the number of people engaged in this kind of non-farming activity and of their incomes are given in Table III. 14.

Trading

At the end of last century the trade in local produce between the coastal tribes and the towns was gradually taken over by Asians. This situation reversed in the fifties and the sixties when the marketing of cash crops like cashew-nuts, coconuts, chilies, citrus fruits etc. was taken over by local

Table III.14. *Estimate of people permanently employed and their income in non-farm rural enterprises in Kwale district 1975.*

	Number of enterprises	Self-employed Number	Self-employed Average yearly income per head (K. shs.)	Employed Number	Employed Average yearly income per head (K. shs.)	Total number in work
Posho mills	33	33	4,000	33	1,200	66
Hides and skins	15	15	1,200	15	600	30
Sugar factories	1			615	4,513	615
Blacksmithing	80	80	3,000			80
House-building	200	200	3,000	200	1,200	400
Tailors	180	180	2,400	180	1,500	360
Carpenters	60	60	1,400	40	600	100
Bicycle repairers	40	40	2,400	40	600	80
Grinder makers	50	50	600			50
Hotels and tea shops	65	65	9,000	65	600	130
Shops in rural markets	160	160	1,200	160	600	320
Total	884	883	2,360	1,348	2,460	2,231

Source: Field surveys undertaken in 1975.

co-operatives. Today most of the marketing of cash crops is undertaken by co-operative societies. But also a significant number of individual male petty traders are engaged in this business.[36]

The relatively late development of the monetary economy in the district has also meant that the establishment of shops in planned rural markets started later in Kwale district than in most other places in Kenya. From our field-work we estimate that there are approximately 65 hotels and tea shops employing 130 people and 160 small shops employing approximately 320 people in the district.

The number of people employed in non-farming activities is summarized in Table III. 14.

A total of 2,231 people were permanently occupied in non-farm rural enterprises in the district in 1975. That is equivalent to 2.35 per cent of the adult population. When employment at Ramisi sugar factory is excluded this proportion falls to 1.7 per cent.

Part-time activities like petty trade in tree crops and in dried fish are important sources of income which in Kwale District, in contrast to most other parts of Kenya, are undertaken mainly by the male population.[37]

[36] See Gillette, C., *A Test of the Concept of Backwardness: A Case Study of Digo Society in Kenya.* Ph.D. thesis, Cornell University, U.S.A., 1978, p. 157, table 8.
[37] *Ibid.* p. 154, 157.

Table III.15. *Employment and incomes in selected small-scale rural enterprises* in the four districts.*

	Employment		Average yearly incomes (K. shs.)	
	Number	% of adult population	Self-employed	Employed
Kisumu	2,964	1.7	2,759	1.604
Kisii	4,445	1.7	2,536	1.765
Taita	7,455	4.7	2,735	815
Kwale	1,626	1.7	2,360	739

Source: Surveys undertaken in 1975.

* The table excludes the large-scale sugar factories in Kisumu and Kwale Districts and the sisal factories in Taita Hills.

NB. The women brewing beer in beer halls in Kisumu District are excluded from this table in order to get comparable data for the four districts.

Comparative data on employment and incomes in *small-scale rural enterprises* in the four districts are given in Table III. 15. The big sugar factories and sisal factories are excluded from this table because to a large extent they employ people coming from other parts of Kenya and thus in terms of employment are not local industries. The most important of the non-farm rural enterprises are included in this table but the table is not all inclusive. Therefore, comparisons of the level of non-farm employment should be undertaken with care.

According to Table III. 15, employment in non-farm enterprises is more important in Taita Hills than in the other districts. On the other hand the workers in the rural enterprises are getting higher incomes in Kisii and Kisumu, whereas income of the self-employed is almost at the same level.

The differences in the sectoral composition of non-farm rural employment partly explain these regional differences. In Table III. 16 employment in rural non-farm enterprises is shown by sector.

The relative position of Taita Hills is due partly to the resource based activities like timber cutting and sawmilling, partly to the relatively large number of small shops, hotels, etc.

Also Kisumu district is characterized by the predominance of trade and services and the insignificance of manufacturing activities based upon processing of agricultural production.

In Kisii District, on the other hand, the processing of agricultural output dominates. In Kwale, the demand-based activities with a local tradition such as house building and tailoring dominate.

Table III.16. *The composition of employment in rural small-scale enterprises in the four districts (Percentage).*

	Kisumu	Kisii	Taita	Kwale
Resource based			*17.6*	
of which				
timber cutting and saw-mills			16.4	
brick makers			1.2	
Output based	*8.3*	*25.2*	*3.3*	*6.0*
of which				
maize mills	5.1	4.1	1.1	4.1
hides and skins	1.7	2.7	0.8	1.9
cotton ginning	1.5			
coffee factories		11.3	1.3	
tea factories		6.8		
sugar jaggeries		0.3	0.1	
Demand based	*19.6*	*15.3*	*12.6*	*65.7*
of which				
blacksmithing	3.4	1.8		4.9
house building	1.0	3.4	1.8	24.6
tailoring	10.1	3.4	3.7	22.1
carpentry	3.7	5.6	6.5	9.2
bicycle repair	1.4		0.2	4.9
Shoe-maker/repair		1.1	0.4	
Total processing	27.9	40.3	33.6	72.3
Shops, hotels etc.	72.2	59.7	66.4	27.7
Total employment	100.0	100.0	100.0	100.0

Source: Surveys undertaken in 1975.

In summarizing this chapter, we have seen that rural non-farm activities are important in Kenya as in many other developing countries in terms of employment as well as in terms of incomes. We have argued that it is necessary to make a distinction between productive employment and low productivity activities undertaken by the rural population as means of survival because they have no other alternatives.

We have further argued that in analysing the development potential (i.e., the creation of productive employment and accumulation of capital) of the rural non-farm sector a more disaggregated analysis has to be undertaken and we have suggested that it would be useful as a beginning to distinguish between resource-based, agricultural output-based and rural household demand-based activities.

We have seen that farming and non-farming activities in the rural areas of Kenya are closely interrelated and that income from agricultural production to some extent has been invested in non-farm enterprises during the periods of expansion in agricultural production in various parts of Kenya.

Still, however, in terms of the number of people involved, the significance of the non-farming sector seems to be more as a sector which serves as a source of income for poor rural households who cannot feed themselves from agricultural production alone and therefore take up a variety of low productivity and low income jobs in order to provide money to buy the necessities they need.

In a development perspective, then, the crucial questions seem to be to what extent the number of productive jobs can be expanded in this sector and to what extent the development of the rural non-farm sector can have a positive impact on the process of capital accumulation in the long run.

These questions will be analysed in greater detail in Chapter V.

Chapter IV

The Agricultural Sample Surveys

Sample Areas and Methods[1]

In the previous chapters we have discussed the general development trends in the rural areas of Kenya with specific reference to the four districts in which we conducted our field work.

In this chapter we will discuss the results of the agricultural questionnaire surveys that were conducted in each of the four study areas. From a sublocation in each district a sample of households was randomly selected from already existing official lists of households. The exact location of the four sublocations: Kombura in Kisumu District, Mwogeto in Kisii District, Werugha in Taita Hills District and Bumbani in Kwale District, can be seen from the maps on the following pages.

The population, the landbase and the population density of the four sublocations are given in Table IV.1. Unfortunately we do not have the necessary data to compute high potential land equivalents for the four sublocations. But it should be kept in mind, as argued in Chapter II, that the figures on population density alone cannot be taken as an indicator of the agricultural development potential of the four sublocations, as there are great differences in the fertility of the land.

In Kisumu District the selection of sample households was undertaken from a list of all households in West Kano division which had been prepared by a public health research unit only a few years before. In Kisii District the list from which we selected our sample was taken from the local tax register of the chief of Manga division. This list had been out of use since the abolition of local-tax in the late 1960's, and some replacement was necessary. In the other two districts of Taita and Kwale the sampling list was obtained from the tax register in conjunction with the land register.

The questionnaire survey had to be supplemented by field measurement and yield measurement from subsamples, for close estimation of the important variables of area and output.

This, however, is a very time-consuming task and has therefore, for

[1] I owe most of this description of the sampling methods and the methodology used in the analysis of the agricultural data to an unpublished paper by my colleague Tony Moody.

Table IV.1. *Population and density of population in the sublocations.*

	Population	Square miles	Density
Mwogeto (Kisii)	14007	25	557
Adult	5648		
Kombura (Kisii)	9463	29	331
Adult	4520		
Bumbani (Kwale)	5780	102	57
Adult	3098		
Werugha (Taita)	13697	539	25
Adult	5969		

Source: Kenya Population Census 1969. Central Bureau of Statistics, Nairobi.

practical reasons, only been done for two of the areas, namely Kombura in Kisumu District and Mwogeto in Kisii District.

In Kisii District it was possible to consult the land register for accurate estimations of the total land area occupied by households. The division of these total land areas between different crops was estimated initially for the whole Kisii sample from the questionnaire response. This was checked subsequently over a 20 per cent sub-sample, all of whose different cropped areas were checked by triangulation.

At the same time the yields of the principal grain crops were checked by estimation of the quantities stored in homestead granaries immediately after harvest. The combined results of the main survey and the sub-sampling gave a reasonable level of confidence to the agricultural input/output variables for Kisii District. Additionally it was possible to check the yields of industrial crops with the records of the co-operative marketing societies.

In Kisumu District, by contrast, estimation of areal variables, and output data consequent upon them, was much more difficult. There was no existing land register for the district, multiple cropping was prevalent and non-cultivated land, if not held by several households in common, was difficult to identify in extent. The same sub-sampling procedure was adopted for Kisumu District, and 20% of the original sample was referred to for land measurement. However, the results were so disparate from the original answers given in the questionnaire, with no common definable trends of over- or under-estimation that extrapolation of the sub-sample data was not possible. For the analysis of land use and yields, it was therefore decided to constrain it to this subsample. But it was thought desirable to supplement the size of the sample and this was done by incorporating the results of the

Map 4. *Location of sample areas in Nyanza Province: Kombura and Mwogeto.*

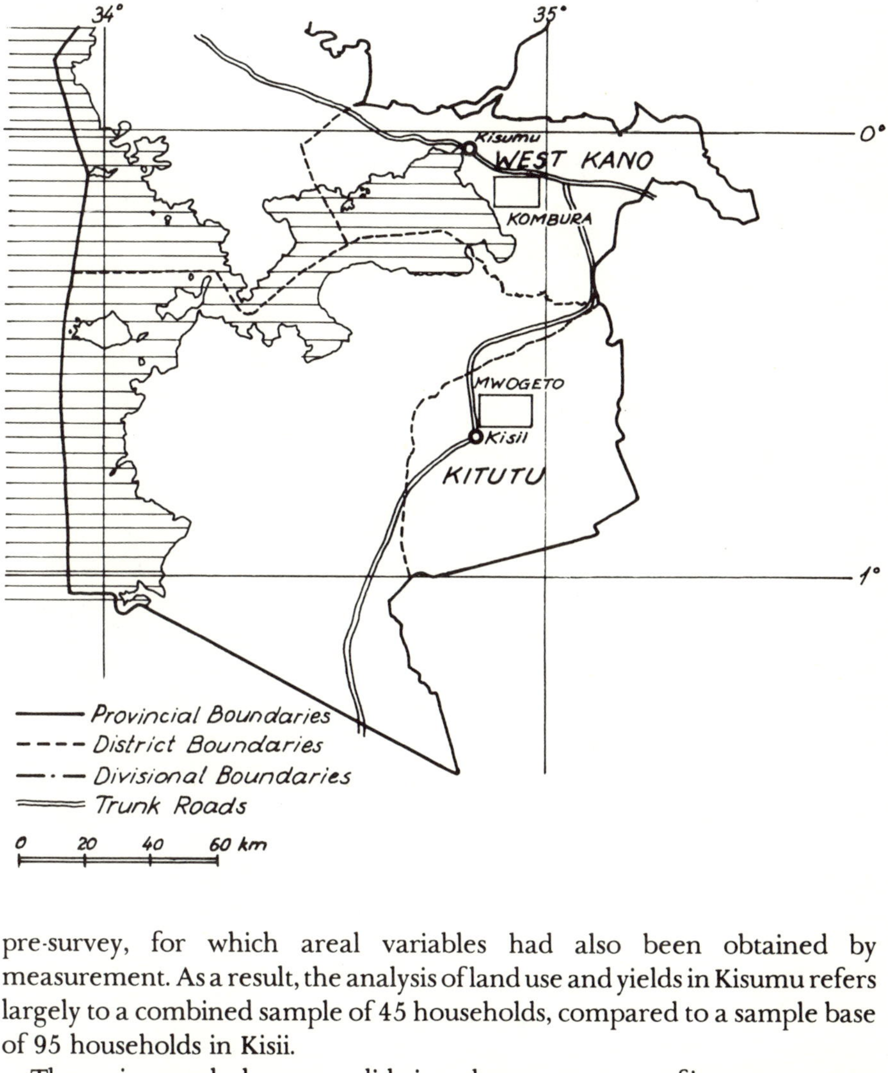

pre-survey, for which areal variables had also been obtained by measurement. As a result, the analysis of land use and yields in Kisumu refers largely to a combined sample of 45 households, compared to a sample base of 95 households in Kisii.

The main sample, however, did give a better coverage of income sources, patterns of expenditure and non-farming occupations and has therefore been used for all but the analysis of land use and yields.

Unfortunately we did not have time to check the quality of the information collected through the questionnaire survey in the same detailed way in Taita Hills and in Kwale District. But we believe that the data on landholding are fairly precise as land adjudication had recently taken place in the districts so that the peasants would know the precise size of their

Map 5. *Location of sample areas in Coast Province: Werugha and Kikoneni.*

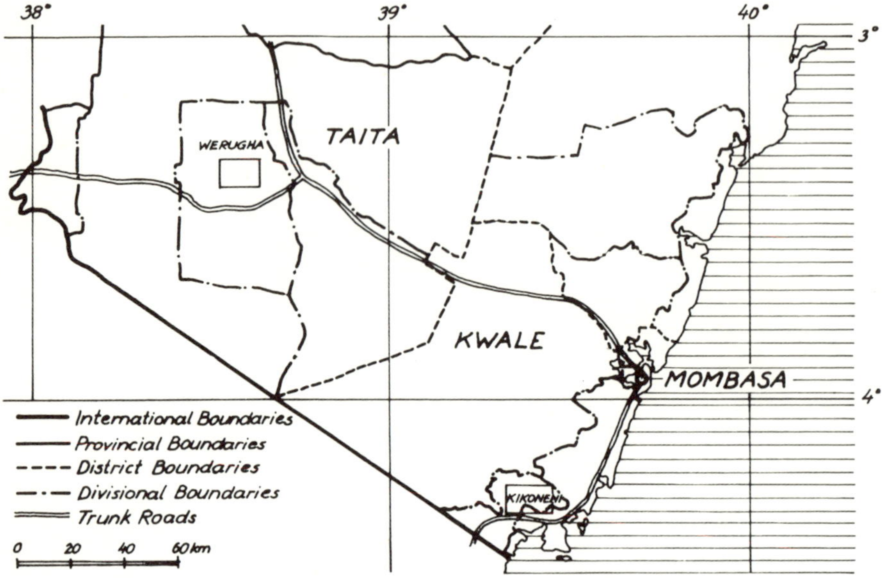

holdings. The size of land cultivated and cropping patterns were checked by research assistants who drew detailed sketch maps of the plots owned by each household. On the other hand we have not been able to check the figures on yields and on cash crop income or any other data collected through interviews in Taita Hills and Kwale Districts where samples of 112 households and 99 households, respectively, were selected.

In interpreting all the sample data one should keep in mind that socio-economic sample surveys, although they often yield more reliable qualitative information than most other sources, do have very important shortcomings in general levels of accuracy.

The sample sizes have been determined by taking into consideration partly the question of representativity and partly the necessity to get a sufficient number of observations in order to study the performance of various subgroups according to for example the size of holding and the size of income. On the one hand, the sample should not be bigger than necessary from a representative point of view, however, we needed a certain number of households in order to get subgroups of a sufficient size for an analysis of stratification.

By assuming average household size of 6 for each of the sublocations we have obtained a measurement of the representativity of the samples. These figures are given in Table IV.2.

Table IV.2. *Representativity of sample surveys.*

	No. of households		
	in sub-location*	in sample	Sample in per cent
Kombura Sublocation	1577	102	6.5
Mwogeto Sublocation	2335	96	4.1
Werugha Sublocation	2283	112	4.9
Kikoneni Sublocation	963	99	10.3

* The figure is calculated from Table IV.1 by assuming an average household size in the four sublocations of 6.

The size of our samples must be said to be of sufficient size to be representative of the households in the sublocation. However, the local variation in rainfall and in soil fertility is so big that we cannot claim full representativity of our samples. This problem is particularly relevant as far as Kombura sublocation in Kisumu District is concerned. Here the households were selected from Masogo village which was found to have very unreliable rainfall and therefore much lower agricultural production than other parts of the sublocation, as for instance the village Nduru, for which a small household survey was undertaken for comparison. This village, Nduru, is located nearer to the lake shore and receives a higher rainfall than Masogo.

The even greater differences in ecology between sublocations and between districts and provinces make generalizations based upon these small sample surveys a rather hazardous task. On the other hand the Districts and the sublocations have been selected in order to include areas of different ecological and demographical characteristics. Therefore, we believe that it will be possible to draw some conclusions of general relevance with regard to the problems of social and economic transformation in rural Kenya.

The Population and Household Size

In estimating the total number of households in the four sublocations we assumed a common household size in the four areas. As a matter of fact we found big differences in household size, sex composition and age distribution in our four sample surveys. Table IV.3 gives figures on the population, sex composition and average household size in the four samples.

We defined a household as the persons who were living and eating together every day. Family members working in other parts of Kenya and living away were not included as members of the household and their

Table IV.3. *Population by sex and average household size in samples.*

	No. of house-holds	Population				Average household size
		Adults				
		male	female	children	total	
Kombura	102	152	143	264	559	5.5
Mwogeto	96	163	162	420	745	7.8
Werugha	112	161	187	245	593	5.3
Kikoneni	99	171	145	157	473	4.8

income was only included in as far as they sent money to contribute to the welfare of the rural household.

The distinction between children and adults is made at the age of 15 although a great number of young people are attending school until their early twenties.

The difference in the sex composition in the samples is due to several factors. First, the age at which the young girls get married and move to the homestead of their husbands influences the sex-ratio. The fact that the young girls marry much earlier than the young men explains that, except in Werugha, there is an excess of men in the rural households. Two other factors pull in the opposite direction. We found that more young men than women are sent to boarding schools to attend further education and secondly that more men than women were working away from home in order to supplement low rural incomes from relatively well-paid urban jobs. Thus a number of the rural households had female heads of households.

We can see that Kombura Sublocation is distinctly different from the other samples in this respect. More than 20 per cent of the households had a female head of household because the agricultural potential of the area is so poor that the adult males are forced to seek employment away from home often in the big urban centres of Nairobi and Mombasa.

Also a number of males from Kikoneni Sublocation in Kwale District are working in Mombasa but some of them live at home and go by bus to work in Mombasa 60 km away every day. Therefore, the number of female heads of households appears rather low although in a number of cases the women are alone responsible for agricultural production.

The migration for wage employment to the urban areas of Kenya also influences the age distribution of members of the rural household as here defined. This can be seen in Table IV.4. We can see that there are important differences in the age distribution of the four samples. Kombura Sublocation, which has a large number of males working away, has less

Table IV.4. *Age distribution in samples (%).*

	Kombura	Mwogeto	Werugha	Kikoneni
0– 4	16.4	15.2	12.4	13.0
5– 9	14.0	19.9	14.4	11.7
10–14	16.5	21.3	14.7	8.7
15–19	10.0	10.7	14.6	9.8
20–24	7.0	5.4	6.8	7.4
25–29	6.0	3.9	7.0	12.1
30–34	3.7	5.9	5.3	9.6
35–39	4.4	4.7	5.3	6.6
40–44	3.5	3.5	3.7	6.8
45–49	5.5	2.7	4.8	5.5
50–54	3.5	2.6	2.4	3.4
55–59	4.4	1.9	3.9	0.9
60–64	2.4	1.3	2.0	2.1
65–69	1.7	0.5	1.2	0.9
70–74	0.9	0.4	1.2	0.2
75–	0.1	0.1	0.3	1.5
	100.0	100.0	100.0	100.0
0–14	46.9	56.4	41.5	33.4
15–24	17.0	16.1	21.4	17.2
25–59	31.0	28.9	32.4	44.9
60–	5.1	2.3	4.7	4.7

Table IV.5. *Rural households with female heads of household.*

	Number of households	Per cent
Kombura	22	21.6
Mwogeto	6	6.3
Werugha	7	6.3
Kikoneni	5	5.1

people in the productive age groups than Werugha and Kikoneni. A comparison of Kombura and Mwogeto Sublocation becomes clearer in Fig. 1 which shows the population pyramids for the two samples.

The average age of heads of household was much higher in Kombura in Kisumu District (52.6 years) than in Mwogeto (44.8), Werugha (45.1) and Kikoneni (44.1).

Fig. 1. *Age distribution in Kombura and Mwogeto.*

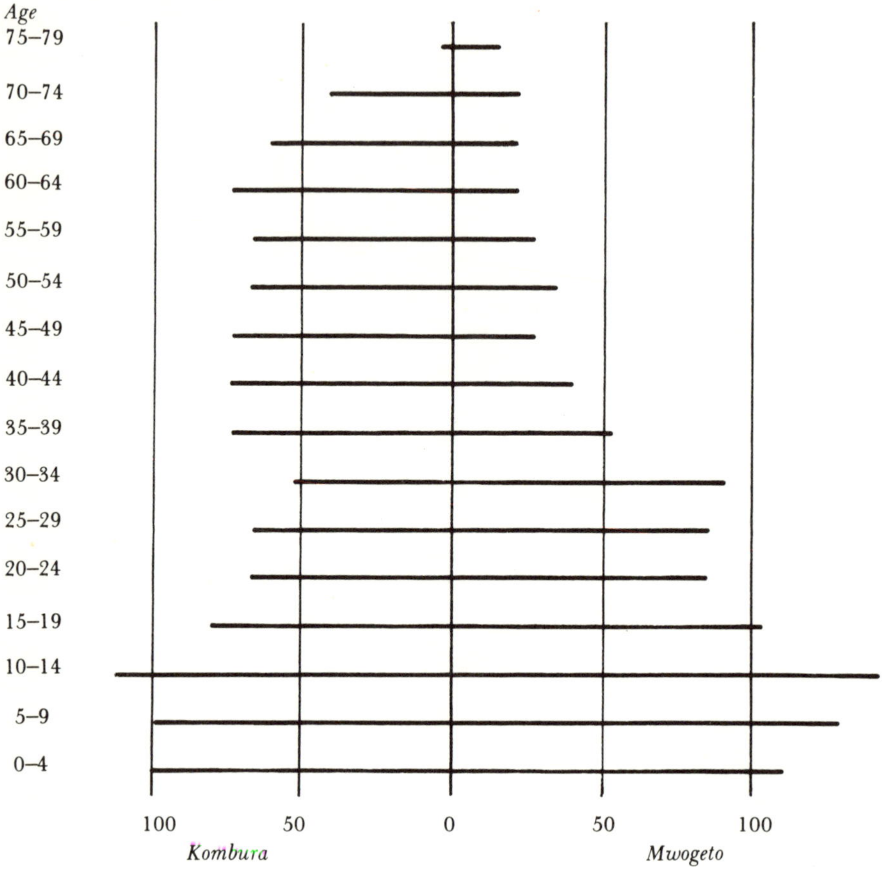

The population figure in Figure 1 shows the tendency for young men to leave the rural areas for work in the urban areas while leaving one wife at home to take care of the younger children and the land.

The fact that a great number of young men are leaving the rural areas is, as we have argued, a result of low agricultural potentials, but on the other hand the lack of labour at land preparation and weeding time may have a negative impact on the agricultural production.

The landbase

The average size of landholding per household in the four sample areas is shown in Table IV.6.

Land tenure was in a transitional stage in Kombura when we did our field work in 1975. Land adjudication had at the time of our field research been

Table IV.6. *Average size of landholding by sample households.*

	Size of holding (acres)
Kombura	5.0[1]
Mwogeto	4.8
Werugha	4.0
Kikoneni	8.8

[1] Estimation based upon cultivated area of 2.7 acres and cultivation percentage of 54%.

carried out in Mwogeto, Werugha and Kikoneni and was being carried out in Kombura Sublocation. But in the pilot survey we made before adjudication we could only identify *cultivated* plots to individual households. We do not have precise figures of the total owned area since we could not estimate individual rights to *uncultivated* land. In general, for Kombura location, using the gross measured area of the location, and sample-based estimates of cultivated land per household, we estimated the cultivation percentage as 54% and from this we have estimated the total owned area in Table IV.6.

We can see from this table that the average size of holding does not differ much in the four samples. Only the households in the Kikoneni sample have a markedly higher average landholding than in the other areas. Kikoneni is also the only one of the sample areas in which shortage of land has not yet become perhaps the most serious of all problems.

There is more variation in the distribution of land within each sample. This can be seen from Table IV.7.

By using the estimates of minimum size of holdings for subsistence from Kisumu, Kisii, Taita Hills and Kwale District shown in Table II.5 we find the percentage of sample households with less than minimum size holdings in the four samples. The result is shown in Table IV.8.

We find that for Kombura, Werugha and Kikoneni more than half of the sample households have less land than the necessary minimum size for average size families as estimated by agricultural economists in the regional development plans for the districts. In Mwogeto only 20 per cent of the sample households were found to have less than the minimum size of land for subsistence.

We can see from the calculation of Table IV.8 that only very few families could be expected to have more than 2.000 K.shs in cash income in addition to a subsistance income. In Kikoneni and Mwogeto approx. 30 per cent of the households had sufficient land to obtain cash incomes of 2.000 K.shs a

Table IV.7. *Size distribution of land in the sample.*

Acres	Kombura[1] No. of households	Kombura[1] %	Mwogeto No. of households	Mwogeto %	Werugha No. of households	Werugha %	Kikoneni No. of households	Kikoneni %
0– 0.9	12	25.0	2	2.1	7	6.3	0	
1.0– 1.9	10	20.8	12	12.6	27	24.1	0	
2.0– 2.9	7	14.6	28	29.9	15	13.4	13	13.3
3.0– 3.9	9	18.7	11	11.6	18	16.1	20	20.4
4.0– 4.9	5	10.4	9	9.5	10	8.9	9	9.2
5.0– 5.9	1	2.1	10	10.5	8	7.1	9	9.2
6.0– 6.9	2	4.2	5	5.2	5	4.5	6	6.1
7.0– 7.9	0	0	6	6.3	7	6.3	7	7.2
8.0– 8.9	0	0	3	3.2	2	1.8	4	4.1
9.0– 9.9	1	2.1	2	2.1	3	2.7	2	2.0
10.0–11.9	0	0	3	3.2	2	1.8	2	2.0
12.0–13.9	0	0	2	2.1	2	1.8	9	9.2
14.0–15.9	1	2.1	1	1.0	2	1.8	1	1.0
16.0–17.9			0	0	1	0.7	4	4.1
18.0–19.9			0	0	0	0	1	1.0
20.0–			1	1.0	3	2.7	11	11.2
	48	100.0	95	100.1	112	100.0	98	100.0

[1] Based upon cultivated area only.

Table IV.8. *Estimated number of households with less than minimum holding sizes in the four samples.*

	Subsistence			Subsistence + 2.000 shs.		
	Estimated min. size (acres)	No. of holdings with less	Holdings with less, %	Estimated min. size (acres)	No. of holdings with less	Holdings with less, %
Kombura	5.0	25	52.1	11.1	47	97.9
Mwogeto	2.5	19	20.0	5.6	69	72.6
Werugha	5.0	77	68.8	8.7	99	88.4
Kikoneni	5.6	51	52.0	8.7	68	69.4

[1] Size of holdings are estimated as cultivated area (54%) plus uncultivated area (46%).

year or more, in Werugha this proportion was 12 per cent while in Kombura only 2 per cent of the households had that much land available.

The Lorenz-curves of distribution of land have been calculated on the basis of accumulated percentage figures for households and their landholding. For Kombura the figures used include only cultivated area. The percentage distribution is given in Table IV.9 and the Lorenz-curves of land distribution are shown in Figure 2.

Table IV.9. *Distribution of land in the samples. Accumulated percentages of no. of households and percentages of total area owned.*

Kombura[1]		Mwogeto		Werugha		Kikoneni	
% of house-holds	% of land	% of house-holds	% of land	% of house-holds	% of land	% of house-holds	% of land
		2.1	0.3	6.3	1.0	13.3	3.0
25.0	6.3	14.7	3.9	30.4	8.8	33.7	9.9
45.8	16.7	44.7	19.2	43.8	15.6	42.9	14.1
60.4	29.4	55.8	27.2	59.9	27.1	52.1	19.3
79.1	52.4	65.3	36.1	68.8	35.3	58.2	23.5
89.5	68.6	78.8	48.0	75.9	43.3	65.4	29.2
91.6	72.4	81.0	55.2	80.4	49.4	69.5	32.9
95.8	82.5	87.3	65.2	86.7	59.2	73.5	37.6
97.9	89.4	90.5	70.7	88.5	62.5	82.7	50.5
		92.6	75.0	91.2	67.9	87.8	59.7
		94.7	79.6			88.8	61.8
100.0	100.0	100.0	100.0	100.0	100.0	100.0	100.0

[1] Based upon cultivated area only.

The nearer the curve is to the 45° line, the greater is the equality of land distribution represented by the curve. The inequality of land distribution is quite conspicuous in all four samples. By extrapolation we find for instance that 30 per cent of the households own only between 7 and 12 per cent of all the land, 60 per cent own only between 25 and 31 per cent while the big landowners own a very large share of all land. Ten per cent own between 28 and 35 per cent while 20 per cent of the big landowners own between 48 and 53 per cent of all land.

It should be emphasized at this point that this stratification in size of landholding is not a "Chayanov case"[2]. The size of holding is not determined by the relationship between "mouth" and "hands" in each family and it would not generally be possible to expand the size of holding as the family size increases in the family life cycle due to the severe shortage of land and the high land prices. On the other hand, the ratio of cultivated to uncultivated land might be explained by the size of the work force but only as one among several factors.

[2] Chayanov explains the differentiation in peasant societies as a result of changes over the life cycle of peasant households and not as a result of a capitalist development process. See A.V. Chayanov, *The Theory of Peasant Economy,* in *D. Thorner et al. (eds.).* Chayanov's theory of the peasant economy has been criticized by a number of people, e.g., G. Littlejohn, Peasant Economy, in *B. Hindes, (ed), Sociological Theories of the Economy, London 1977.*

Fig. 2. *Distribution of land in samples.*

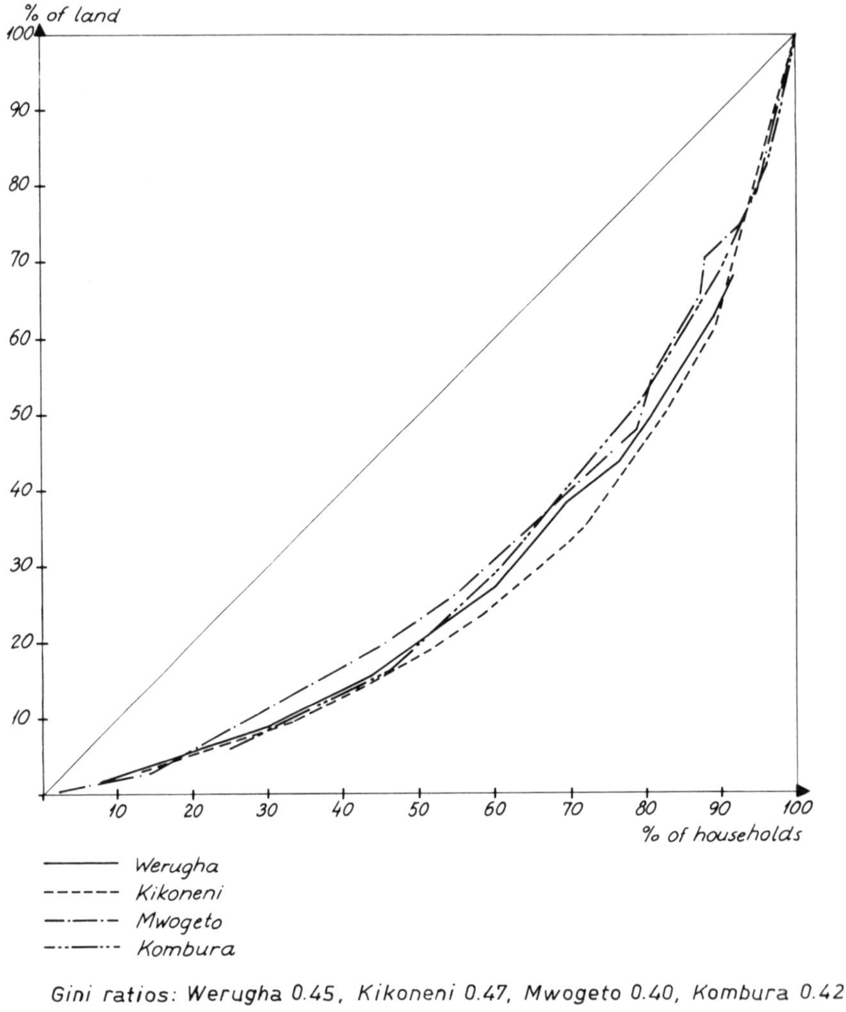

We can see from the Lorenz-curves in Figure 2 that land distribution is more unequal in Kikoneni than in the other three samples. But in order to rank the other samples we need a measurement for the inequality of distribution. This is obtained by the calculation of the so-called Gini concentration ratio which is the ratio of the area bounded by the Lorenz-curve and the diagonal to the area of the triangle. Thus the higher the inequality the higher the value of the Gini ratio. Defined in this way and calculated by the method of approximate triangles we find the Gini

Table IV.10. *Gini ratios of land distribution in sample areas.*

Sample area	Gini ratio
Kombura	0.42
Mwogeto	0.40
Werugha	0.45
Kikoneni	0.47

coefficients shown in Table IV.10. We get the following ranking in inequality in land distribution: Kikoneni 0.47 with the highest inequality, Werugha 0.45, Kombura 0.42 and Mwogeto 0.40 with the lowest inequality in land distribution

Most households in the four samples got access to land by inheritance and in that respect ownership of land and also land distribution reflects the accumulation of land by the ancestors.

But as in the rest of Kenya the adjudication of land has opened up for buying and selling of land and a rural land market has emerged.

Since land adjudication was being undertaken at the time of our field work in Kombura Sublocation no buying and selling of land had yet started in this area. But in the other samples we found cases of buying and selling of land.

As a substitute for this kind of land transfers renting and leasing of land was used as a way of getting access to more land in Kombura Sublocation. But also in Mwogeto we found that renting of land was often used as a way of acquiring more land for cultivation. We believe that renting has become a substitute for purchasing in Mwogeto partly because the price of land is extremely high in the overpopulated fertile area, and partly because there is a strong resistance against selling of land because land is a very valuable asset in Mwogeto and therefore is only sold under circumstances of extreme need for cash. But we also suspect that a number of the people who said that they rented land had actually bought. At the time of our interviews in Mwogeto some people feared that a tax on landownership would be introduced and therefore some of the sample households might have given us wrong information about landownership. Likewise, people would be ashamed to admit they were leasing out land. This explains the discrepancy between renting and leasing of land in Mwogeto sublocation.

Table IV.11 summarizes our findings on land transfers as a way of getting access to land. It should be emphasized again that inheritance is still by far the most important source of access to land. Thus all households in our samples have inherited land. However, as we can see from Table IV.8 the further subdivision of holdings by inheritance will lead to a majority of

Table IV.11. *Land transfers in samples.*

	Buying		Selling		Renting		Leasing		
	No. of households	%	No. of households	%	No. of households	%	No. of households	%	Total transactions, %
Kombura	3	3.0	.	.	2	2.0	27	26.4	28.4
Mwogeto	4	4.2	.	.	26	27.1	4	4.2	35.4
Werugha	23	21.5	.	.	3	2.7	.	.	23.2
Kikoneni	7	7.1	11	11.1	.	.	.	.	18.1

Table IV.12. *Proportion of land cultivated in samples.*

	Percentage
Kombura	54
Mwogeto	71
Werugha	47
Kikoneni	85

holdings too small to support average sized families and are therefore likely to create a class of agricultural labourers as foreseen in the Swynnerton plan.

We can see from Table IV.11 that a relatively high proportion of households in the samples have been engaged in some kind of land transaction. It might seem paradoxical that we get different frequences of buying/selling and renting/leasing, respectively. As far as buying is concerned the reason is that households in Mwogeto and Werugha mostly bought land outside the sublocation. The differences between renting and leasing is more difficult to explain but is probably partly due to the factors mentioned above. We should like to add that recent studies of Mwogeto and of Kikoneni sublocations found higher frequencies of land purchase as a means to acquire access to land.[3]

Agricultural Production. Land Use

There are big differences in land use and yields between the four samples as one would expect due to the differences in soil and climate. In Table IV.12 we have estimated land use ratios in the four samples but it should be recalled that interviews have only been checked against actual measurement for subsamples in Kombura and Mwogeto.

[3] See T. Bager's study of committee members in Cooperative Societies in Mwogeto Sublocation, Kisii and C. Gilette, A Test of the Concept of Backwardness: A Case Study of Digo Society in Kenya, *op.cit.* p. 125–154.

Table IV.13. *Cropping pattern in Kombura sample*[1].

Crop	Cropping pattern acres	%	No. of growers	Average area per grower
Maize/sorghum	65.3	51	33	1.9
Maize/sorghum/cotton	22.3	18	22	1.0
Pure maize	7.3	6	9	0.8
Pure sorghum	27.0	21	27	1.0
Pure cotton	5.2	4	9	0.6
Total	127.1	100	50	2.5

[1] Grazing is not included.

The differences in cultivation percentages are partly due to the significance of livestock in the four sublocations. Thus livestock owned by households in Kikoneni are always kept by a Duruma herdsman living away from the Digo village often in the drier Kwale Ranch Lands west of the Kwale Crop Lands and there is no land for grazing in Kikoneni. The high cultivation percentage in Mwogeto is a consequence of high population pressure.

But the difference in cropping patterns also makes it difficult to compare cultivation ratios. For example, the dominance of tree crops in the Kikoneni sample makes it difficult to estimate uncultivated area in this sublocation.

The pattern of *land use in the Kombura sample* is given in Table IV.13 based upon the two sub-samples referred to above.

One predominant feature in the land use in Kombura sublocation which influences the planting of maize and sorghum is the drainage problem. Maize is mostly planted on the better drained higher land, while sorghum which is more resistant to waterlogging is mostly planted on the lower land. The difference in altitude in the area, however, is only slight, 5–10 meters, but big enough to influence the cropping pattern on high altitude and low altitude land.

Another dominant feature of the land use in Kombura is evident from Table IV.13, namely the predominance of mixed cropping. In our two sub-samples the average proportion of land under crop-mixtures was 69 per cent. The mixtures are any combination of maize and sorghum with cotton, green-grams, cowpeas and beans. In all mixtures maize and sorghum predominate. As we can see from the table very little pure maize is cultivated, but sorghum is often planted by itself when planted in lower areas. Most of the planted cotton is found in mixtures. It is generally planted in maize/sorghum plots when the latter have tasselled. This is late planting

Table IV.14. *Cropping pattern by size of cultivated land (acres), Kombura sample (%).*

	0–1.25	1.25–2.5	2.5–3.75	3.75–6.25	6.25–	Total
Maize/sorghum	40	57	24	54	70	51
Maize/sorghum/cotton	39	7	26	17	12	18
Pure maize	10	2	2	14	0.5	6
Pure sorghum	11	31	39	15	9	21
Pure cotton	0.5	3	9	0.5	8	4
Total	100.5	100	100	100.5	99.5	100

Table IV.15. *Cropping pattern in Mwogeto sample.*

	Cropping pattern			Average area per
	acres	%	growers	grower
Maize	115.3	27.7	90	1.3
Finger millet	43.7	10.5	76	0.6
Potatoes	3.2	0.8	7	0.5
Sweet potatoes	3.2	0.8	2	1.6
Bananas	2.2	0.5	11	0.2
Coffee	51.0	12.5	68	0.8
Tea	33.8	8.1	50	0.7
Pyrethrum	40.8	9.8	52	0.8
Other	1.0	0.3	4	0.3
Total cultivated	294.2	70.9	94	3.1
Grazing	120.8	29.1	90	1.3
Total area	415.0	100.0	94	4.4

according to recommendations from agricultural advisers and late planting damages the potential yields of the cotton. But the late planting of cotton reflects the priority given to foodcrops. In Table IV.13 we have only defined two types of crop mixtures and we have excluded the minor crops.

When the sample is stratified according to the size of cultivated area we get the figures shown in Table IV.14.

There does not seem to be any clear relationship between the size of cultivated area and cropping pattern in the Kombura sample, and we must conclude that other factors than available land determine the cropping patterns in Kombura.

The cropping pattern in the Mwogeto sample is shown in Table IV.15. By comparing with Table II.23 we can see that the cash crops take up a larger

Table IV.16. *Cropping pattern by size of holding in Mwogeto sample (acres).*

	0–2.5		2.5–5.0		5.0–7.5		7.5:		Total	
	% of area	% of growers	% of area	% of growers	% of area	% of growers	% of area	% of growers	% of area	% of growers
Maize	34	92	29	97	27	100	28	100	28	96
Finger millet	13	69	11	83	10	94	9	77	11	81
Pyrethrum	5	38	11	53	10	72	10	85	10	55
Tea	2	12	7	28	13	56	7	38	8	53
Coffee	17	65	14	75	14	72	7	77	· 13	72
Grazing	28	85	28	97	21	100	35	100	29	96
Total planted	100	100	100	100	100	100	100	100	101	100
n =		26		36		18		13		94

area than the average for the Kisii District (43 per cent of cultivated land in Mwogeto against 20 per cent of cultivated land in the Kisii District). On the other hand maize, which accounted for 53 per cent of cultivated area in the Kisii District in 1974, only takes up 39 per cent of cultivated land in our sample, while finger millet was more important in our sample – 15 per cent of cultivated land – than in Kisii District in all (9 per cent).

Only one of the 95 households that responded on land use did not grow either coffee, tea or pyrethrum. Coffee was still in 1975, when we did our field work, the most important crop in terms of acreage planted and number of growers. 72 per cent of the households in our sample were growing coffee against 55 per cent for pyrethrum and 53 per cent for tea. But still the food crops are more important in our sample than the cash crops both in terms of number of growers and area cultivated.

In Table IV.16 we have stratified land use according to size of holding and for each subgroup we show the proportion of the growers that grow the various crops.

It is interesting to note that there is a fairly constant proportion of land under grazing at all levels of size of holdings. Even the smallest contain 28 per cent of grazing land. The proportion of land under food crops decreases with increasing size of holding from 47 per cent on small holdings to 37 per cent on the large holdings. Also the proportion of coffee decreases with increased size of holding although the proportion of households growing coffee increases with increasing size of holding. This is due to the fact that the largest holdings had only very small plots planted with coffee.

For pyrethrum and tea the proportion of area planted as well as the proportion of households growing them increases with the size of holding.

Table IV.17. *Cropping pattern in Werugha sample.*

	Cropping pattern			
	acres	%	No. of growers	Average area per grower
Maize	144.5	28.6	110	1.3
Beans	22.1	4.4	58	0.4
Onions	2.5	0.5	10	0.3
Potatoes	4.7	0.9	11	0.4
Tomatoes	15.0	2.9	52	0.3
Cabbage	17.1	3.4	55	0.3
Coffee	17.8	3.5	25	0.7
Other	14.4	2.9	42	0.3
Total cultivated	238.1	47.1	112	2.1
Grazing and home	266.9	52.9	112	2.4
Total land	505.0	100.0	112	4.5

The greater the amount of land available, the greater the amount of tea and pyrethrum that was planted on holdings. Both these crops increased in planted area, with size of holding, to a greater extent than maize, finger millet and coffee.

Although more holdings had coffee than either of the other cash crops, and coffee was grown by almost the same proportion of small and large holdings, one must conclude that primarily the large holdings benefited from the high priced cash crops, which were pyrethrum and tea in 1975. Thus only 12 per cent of the smallest holdings were growing tea in 1975.

The land use in the Werugha sample as shown in Table IV.17 is strongly influenced by the location of the sample area on the steep hill sides of Taita Hills where it is only possible to cultivate the terrassed slopes. Therefore, the cultivation ratio is lower in the Werugha sample than in the other sample areas. Only 47 per cent of the total owned area of the sample households was cultivated.

Another dominating factor is the relatively low frequency of mixed cropping in the area. This is a result of intensive extension services from district agricultural officers who have been concerned with the yield of food crops.

Maize and beans are the dominant food crops, covering 70 per cent of the cultivated area. Among the cash crops various kinds of vegetables dominate over coffee both in terms of acreage grown and the proportion of households that have planted. Only 25 per cent of the households in the sample grew coffee while 70 per cent were growing one or more kinds of

Table IV.18. *Cropping pattern by size of holding in Werugha sample (acres).*

	0–2.5		2.5–5.0		5.0–7.5		7.5–		Total	
	% of area	% of growers	% of area	% of growers	% of area	% of growers	% of area	% of growers	% of area	% of growers
Maize	49	98	41	100	28	93	15	100	29	98
Beans	8	52	6	53	5	67	2	20	4	52
Onions	0	2	1	18	0	0	0	13	1	9
Potatoes	1	11	1	11	0	0	1	13	1	10
Tomatoes	6	36	6	58	4	67	1	27	3	46
Cabbage	5	41	5	55	5	73	2	47	3	49
Coffee	7	30	6	21	4	20	1	13	4	22
Other	3	25	3	37	2	40	2	40	3	38
Grazing	21	100	32	100	53	100	76	100	53	100
Total	100	100	101	100	101	100	100	100	101	100
n =		44		38		15		15		112

vegetables. The vegetables are grown in small terrassed rifts on the hillside where they are irrigated from the small streams running down the mountain. These small plots are very fertile and make it possible to harvest vegetables 2–3 times a year.

Table IV.18 shows the stratified cropping pattern according to size of holding. The most dominant feature is that the grazing area increases sharply when the size of holding increases. Thus, there is much less difference between the average size of the cultivated area in the different size groups shown in Table IV.18, and there is surprisingly little difference in the cropping pattern of the cultivated area between groups. Of significant differences in land use of the cultivated area it should be noted that the proportion of the cash crops, coffee and tomatoes, decreases with the largest holdings. This is in both cases due to a combined decrease in the proportion of growers in this group growing coffee and tomatoes and a decrease in the size of plots with these crops.

Land use in Kikoneni is characterized by two main features. First, since no cattle are kept in Digo villages the holdings in the Kikoneni sample are not using any of their land for grazing. An uncultivated plot in Kikoneni therefore means a piece of land which has not been cleared for planting. Secondly, the agricultural scenario is dominated by tree crops. Coconut trees, cashew nut trees and a variety of fruit trees dominate the landscape.

Food crops are dominated by mixed planting of maize and cassava and sometimes also maize/cassava mixtures interplanted with various pulses. But also tree crops and food crops are very often interplanted in the same

Table IV.19. *Cropping pattern in Kikoneni sampsample.*

	Cropping pattern			
	acres	% per cent	No. of growers	Average area per grower
Pure maize	18.4	2.1	5	3.7
Maize/cassava mixture	65.0	7.5	19	3.4
Maize/cassava/ other mixtures	28.0	3.2	6	4.7
Maize/tree crops Mixture 1	179.8	20.8	36	5.0
Maize/tree crop mixture 2	199.4	23.1	38	5.2
Rice	1.0	0.1	4	0.3
Sugarcane	62.0	7.2	20	3.1
Tree crops	177.8	20.6	32	5.6
Total cultivated	731.4	84.8	98	7.5
Uncultivated	131.6	15.2	11	12.0
All land	863.0	100.0	98	8.8

fields, which made it difficult to measure the exact acreage under food crops and tree crops, respectively. During our field work we identified the various crop mixtures listed in Table IV.19. Most of the cultivated land is planted with mixtures of maize/cassava and coconut/cashew nut trees (mixture 1) or with mixtures of maize/cassava/and coconut/cashewnut/fruit trees (mixture 2).

But also plots where no food crops are planted between the tree crops cover a large part of the cultivated area. The significance of tree crops can be seen from the fact that only 8 per cent of the holdings had no tree crops of one kind or another.

In addition to the tree crops 20 per cent of the holdings have small plots of sugarcane. The average size of sugar plots in the sample is 3.1 acres which, when harvested and sold at Ramisi sugar factory, makes a significant contribution to the cash income from cashew nuts, coconuts and fruits like oranges, lemons and mangoes.

In Table IV.20, which shows the stratified land use in the Kikoneni sample, we can see that the smallest holdings have the highest cultivation ratio. As much as 28 per cent of the largest holdings had plots that were not cleared for cultivation. These plots, that had an average size of 20.5 acres, made up 21 per cent of their total land or equivalent to 78 per cent of all the uncultivated land in the sample.

Table IV.20. *Cropping pattern by size of holding in Kikoneni sample (acres).*

	0–3.9		4.0–6.9		7.0–13.9		14.0–		Total	
	% of acres	% of growers	% of acres	% of growers	% of acres	% of growers	% of acres	% of growers	% of acres	% of growers
Pure maize	0	0	3	3	6	17	0	0	2	5
Maize/cassava mixture	12	16	14	14	7	21	4	22	8	19
Maize/cassava/other mixtures	0	0	1	3	12	21	0	0	3	6
Maize/tree crops mixture 1	35	34	29	24	19	29	13	44	21	37
Maize/tree crops mixture 2	44	47	30	27	14	29	38	44	24	40
Rice	0	0	0	0	0	4	0	0	0	4
Sugarcane	4	6	5	8	9	33	5	28	6	19
Tree crops	4	6	16	19	28	63	18	56	21	33
Uncultivated	0	3	2	3	4	13	21	28	15	11
Total	99	100	100	101	99	100	99	100	100	100
n =		32		37		24		18		98

Of other features we can see that the proportion planted with "pure" cash crops, i.e., without foodcrops interplanted, increases with the size of cultivated area. We can also see that there is an increase in area planted with foodcrops mixtures alone up to the size of the largest group of holding. On the other hand, the share of cultivated land planted with tree crops either in mixtures or pure decreases up to the size of the largest holdings in which it reaches as much as an average of 87 per cent. But in none of the other groups does the share of cultivated area planted with tree crops fall below two-thirds. This figure clearly demonstrates the dominance of tree crops in the Kikoneni sample.

Agricultural production. Gross value of production

A detailed analysis of yields per acre for different crops in the various areas will not be attempted because we only have accurate actual measured data of sizes of land cultivated and the quanta of crops harvested for small sub-samples in Kombura and Mwogeto sublocations.

Here we will only make an account of the sources of agricultural cash incomes and of the value of foodcrops consumed by the producers themselves in the different sample areas. A more detailed statistical analysis of the relationship between the value of crop production and the size of holding, area cultivated, size of family labour force, hired labour and

Table IV.21. *Gross value of agricultural crop production per holding in sample areas.*

	Kombura			Mwogeto			Werugha			Kikoneni		
	Income		% of hold-ings	Income		% of hold-ings	Income		% of hold-ings	Income		hold-ings
	shs.	%		shs.	%		shs.	%		shs.	%	
Cash income												
Cereals												
Maize	6	0.9	1	76	2.3	25	20	0.8	8	19	1	11
Finger millet	.		.	19	0.6	11	.	.	.	.	.	.
Sorghum	1	0.1	1		.		.	.	.	.	.	.
Temporary industrial crops												
Cotton	64	9.2	34	.	.	.	.	.	.	3	0	5
Sugarcane	.		.		.	.	.	.		430	26	22
Pyrethrum	.			870	26.1	55	.	.	.	.	.	
Other temporary crops												
Cassava	.	.		.	.	.	.	.	.	2	.	2
English potatoes	.	.		.	.	.	46	2.0	7	.		.
Cabbages	.	.		.	.	.	204	8.7	40	.		.
Tomatoes	.	.		.	.	.	453	19.3	42	.		.
Onions	.	.		.	.	.	133	5.7	9	.		.
Permanent crops												
Coffee	.	.		398	11.9	73	196	8.4	22	.		.
Tea	.	.		138	4.1	27	.	.	.	.		.
Coconuts	.	.		.	.		.	.	.	147	9	66
Cashew nuts	.	.		.	.		.	.	.	301	18	76
Mangoes	.	.		.	.		.	.	.	23	1	18
Citrus fruits										144	9	39
Other	.	.		67	2.0	17	163	6.9	31	66	4	24
Total cashcrops	71	10.2	35	1567	47.0	100	1248	53.2	79	1135	68	90
Subsistence crops	626	89.8	98	1764	53.0	100	1097	46.8	99	536	32	99
Total value of crops	697	100.0	98	3331	100.0	100	2345	100.0	100	1671	100	100

purchased inputs has been undertaken, but here it suffices to bring the main conclusion of this complicated analysis, namely that neither the size of holding nor the size of the family labour force can "explain" the differences in the value of crop production per holding shown below. We do find that large holdings generally produce more than small holdings, but the size of holding alone cannot explain the differences in the value of crop production.

In Table IV.21 we have calculated the cash income from sales of various crops and the proportion of the holdings involved in the sales of each crop. We have furthermore calculated the value of produce consumed by the sample households themselves. Together these values make up the gross value of agricultural production in the sample areas.

Let us consider the cash incomes first. The differences between the four samples are quite striking both in terms of the level of total cash income and the composition of cash income.

The level of cash income in the *Kombura* sample is so low that one might question whether the term agriculture should be related to these households.

The total cash income from sale of produce is only 71 shs per household per year in the study year 1974. Almost all of the cash incomes are from sales of cotton – 90 per cent. Only one of the holdings in the sample was selling foodcrops, maize and sorghum. This household did not sell food because it had a surplus, but rather because it needed money to buy other necessities and did not have any other source of income. Of the households in the sample only 35 per cent were receiving cash incomes from agriculture. In evaluating these figures it should be remembered that 1974 was a particularly bad year in Kombura Sublocation. Although Kisumu District received only 14 per cent less than the mean annual rainfall the distribution over the year and the variation within the district was not beneficial to agriculture in Kombura Sublocation. Kombura received much less rain than other parts of the district and at the wrong time of the year in relation to agricultural production.

Especially the cotton yields were low in 1974. Thus from direct measurement in a subsample of 20 per cent we estimated that cotton yields per hectare were only 156 kg in 1974 against 600 kg in 1975 which had above annual mean rainfall in the districts.

Also the fact that the average age of heads of households is very high and that a high proportion of young men have left the rural areas to seek employment may explain the very low level of cash income in the sample. But on the other hand the low agricultural potential in itself is the main reason – the push factor – which forces the rural households to seek other sources of income.

Table IV.22. *Yields of pyrethrum and coffee by size of cultivated area in Mwogeto sample.*

Size of plot	Av. Pyre-thrum yield (kg/ha.)	Coeffi-cient of variation	Av. Cof-fee yield (kg/ha.)	Coeffi-cient of variation
0 –0.2	840	72%	4441	72%
0.21–0.4	903	90%	4557	76%
0.41–0.6	994	67%	5066	65%
0.61–0.8	952	–	1335	56%
0.81–1.0	903	–	2703	88%
1.0 +	824	–	4000	–

Table IV.23. *Composition of agricultural incomes by size of holding (acres), K. shs. Mwogeto sample.*

Size of holding (acres)	0 –2.5	2.5–5.0	5.0–7.5	7.5–
	Average income per member of strata/sample			
Incomes				
Maize sale	15.40	35.40	76.45	120.00
Millet sale	20.40	7.75	44.15	–
Pyrethrum	158.40	1223.30	1207.75	1129.70
Tea	10.60	92.15	469.00	66.50
Coffee	398.05	492.85	392.20	210.45
Other crops	61.55	12.65	175.90	18.45
Total	664.40	2356.05	2365.45	1545.10

The households in the *Mwogeto sample* have higher average levels of cash income from crop production than any of the other samples and the sources are quite diversified.

The average cash income per holding in the sample was 1567 shs in 1974 which was an average year as far as annual rainfall is concerned. Besides the high general average level of cash income, it is quite characteristic for the Mwogeto sample that all the households had some cash income. But this is not to say that cash income is more evenly distributed in Mwogeto than elsewhere. Pyrethrum is the most important source of cash income from crops in the sample. But only 55 per cent of the households were receiving pyrethrum income, getting an average yearly income from this source of 1576 shs.

Coffee income which is the second most important source of cash income is shared among more households, but not therefore necessarily more evenly distributed. 73 per cent of the sample households were receiving on average 545 shs annually from coffee sales.

Table IV.24. *Production and consumption of food-grains by size of holding in Mwogeto.*

	Size of Holding (Acres)			
Kilograms maize and millet	0 –2.5	2.5–5.0	5.0–7.5	7.5–
Production per household	1300	1250	1850	1850
Consumption per household	1200	1200	1550	1700
Surplus sold	100	50	300	150

Only 27 per cent of the households received tea incomes although as many as 53 per cent had planted tea. This is because tea has been introduced as a cash crop only recently and a number of holdings only just planted and are not yet harvesting. The average income per grower receiving income from tea is somewhat lower than for coffee, namely 510 shs which is partly due to the lower average size of plots cultivated for tea, partly due to the age of the tea.

Therefore we have not been able to compute the yields of tea, but for pyrethrum and coffee we found that yield per hectare did not vary greatly according to the area planted although the individual variations are great (see Table IV.22).

Thus cash income from pyrethrum and coffee is mainly a question of the size of plots planted with these crops. This can be seen from Table IV.23 which shows the composition of cash income from sales of croops by size of holding.

Mwogeto is also exceptional in the sense that it is the only area where sales of foodcrops are important. As many as 25 per cent of the sample holdings in Mwogeto were selling maize and 11 per cent were selling finger millet, all in the local market. But Mwogeto was also the only sample area in which there was a surplus production of maize as indicated in Table IV.24. We can see that there is a surplus production in all subgroups.

The average yield of maize in the sample is quite high, approx. 2700 kg per hectare, but decreases as the size of plot increases indicating that small plots are cultivated more intensively than larger plots by for example more use of labour and fertilizer.

The level of agricultural cash income in *Werugha* comes second only to Mwogeto. The average annual income from sales of crops was 1248 shs in 1974 which was a year with much below average annual rainfall. But as many as 21 per cent of the households in the Werugha sample had no income from sales of crops at all. Thus, those with cash income had higher levels of income – 1588 shs annually on average – than in Mwogeto.

Various kinds of vegetables dominate the cash income. Together they account for 80 per cent of all cash income, while coffee contributes 16 per cent to total cash income from crops. Tomatoes and cabbage are by far the two most important crops. Tomatoes alone account for 36 per cent of the cash income, more than double the income from coffee. Forty-two per cent of the holdings sold tomatoes for which they received an average annual income of 1080 shs.

But also cabbage yields high cash income to the growers. Forty per cent of the holdings sold cabbage for which they received annual average incomes of 507 shs.

The relatively few holdings growing coffee receive relatively higher incomes. The average annual income for the households growing and selling coffee was 880 shs from this source.

Taita Hills is still a deficit maize producing area and only 9 per cent of the households were selling maize. Most of these were households that had planted hybrid maize and received high yields. Generally, however, judging from the interviews alone, as no measurements of area planted or of yields were undertaken, we found very low yields of maize. Only 8–10 bags of unshelled maize were harvested per acre on average (equivalent to 1400–1700 kg shelled maize per hectare). These are yields which are no better than maize yields in Kombura. However, we should remember that 1974 was a very dry year for Taita Hills. The households that had the highest maize yields in the Werugha sample still had only about 50 per cent of the average maize yields obtained in Mwogeto.

Kikoneni ranks third in terms of the average value of cashcrops per household. The average income from sales of crops was 1135 shs per household in the sample. As many as 90 per cent of the households had cash incomes at an average level of 1264 shs.

The tree crops dominate in the sense that they provide 54 per cent of all incomes from sales of crops. But also sugarcane is very important. It accounts alone for 38 per cent of all cash income from crops and thus is the single most important source of income from crops. However, only 22 per cent of the holdings are selling sugarcane from which they receive as much as 1934 shs per grower. On the other hand, there are also great costs of cultivation involved so that the net value of production is somewhat less.

Among the tree crops cashew nuts are the most important both in terms of the contribution to total average cash income per holding (27 per cent) and in terms of the proportion of households receiving income from this source. Seventy-six per cent of the households received an average income of 397 shs from sales of cashew nuts. Coconuts are almost as important as cashew nuts in terms of the proportion of growers selling this product but the average income they receive is somewhat lower.

A somewhat smaller proportion of the households are receiving income from fruit trees like oranges, lemons and mangoes but since many of the trees planted are still young this source of income will increase in importance in the future and contribute to the diversification of cash crop incomes.

The food crop yields are generally low in Kikoneni and were particularly low in the 1974 season since rainfall in the growth period was only 50 per cent of the annual mean for the Kikoneni area.[4] Only 11 per cent of the households are selling maize. However, all but one of these households are deficit producers getting only a few bags of maize per year from their maize fields. They are selling maize because they had very little cash income from other sources to pay for various necessities which had to be purchased. In order to prevent the selling of maize in order to buy "luxuries", the sale of maize was prohibited while we were still conducting our interviews in the area.[5] But most Digo farmers were simply not concerned about these regulations since they did not plan to sell maize in any case.

There is little to say about the value of crops produced for own consumption. The figures in Table IV.21 have been calculated as the value of produce not sold, valued at average local market prices over the year.

It is obvious that these figures involve very big elements of inaccuracy and that it is impossible to interview the peasants on every single item that has been produced for home consumption. We are particularly aware that the amount of various pulses like beans, pigeon peas, cowpeas and grams has been grossly underestimated. But it has been even more impossible to get figures on the home consumption of cassava which is for instance in Kikoneni the staple food, which is being dug up every day for daily consumption. The value of this consumption is most likely underestimated in the Kikoneni sample as is the value of fruits and coconuts consumed in this area. It should also be remembered, when comparing the four samples, that there was almost no rain in Kikoneni in 1974 when the main food crop, maize, needed it mostly. We would think that approx. 1000 shs as value of annual crop production consumed at home in Kikoneni would be a better indication of the comparative position of rural households in the four sample areas.

It should also be noted that at least some of the differences in levels of consumption of own produce might be caused by differences in household

[4] See C. Gilette *op.cit.* p. 58.
[5] *Ibid* p. 224.

Table IV.25. *Use and cost of purchased inputs per holding in samples (K. shs.)*

	Kombura			Mwogeto			Werugha			Kikoneni		
	Cost		no. of holdings,	Cost		no. of holdings,	Cost		no. of holdings,	Cost		no. of holdings,
	shs.	%	%	shs.	%	%	shs.	%	%	shs.	%	%
Tractor hire	27	33	23	6	5	1	1	0	1	46	28	11
Oxplough hire	20	24	25	0	0	0	0	0	0	5	3	1
Hired labour	34	41	38	82	70	56	199	57	58	113	69	67
Insecticide	0	0	1	3	3	16	24	7	53	0	0	0
Fertilizer	1	1	1	26	22	38	95	27	56	1	1	1
Manure	0	0	0	0	0	0	31	9	10	0	0	0
Total cost	82	99	50	117	100	76	350	100	84	165	101	68
As percent of gross production		12%			4%			15%			10%	

size in the four samples. Kombura and Kikoneni have the lowest average size of households (see Table IV.3).

Otherwise, Table IV.21 shows that there is a good correspondence between income from sales of crops and the value of food consumed at home. Mwogeto, which has the highest income from sales of crops, also has the highest value of crops consumed by the household while the Kombura sample, which has the lowest cash income also has the lowest value of subsistence crops.

It is often assumed that there is also a positive correlation between the level of agricultural food production and the level of food marketed within the individual household. However, evidence from Central Province of Kenya and also from Nyanza Province has shown that at very low levels of agricultural production this relationship might turn negative. The explanation seems to be that although the agricultural production is not sufficient to feed the members of the individual households they have to sell some of their foodcrops in order to get money for paying school fees and for buying other necessities such as cooking oil, kerosine, salt and sugar.[6]

For the four sample areas we find a positive correlation between the ratio

[6] See for example David, Martin, "Marketing of foodcrops and purchase of industrial commodities by Nyanza smallholders, 1970–71". *Working Paper No. 247, Institute for Development Studies, University of Nairobi. December 1975.*

Table IV.26. *Cost of purchased inputs by crops. Mwogeto. Percent.*

	Hired labour	Ferti-lizer	Insecti-cides	Total
Food crops	7	100	100	41
Coffee	47	.	.	30
Tea	22	.	.	14
Pyrethrum	24	.	.	15
Total	100	100	100	100

of agricultural produce marketed and the level of agricultural production.[7] It should however be noted that there is a tendency for households at very low levels of agricultural production to market a relatively large proportion of their produce. Thus we find that Kombura households with an agricultural production below K.shs 200 yearly, marketed as much as 23 per cent of their agricultural produce.

Agricultural Production. Purchased Inputs

The gross value of agricultural production does not of course give the real picture of the significance of the various crops in the total net value of agricultural production since hired labour, insecticides and fertilizers are used in different degrees for the various crops. The aggregated figures of use of various inputs in the four samples are shown in Table IV.25.

Again we can see that there are big differences in the total cost of purchased inputs in the four samples. On the other hand, there seems to be no direct relationship between the average value of crop production in the four samples and the use of purchased inputs. Thus in terms of the cost of purchased inputs expressed as a percentage of the value of crop production, Werugha ranks highest followed by Kombura, Kikoneni and lastly Mwogeto. It might be surprising at the first instance to note that Mwogeto which is most dominated by the cash crops coffee, tea and pyrethrum ranks lowest in relative sense, and even in absolute figures on money spent ranks lower than both Werugha and Kikoneni. But since the expenditure on hired labour is far the most important single item in each of the samples the size of the family labour force explains part of the difference in cost levels. Thus the absence of young men in Kombura sublocation explains the relatively high

[7] The model $\log S = a + b \cdot \log A + c \cdot \log P$ was used for testing our hypothesis and estimating the parameters b and c; where S = percentage of agricultural production marketed; A = agricultural production and P = family size.

Table IV:27 *Cost of purchased inputs by crops. Werugha. Percent.*

	Hired labour	Ferti-lizer	Insecti-cides	Total
Food crops	73	77	5	69
Coffee	5	0	18	5
Vegetables	22	23	77	27
Total	100	100	100	100

Table IV.28. *Cost of purchased inputs by crops. Kikoneni. Percent.*

	Tractor hire	Hired labour	Total
Food crops	3	19	14
Sugarcane	97	43	60
Tree crops	0	38	26
Total	100	100	100

expenses on land preparation by the use of tractor hire and oxplough hire. Likewise, the size of the family labour force explains the differences in absolute levels of cost of hired labour in Mwogeto and Werugha where neither tractor ploughing nor oxploughing is used due to the steepness of the hillsides where the crops are planted. But also the cropping patterns and the soil composition are important determinants of the levels of cost spent on various inputs in the four samples.

In Kombura all the expenditures on inputs, i.e., tractor hire, oxplough hire and hired labour are spent on food crops, but in the other samples the pattern is more diversified.

Table IV.26 shows the utilization of the various purchased inputs by crop in the Mwogeto sample. We can see that almost all the hired labour, which accounts for as much as 70 percent of the total cost of inputs in Mwogeto, is used for the labour intensive cash crops while family labour is predominant for the food crops. On the other hand, and a bit surprising, all the chemical inputs, of which fertilizers are by far the most important, are used for foodcrops.

In Werugha the picture is quite the reverse. As can be seen from Table IV.27 most of the hired labour is used for food crops and only very little for coffee. Most of the fertilizers are also here used for the foodcrops although 23 percent are for vegetables. On the other hand, most of the insecticides are used on vegetables and coffee.

Table IV.29. *Net Value of crop production in samples.*

	Kombura		Mwogeto		Werugha		Kikoneni	
	shs.	%	shs.	%	shs.	%	shs.	%
Food crops	551	89.6	1.877	58.4	913	45.8	600	39.8
Cotton	64	10.4	.		.	.	3	0.2
Sugarcane	.		.		.	.	331	22.0
Pyrethrum	.		852	26.5	.	.	.	.
Vegetables	.		.		904	45.3	.	.
Coffee	.		363	11.3	178	8.9	.	.
Tea	.		122	3.8	.	.	.	.
Tree crops	.		.	.	.	.	572	38.0
Total	615	100.0	3.214	100.0	1.995	100.0	1.506	100.0

Almost all expenditures in Kikoneni were spent on tractor hire and hired labour, and for both categories the use for sugarcane was dominant. This was particularly the case for tractor hire which was almost exclusively used for sugarcane. Forty-three percent of the cost of hired labour was spent on sugarcane and another 38 percent was spent on tree crops while foodcrops take up a much smaller proportion (Tab. IV.28).

While we find no correlation between the value of agricultural production and the cost of purchased inputs when comparing the four samples, the result is the opposite when the analysis is conducted at the household level within each sample area. Then we generally find positive returns to all inputs and the other way round we also find a strong correlation between the use of various inputs and the level of total income per household. On the other hand, although the use of the various inputs increases with the size of holding, this factor alone cannot explain the differences in the use of purchased inputs.

Agricultural Production. Net Value of Crops

When the cost of purchased inputs are deducted from the value of gross production we get the net value of agricultural production. The net value of food crops and of cash crops are shown for the four samples in Table IV.29.

As we can see by comparing Table IV.21 and Table IV.29, neither the relative position of the various crops within each sample nor the relative size of total income from crops in the four samples change very much when we go from gross to net values.

In general the same proportion of expenditures on total inputs are spent on the various crops so that the relative significance of the various crops are not altered.

Table IV.30. *Distribution of crop income in the samples. Accumulated percentages of number of households and percentage of total crop income owned and Gini ratios.*

Kombura		Mwogeto		Werugha		Kikoneni	
% of house-holds	% of income	% of house-holds	% of income	% of house-holds	% of income	% of house-holds	% of income
9.9	1.2	10.4	1.9	8.9	0.7	10.1	0.3
19.8	4.1	20.8	5.5	17.8	2.3	20.2	2.2
29.7	7.6	31.2	10.6	26.8	4.5	30.3	5.3
39.6	13.1	41.6	16.6	35.7	8.0	40.4	9.1
49.5	19.7	52.0	24.4	44.6	12.4	50.5	13.8
59.4	27.7	62.4	34.7	53.5	18.0	60.6	19.7
69.3	37.0	72.8	47.6	62.4	25.5	70.7	28.4
79.2	48.5	83.2	63.3	71.4	35.5	80.8	39.7
89.1	62.2	93.6	82.9	80.3	47.3	90.9	55.9
96.0	76.9			89.2	65.0	98.9	78.9
98.0	83.3			98.1	92.1		
100.0	100.0	99.9	99.9	99.9	100.0	100.0	100.0
Gini ratio 0.46		Gini ratio 0.37		Gini ratio 0.49		Gini ratio 0.57	

Also the relative size of total crop production pertains, although the gap between the richest area, Mwogeto, and the other areas increases since the average holding in Mwogeto spends relatively less on purchased inputs than the average holding in the other sample areas.

The differences in incomes from various crops between households within each group was briefly discussed in the chapter on gross value of production.

Here a more detailed analysis of the distribution of income from crop production within each of the samples will be undertaken. For the purpose Lorenz curves of value of crop production and Gini ratios have been calculated for each sample.

Table IV.30 shows the accumulated percentage figures upon which the Lorenz curves in Figure 3 have been drawn.

There are big differences in income distribution of crop incomes within each sample but also between the four sample areas. The poorest 30 per cent of the households receive only between 5 per cent (in Kikoneni) and 10 per cent (in Mwogeto) of total crop income. The poorest 50 per cent receive between 12.5 per cent (Kikoneni) and 23 per cent (Mwogeto) of total crop income. On the other hand, the richest 5 per cent of the households receive between 14 per cent (Mwogeto) and 32 per cent of total crop income, while

Fig. 3. *Distribution of agricultural production in samples.*

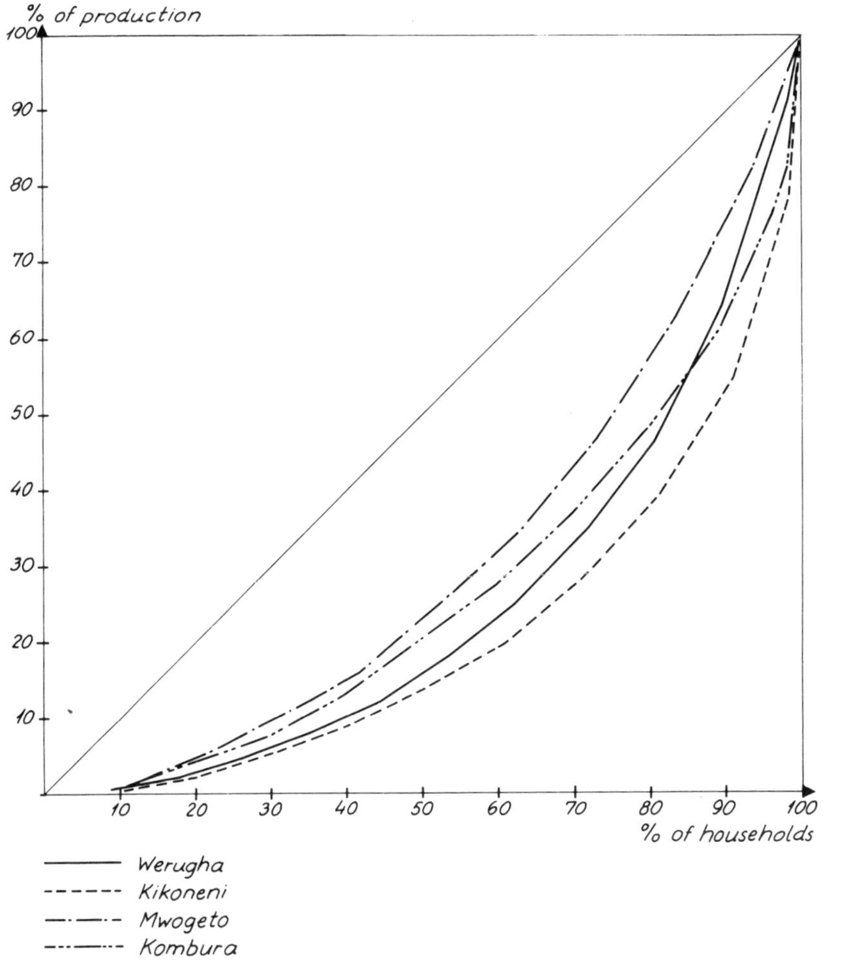

the richest 10 per cent receive between 24 per cent (Mwogeto) and 46 per cent (Kikoneni) of total cash income. The calculation of Gini ratios quantifies the inequality in the distribution of crop income and we get the following ranking of sample areas according to inequality. Crop incomes are most unevenly distributed in Kikoneni (Gini ratio 0.57), then follows Werugha (0.49), Kombura (0.46) and Mwogeto (0.37).

It is quite interesting to note that we get the same ranking of samples according to distribution of crop income as we found for the distribution of land and that for all samples, except Mwogeto, we find higher inequalities in crop income distribution than in the distribution of land. On the other hand, there seems to be no clear relationship between the average level of household crop income and the distribution of land and the distribution of crop income (see below).

Ranking according to distribution of land, crop income and distribution of crop income.

	Kombura	Mwogeto	Werugha	Kikoneni
		Rank		
Distribution of land	3	4	2	1
Crop income	4	1	2	3
Distribution of crop income	3	4	2	1

In Mwogeto the distribution of income from crops is more equal than the distribution of land. The main reason for this seems to be partly the general high fertility of soils which makes it possible with labour intensive cultivation of food crops to get relatively high yields, partly the fact that total cash crop income, in particular coffee income, is fairly evenly distributed among the households in the sample. When the tea bushes that have been planted in the years previous to our fieldwork start to yield, cash crop income will be even more affected in direction of more equality.

On the other hand, the very uneven distribution of crop income in Kikoneni, partly a consequence of the unequal distribution of land, is due to the fact that the sample included relatively many young families that had just started planting various tree crops, but were not yet receiving a cash return. In this way the average age of the sample households may influence the distribution of income since crop income as well as other sources of income varies over the life cycle of the households.

Income from Animal Husbandry

Cattle-keeping is quite an important part of agriculture in all the samples and in addition to crop production a number of households in three of the four sample areas get a significant contribution to consumption and in a few cases also to cash income from sale of milk. Also the sale of livestock and hide and skins contributes to incomes but is of a different nature, since livestock is only rarely sold and then often in relation to an urgent need for cash income, while milk production and income is a more continuous flow. But cattle-keeping has not been studied in any detail in any of the areas. Thus for

Table IV.31. *Value of annual animal production per household in samples.*

	Kombura			Mwogeto			Werugha			Kikoneni		
	Value		% of holdings	Value		% of holdings	Value		% of holdings	Value		% of holdings
	Shs.	%		Shs.	%		Shs.	%		Shs.	%	
Milk sales	2	1	1	186	18	15	227	32	11	2	29	1
Value of milk consumed	93	37	18	610	59	75	311	44	34	2	29	2
Livestock sales	155	62	25	233	23	49	164	23	46	3	43	12
Husbandry	250	100	34	1.029	100	82	703	99	47	7	101	13

example we have not been able to study the introduction of grade cattle and its impact on milk production in the different areas.

The value of annual dairy and livestock production per household in the four samples is shown in Table IV.31. The low figure for Kikoneni is due to the fact mentioned previously that no cattle are kept in the Digo villages. This, of course, does not mean that Digo do not keep cattle or receive income from animal husbandry. However, they do not get milk every day. And as we can see from the table the value of milk production is quite important in the other three samples. With Kikoneni as the exception, the relative levels of production in the samples follow the same pattern as we have seen for crop production. The production is highest in Mwogeto and lowest in the Kombura sample.

The figures for *Kombura* are influenced by the drought in the survey year, 1974. Due to the low value of crop production, a number of people who does not keep cattle as a business, but mainly as a form of savings bank, have been forced to sell cattle in order to obtain cash to buy food. The figure for sales of livestock might therefore be somewhat higher than in an average year, while the figure for milk production will most likely for the same reason be somewhat lower.

Only one per cent of the holdings were selling milk, but in addition 18 per cent of the households were getting milk for their own consumption. The yields are very low and none of the holdings had any grade cattle. But altogether animal husbandry contributes more to total agricultural income than in the other 3 sample areas.

Cattle-keeping is more commercialized in Mwogeto and in addition to the income from production a number of households get a business income from trade in cattle, 15 per cent of the households are involved in commercial dairy production in the sense that they sell milk every day. The average yearly income received by these holdings are quite high, 1200 shs., which means that the average daily sales of milk is approx. 3 litres per household. Income from milk is quite unevenly distributed and as cattle keeping depends on having grazing land the large holdings get higher milk income than the small holdings who have less cattle and therefore only get milk for own consumption. Using the same stratification according to size of holding as used above, we find the following average incomes from milk sales by size of holding (acres).

Mwogeto sample

	Size of holding (acres)			
	0–2.5	2.5–5.0	5.0–7.5	7.5–
Milk sales (shs.) per holding	0	137	324	334

On the other hand, a large proportion of all the sample holdings are getting milk for their own consumption. Seventy-five percent of the holdings got an average of 813 shs. value of milk for their own consumption equivalent to approx. two litres of milk daily. Also cattle sales are quite important in Mwogeto. Almost 50 per cent of the households received an average annual income of 475 shs. from this source. Altogether 82 per cent of the households had some animal husbandry production which altogether contributed significantly to total agricultural income.

Animal husbandry is also quite important in Werugha. Forty-seven percent of the holdings had some income from this source yielding an average annual income of 1.485 shs. Most of this came from milk and the small proportion of the households that were selling milk received quite high incomes. The average annual income from milk sales for the 11 per cent of the households that were selling milk were 2.121 shs. which means that on average approx. 4.5 litres of milk was sold daily by these holdings.

The high average of milk sales is due to the impact of grade cattle kept on four of the holdings. Grade cattle also influences the relationship between income from milk sales and size of holding (acres) (see below).

Werugha sample

	Size of holdings (acres)			
	0–3	3–5	5–7	7–
Milk sales per holding (shs.)	60	560	451	234
Excl. grade cattle	60	76	91	234

Grade cattle kept on holdings of size 3–5 acres (2 holdings) and 5–7 acres (1 holding) influence the average income from milk sales in these groups in a positive direction. When grade cattle is excluded we find the same relationship between size of holding and income from milk sales as above for Mwogeto.

In comparison to Mwogeto few holdings get milk for their own consumption (34 per cent). But almost the same proportion of the holdings receive income from sales of livestock. The average value of sales for holdings involved in livestock sales, however, is much lower in Werugha than it is in Mwogeto. But altogether the contribution of animal husbandry to total agricultural incomes is higher in Werugha than in Mwogeto.

Total Agricultural Incomes

In order to get total agricultural incomes from the four samples the cost of renting land has to be deducted from the combined value of crop and animal production.

We have seen that only in the Mwogeto sample is the renting of land a significant feature, 30 per cent of the households rented land in Mwogeto compared to only 1 per cent in Kombura and 2 per cent in the Werugha sample. None of the households in Kikoneni rented land as land is still relatively abundant in this area. The holdings renting land in Mwogeto spend an average of 94 shs. or equivalent to 187 shs. per acre annually for renting land. This relatively high cost of renting land should of course be seen in relation to the fertility of land (the high potential cash returns per acre) and the extreme shortage of land in Mwogeto sublocation.

As one would have expected the cost of renting land is greater on the small holdings than on the large holdings (see below).

Land rent by size of holding in Mwogeto (acres).

	0–2.5	2.5–5.0	5.0–7.5	7.5–
Land rent (shs.)	30	28	18	13

When the cost of renting land is deducted we get the pattern of agricultural income in the four samples as shown in Table IV.32. By including animal husbandry we get even greater inequality in incomes between the samples as well as between households within each sample.

The level of total agricultural incomes in Mwogeto is 4.8 times higher than in Kombura, 2.8 times higher than in Kikoneni and 1.6 times higher than total agricultural income in Werugha.

Table IV.32. *Value of annual agricultural income per holding in samples.*

	Kombura		Mwogeto		Werugha		Kikoneni	
	Shs.	%	Shs.	%	Shs.	%	Shs.	%
Crop production	615	71	3.214	76	1.995	74	1.506	100
Animal husbandry	250	29	1.029	24	703	26	7	0
Land rent	.	.	28		1	.	.	.
Total Agr. Income	865	100	4.215	100	2.697	100	1.513	100

Since income from animal husbandry is more uneven distributed than value of crop production, total agricultural income is more unequally distributed. We have calculated the following Gini ratios for the four samples.

Kombura : 0.47
Mwogeto : 0.40
Werugha : 0.52
Kikoneni : 0.57

The general level of agricultural income is so low in at least two of the four samples that it would be impossible to survive if agricultural income was not supplemented by income transfers from family members working and living in the urban areas of Kenya and by various kinds of non-farm income.

Remittances

We have seen in the section on population in the samples that a large proportion of the young men, especially in Kombura, were living away from home because of the poor agricultural potential in the sublocation. But also the so-called "pull factor", i.e., the relatively high urban incomes, are an important factor in rural-urban migration in Kenya. This motivates most of the men from the rural areas at some point in their lives – mostly in the age of the twenties and thirties – to look for highly paid jobs in the towns. This had also been the case for almost all the men in the four samples that we interviewed as heads of households. They had now returned to live in their rural homes. This factor is of great importance when one considers the composition of income from various sources over the life cycle of the rural families.

The contribution received from family members working away from the home is shown in Table IV.33.

Table IV.33. *Remittances in the samples (shs.)*

Kombura	Mwogeto	Werugha	Kikoneni
948 n = 54	113 n = 32	1.075 n = 53	340 n = 46

We would have expected an inverse relationship between agricultural incomes and remittances due to the "push factor", i.e., men from low potential agricultural areas seeking alternative sources of income. We can see that the push factor has been in work as far as *Kombura* is concerned. The average contribution to income from family members living elsewhere is bigger than agricultural incomes in the sample. In this sense Kombura should be considered a labour reserve area rather than an area of agricultural producers. The average sum received as remittances per family is 948 shs. a year, 54 per cent of the households receive this kind of income at the very high relative level of 1.773 per household.

Income remittances are of less significance in *Mwogeto* than in any of the other areas. The high return to labour on food as well as cash crops yield good income opportunities for the rural labour force. Nonetheless, 33 percent of the households receive small sums monthly from family members living and working outside the district. On average these income transfers contribute 339 shs. to the income of these households.

The high level of remittances in *Werugha* is due to the high educational level of the people living in Taita Hills. A large number of young men are employed in civil service positions in Nairobi or work as qualified professionals in various types of skilled jobs yielding high incomes. But also the shortage of land in the fertile part of the sublocation acts as a push factor for the families in the Werugha sample. The average value of remittances for households in the sample is as high as 1075 shs. and 47 per cent of the households had this kind of income which on average contributed 2.272 shs. to the already high level of agricultural incomes.

A great number of young men in *Kikoneni* are working in either Mombasa or other small towns in Kwale District, but since some of them are still living in Kikoneni their income has been recorded as non-farm income and not as remittances. This procedure could of course be questioned since they only contribute part of their income to the household consumption unit, partly due to transport cost, partly due to food expenses during the day. However, we believe that they contribute most of their income and also undertake most of their consumption in their "home" in Kikoneni. Therefore they are recorded as family members living *here,* i.e., members of the rural households. The average level of remittances is 340 shs. a year. But almost

Table IV.34. *The significance of the rural non-farm sector for total income and employment in samples.*

	Kombura (k. shs.)	Mwogeto (k. shs.)	Werugha (k. shs.)	Kikoneni (k. shs.)
1. Income from agriculture	865	4.215	2.697	1.513
2. Land rent (income from leasing)	113	5	0	0
3. Income from non-farm activity	1.815	3.367	3.676	1.969
4. Remittances	948	113	1.075	340
5. Total income	3.741	7.700	7.448	3.822
6. Income from non-farm activity, %	48.5%	43.7%	49.4%	51.5%
7. Employment of women in non-farm activity, %	42.0%	16.1%	10.2%	11.7%
8. Employment of men in non-farm activity, %	44.1%	19.6%	23.6%	29.8%
9. Share of adult population with non-farm occupation, %	43.1%	17.9%	16.4%	21.5%

the same proportion of the households in Kikoneni (46 per cent) as in Mwogeto are receiving money from this source of income. On average they get 732 shs. a year.

Non-agricultural Income by Sample Holdings

As we have seen in Chapter III, a large number of rural households are receiving income from a great variety of non-farming activities. This was also the case in the sample households.

Figures on employment and incomes from non-farming activities in the four samples are given in Tables IV.34, IV.35 and IV.36.

Table IV.34 shows the absolute level of non-farm activity in the four samples. We can see that the pattern that we saw for remittances is partly repeated for non-farm incomes. The highest absolute level of non-farm incomes is in Werugha followed by Mwogeto, Kikoneni and Kombura. But in terms of the relative contribution of non-farm income to total income (line 6 in Table IV.34) Kikoneni ranks highest (followed by Werugha, Kombura and Mwogeto.)

In terms of employment we get yet another pattern. As many as 43.1 per cent of the adult population in Kombura was engaged in non-farm activity, while this percentage was only 16.4 per cent in Werugha, 17.9 per cent in Mwogeto and 21.5 per cent in Kikoneni, (line 9 in Table IV.34). There are little differences between the participation in non-agricultural activities between men and women in Kombura and Mwogeto, but in Werugha and Kikoneni there are big differences between the proportion of men and women who are engaged outside agriculture. The reason for this as far as

Table IV.35. *Employment and income in the rural non-farm sector in Mwogeto and Kombura samples.*

	Kombura				Mwogeto			
	Employment			Average yearly income (K. shs.)	Employment			Average yearly income (K. shs.)
	Men	Women	Total		Men	Women	Total	
Fishing	5	0	5	1.012	0	0	0	
Cattle trade	1	0	1	2.000	3	0	3	3.720
Petty trade	6	13	19	1.125	0	12	12	905
Beer brewing	0	3	3	460	0	10	10	1.272
Home craft	23	43	66	922	1	1	2	900
Restaurant/retail trade	3	0	3	2.400	6	3	9	5.033
Transport	0	0	0		5	0	5	4.464
Small-scale industry	12	0	12	2.898	8	0	8	5.169
Woodcutting	0	0	0		1	0	1	600
Public service (teachers)	17	1	18	5.753	8	0	8	7.577
Total	67	60	127	1.860[1]	32	26	58	3.367[1]

Source: Interviews of sample households in the two sublocations in 1975.

[1] weighted average.

Table IV.36. *Employment and income in the rural non-farm sector in Werugha and Kikoneni sample.*

	Werugha				Kikoneni			
	Employment			Average yearly income (K. shs.)	Employment			Average yearly income (K. shs.)
	Men	Women	Total		Men	Women	Total	
Fishing	–	–	–	–	1	–	1	2.400
Cattle trade					–	–	–	–
Petty trade	4	–	4	2.790	25	–	25	460
Beer brewing[1]		11	11	1.200	–	5	5	1.200
Home craft	–	–	–	–	–	9	9	654
Restaurant/ retail trade	8	5	13	3.831	5	–	5	3.720
Transport	1	–	1	6.000	3	–	3	3.800
Small-scale industry	6	–	6	2.900	7	–	7	4.029
Woodcutting	–	–	–	–	1	–	1	3.000
Public service (teachers, civil servants)	18	3	21	4.989	9	3	12	3.910
Total non-agricultural	38	19	57	3.676[2]	51	17	68	1.969[2]

[1] Estimated from the use of sugar in the individual households as the questionnaire survey did not reveal this "illegal" activity.
[2] Weighted average.

Kikoneni is concerned, is that Moslim women are prohibited against buying and selling in the market-place according to the local tradition.[8] For Werugha the reason for the low participation of women in non-farm activity is caused by the total absence of women participation in petty trade and home craft. A phenomenon which can also be explained by religion.

It might seem paradoxical that Kombura, having the highest ratio of non-farm occupation, also has the lowest level of non-farm income while at the same time Werugha has the lowest level of non-farm occupation and the highest absolute level of non-farm income. The explanation for this is simply that there are big differences in the composition of non-farm activities in the four samples. This can be seen from Table IV.35 and Table IV.36.

Non-farm occupation in the Kombura sample is dominated by low income part-time occupations undertaken as "subsistance activities" such as petty trade and home craft, which together account for more than two-thirds of all non-farm occupation. On the other hand, very few are involved in the highly paid permanent full time occupations such as rural industries and public services, which only accounted for 23.6 per cent of total non-agricultural occupation in Kombura.

The relatively high level of non-farm income in Mwogeto (3.367 shs.) in spite of the fact that only 17.9 per cent of the adult population of the sample had this kind of occupation, is due to the high ratio of people engaged in ownership of shops and smallscale rural industry or employed as civil servants (teachers). These groups accounted for 43.1 per cent of all non-farm occupation, but in addition yielded higher incomes than in Kombura. Conversely, low income activities like petty trade and home-craft are of less importance in the Mwogeto sample.

The Werugha sample is even more dominated by high income permanent occupations than we saw for Mwogeto. The relatively high levels of education in Werugha, which we saw had an influence on the level of remittances from people working outside the sublocation, is also likely to influence the level of non-farm income. Thus we see that as many as 36.8 per cent of the people having non-farm occupations are employed as civil servants with relatively high income. But we also see that a relatively high proportion are getting high incomes from shops. As mentioned previously, no women are involved in subsistence type activities and the men involved in vegetable trade receive relatively large incomes. But we can also see that incomes from shops, smallscale industries and public employment is generally lower than in Mwogeto.

The most characteristic feature of Kikoneni is the great number of men

[8] See C. Gilette *op.cit.,* p. 74.

involved in petty trade. As mentioned above, this is because according to Muslim tradition the women are prohibited from participating in this business. The only women activities are mat making and a little illegal beer brewing undertaken at home. The differences in level of income and occupation between the four sample areas are more thoroughly discussed in Chapter V.

Income and Income Distribution in Samples

Remittances and non-farm income, which make it possible for the poor households in the low potential agricultural areas to survive, have an equalizing effect upon differences in income levels between the four sample areas. When the average income in the "richest" sample, Mwogeto, is expressed as a proportion of incomes in the other samples we get the following picture for agricultural and total rural household income:

	Agricultural income	Total Household Income
Kombura	4.87	2.06
Kikoneni	2.79	2.01
Werugha	1.53	1.03

We can see that, while agricultural incomes in the Mwogeto sample are 4.87 times higher than in the Kombura sample the ratio is only 2.06 when income from remittances and non-agricultural activities are added to agricultural incomes in order to get the total income of the rural households. The same tendency exists for the relationship between Mwogeto and the other two sample areas, Kikoneni and Werugha.

In the following we will investigate whether the inclusion of remittances and non-agricultural incomes have a similar equalizing effect upon the distribution of income within each of the four sample areas.

Table IV.37 gives the accumulated percentages of households and the percentages of total income received by the different income groups and based upon these figures the Lorenz curves of income distribution have been drawn in Fig. 4.

The big inequalities in income distribution between the households within each sample as well as between the four samples is clearly seen in Figure 4.

The poorest 30 per cent of the households only receive between 3 per cent (Kikoneni) and 10 per cent (Kombura) of total incomes in the samples, and the poorest 50 per cent of the households only receive between 12 per cent (Kikoneni) and 22 per cent (Kombura) of total income.

Table IV.37. *Distribution of income (accumulated %).*

Mwogeto	Percent of Households		5.20	10.41	20.83	30.21	40.62	50.00	60.41	70.83	80.21	90.62	95.83	100.0
	Percent of Income		0.84	2.04	5.29	9.23	14.74	20.50	28.51	38.26	48.57	65.84	79.74	100.0
Kombura	Percent of Households		5.47	10.16	20.31	30.47	40.63	50.00	60.16	70.31	80.47	90.63	95.31	100.0
	Percent of Income		1.11	2.43	6.02	10.55	16.00	21.84	29.09	37.67	48.21	63.40	73.99	100.0
Werugha	Percent of Households		12.5	20.5	31.2	44.6	53.5	60.7	72.3	80.3	84.8	89.3	94.7	100.0
	Percent of Income		1.2	3.2	8.1	16.4	23.4	30.4	44.0	54.8	61.7	69.3	80.8	100.0
Kikoneni	Percent of Households	13.2	25.3	37.4	54.6	66.7	73.8	79.8	86.9	90.9	91.9	92.9	96.9	99.9
	Percent of Income	0.7	2.6	5.5	13.4	22.8	30.5	38.7	50.4	58.4	60.9	63.5	79.2	100.0

Fig. 4. *Distribution of income in samples.*

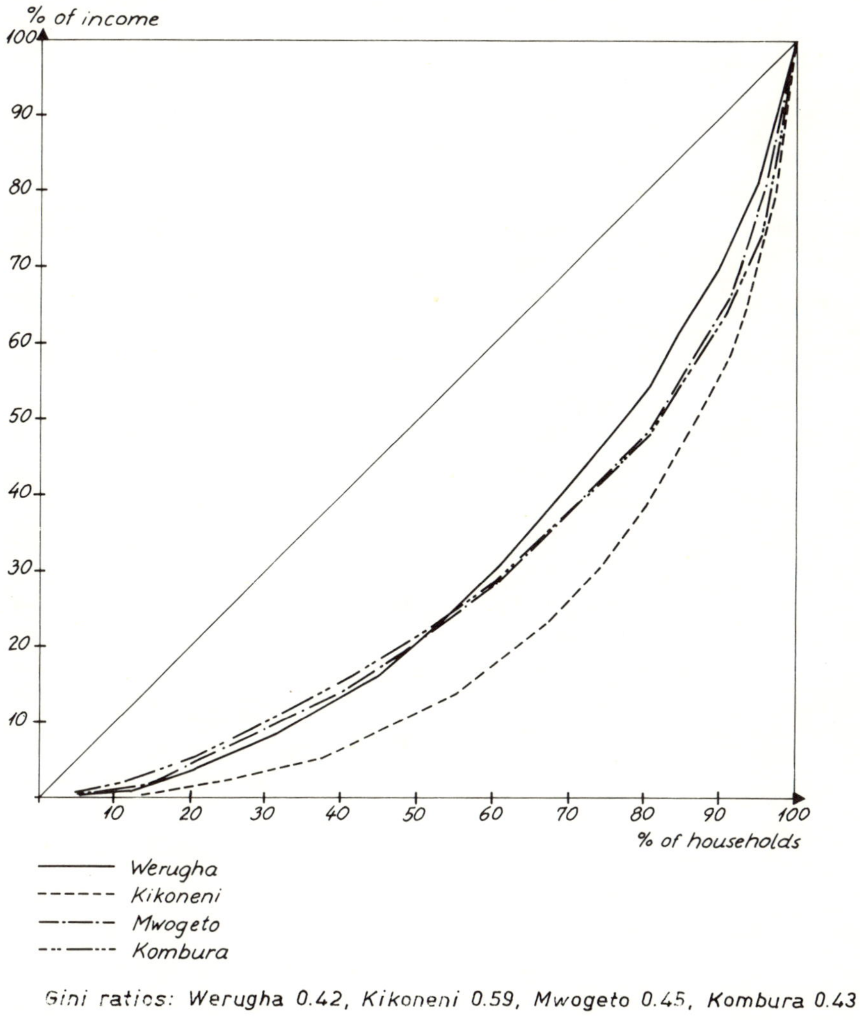

At the other end of the income scale the richest 5 per cent of the households receive between 19 per cent (Werugha) and 29 per cent (Kikoneni) while the richest 10 per cent received as much as between 29 per cent (Werugha) and 44 per cent (Kikoneni) of total income.

The Gini ratios give a clearer picture of the relative levels of inequality of income in the four samples:

Sample	Gini ratio
Kombura	0.43
Mwogeto	0.45
Werugha	0.42
Kikoneni	0.59

The impact of income transfers and non-agricultural incomes on the distribution of wealth is quite different in the four samples. By comparing with the Gini ratios computed for crop income and total agricultural income we find that remittances and non-farm incomes reduce inequality in the Kombura sample and in the Werugha sample while they increase the inequality in Mwogeto and in Kikoneni. This is so because income transfers in Werugha are mainly benefitting the poorer households and because non-farming activities in Kombura are very much of a subsistence nature which are of course dominated by the poorer households.

By comparing with Table II.32 in Chapter II we see that average inequality in our combined four samples is less (0.47) than the Kenya smallholder average (0.49), only in Kikoneni do we find above average inequality. But we can also see that our Nyanza Province samples, Kombura and Mwogeto, have a more unequal distribution of income than the smallholders in Nyanza Province sampled for the integrated Rural Survey 1974/75. The same is the case as far as our Coast Province samples, Werugha and Kikoneni are concerned. The income distribution found in our samples is much more unequal than in the Coast Province households sampled for the Integrated Rural Survey.

Household Consumer Expenditure

The level of average income per capita as well as the distribution of income determines the level and the composition of consumption within each of the samples.

Table IV.38 shows the level of yearly consumption of non-durables and the average consumer pattern in the four samples. The figures include purchased items as well as consumption of the household's own produce. The yearly consumption of purchased items is based upon information about expenditures in the month in which the interviews were undertaken. Monthly consumption, of course, varies over the year since the households usually buy maize only when the granaries are empty. The yearly consumption of those items which are only purchased when the household's own produce has been consumed, has therefore been calculated as the sum

Table IV.38. *Average yearly consumption of non-durables in the four samples.*

	Kombura		Mwogeto		Werugha		Kikoneni	
	K. shs.	%	K. shs.	%	K. shs.	%	K. shs.	%
Cereals	1033	46.7	1136	33.4	1203	28.6	1272	36.1
Pulses	61	2.8	33	1.0	120	2.9	297	8.4
Vegetables	34	1.5	31	0.9	68	1.6	21	0.6
Fruit	0	0	12	0.4	0	0	53	1.5
Fish	212	9.6	2	0.1	21	0.5	557	15.8
Meat	197	8.9	222	6.5	365	8.7	720	20.4
Sugar	121	5.5	174	5.1	505	12.0	385	10.9
Milk	117	5.3	639	18.8	467	11.1	9	0.3
Cooking oils & fats	54	2.4	97	2.9	228	5.4	49	1.4
Total food	1819	82.2	2346	69.1	2977	70.7	3291	93.4
Soft drinks	8	0.4	17	0.5	59	1.4	7	0.2
Bottled beer	2	0.1	31	0.9	59	1.4	19	0.5
Local beer	38	1.7	256	7.5	120	2.9	5	0.1
Total drinks	48	2.2	304	9.0	238	5.7	31	0.8
Fuel	73	3.3	102	3.0	303	7.2	108	3.1
School fees	181	8.2	514	15.1	320	7.6	48	1.4
Harambee contrib.	38	1.7	103	3.0	350	8.3	24	0.7
Funerals, etc.	54	2.4	28	0.8	26	0.6	19	0.5
Total non-durables	2213	100.0	3397	100.0	4214	100.1	3522	99.9

of home produce consumed by the household plus monthly expenditures in the part of the year when food is purchased.

The consumption of the household's own produce is valued at local selling prices at the market, while purchasing, naturally, is valued at the actual cost of buying. Therefore, the average level of consumption per household depends not only upon disposible income and average family size, but also upon the ratio between the consumption of its own produce and the consumption of purchased items.

From Table IV.38 we can see that Werugha had the highest absolute level of consumption (4.214 shs. a year) followed by Kikoneni (3.522 shs.), Mwogeto (3.397 shs.) and Kombura (2.213 shs.). But measured as proportion of income, consumption was relatively highest in Kikoneni (111 per cent) followed by Werugha (76 per cent), Kombura (59 per cent) and Mwogeto (55 per cent). The same ranking of the four sample areas results when consumption per capita is considered.

These differences in the level of consumption in the four sample areas can to some extent be explained by the degree of self-sufficiency in food.

Food consumption makes up the most important part of non-durable

Table IV.39. *Dependency on purchased food in samples.*

	Kombura	Mwogeto	Werugha	Kikoneni
Purchased food as percent of all food consumption	59.2	33.0	53.0	83.7

consumption in all samples. But it varies between 93.4 per cent in Kikoneni, 82.2 per cent in Kombura, 70.7 per cent in Werugha and 69.1 per cent in Mwogeto. Differences in the cost of food consumption can therefore explain much of the difference in total non-durable consumption.

Table IV.39 gives the ratio of purchased food to total food consumption.

We can see that the sample households in Kikoneni buy 83.7 per cent of their food while on the other hand the sample households in Mwogeto only purchase 33.0 per cent of their food. Differences in self-sufficiency ratios in food consumption, together with the high opportunity cost of growing cash-crops instead of foodcrops, i.e., the cost difference between food produced at home and food purchased, explains most of the differences in consumption cost levels in the four samples.

Also the composition of consumer expenditures varies greatly in the four samples. Of noticeable differences we should like to point at the high expenditures on fish and meat in Kikoneni. This is partly due to the fact that the households in Kikoneni do not keep cattle in their own village. Therefore, the home slaughtering of livestock does not exist, and people have to buy most of their meat. Due to the low level of local slaughtering the meat prices are also higher in Kikoneni than in the other sample areas.

Also the high sugar consumption in Werugha should be mentioned. This is probably explained by the significance of home-brewing of changaa, the local gin.

Finally, we should like to point at the very large amounts spent on school fees in all the samples, but in particular in Mwogeto, where as much as 514 K.shs. is spent annually per household.

It should be emphasized that expenditures on durables are not included in this table of yearly consumer expenditures.

Durables are often bought by family members working in the urban areas and brought back as gifts. Or they are purchased by the household just after a high cash payment has been received. Furthermore, the consumption of durables should not be related to average income in one single year, as durables are not usually consumed in one year, but last for a number of years. Thus, the consumption of durables must be seen in relation to the level of total income over a longer period of time. Expenditures on durables in the survey year 1975, therefore, should be considered in the light of past (and future) incomes of the rural families.

In order to get a more representative picture of the value of the consumption of durables in the sample households, an inventory of household durables was undertaken for a 20 per cent sub-sample. The price and the year of purchase was noted for each item and the present day value was calculated by taking into account inflation and wear and tear. The durability was finally taken into account by dividing the present day value of the items by the number of years they could be assumed to last. By adding together the yearly share of the present day values of various durables including housing the total value of durables was calculated.

In this way we found that total durables made up approximately 10 per cent of total consumption in the four samples. The variations in this proportion between the different samples are so small that they are not statistically significant.

A more thorough statistical analysis was undertaken in order to explain the differences in consumer patterns between the households within each sample.

The correlation between rural household expenditures on some major items and the disposable incomes of rural households has been tested. The model is:

$$C_{ij} = \alpha_i + \beta_i \cdot Y_j + \gamma_i \cdot P_j$$

where C_{ij} is the yearly consumption of commodity i by household j; Y_j is the disposible income of household j; P_j is the family size of household j (measured in consumer equivalents), and α_i, β_i and γ_i are the parameters that we have to estimate. Thus β_i is the income elasticity, and γ_i the household size elasticity of demand for commodity i.

The double log function

$$\log (C_{ij}) = \alpha_i + \beta_i \cdot \log (Yj) + \gamma_i \cdot \log (P_j)$$

was used for estimating α, β and γ because of its relative simplicity.

We found a positive correlation between disposible income and the consumption of major groups of commodities as well as between family size and consumption, i.e., that consumption increases as income and size of household increases. But there are important differences between the size of the income elasticity of demand and the household size elasticity of demand. For food, for example, we find that the income elasticity of demand is greater (approx. 0.5) than the household size elasticity of demand (approx. 0.2). The difference between the income elasticity of demand and the household size elasticity of demand is generally higher for "luxury items" such as meat, sugar, cooking oils and drinks (for which the income elasticity of demand becomes higher than one, while the household size elasticity turns negative), than it is for consumer goods satisfying basic needs, such as basic food (maize, beans and milk), fuel and housing.

But only for one item, school fees, do we find that the family size elasticity is significantly higher than the income elasticity of demand.

This underlines the extent to which high educational standards are considered a necessity even among very poor rural families. It also follows from this analysis of income and family size elasticities of demand that there are important differences in consumer patterns between relatively poor and relatively rich households. Since income elasticities of demand are greater and higher than one for "luxury items" like bottled beer (approx. 1.0) and most durables, e.g., iron-roof houses (approx. 1.1) and radios etc. (approx. 1.3) than for consumer goods satisfying basic needs like cereals (approx. 0.3), we can conclude that high income groups consume a higher proportion of "luxury items" than the low income consumers.[9]

Savings in Samples

From the figures of total income in Table IV.35 and the figures of consumer expenditures in Table IV.36 we can now calculate the savings of the average household in the four samples. Again we should like to point at the important changes in income levels and levels of consumer expenditures over the life cycle of the rural households. *Ceteris paribus,* young families are likely to be net savers of money which is then usually hoarded for consumption at an older age when the family becomes net de-savers.

Differences in the age composition of the four samples will therefore influence the relative level of average household savings performance. We shall therefore recall that the average age of heads of household was much higher in Kombura (52.6 years) than in Mwogeto (44.8), Werugha (45.1) and Kikoneni (44.1).

The average household savings of the four samples are shown in Table IV.40.

[9] Our findings here seem to be well in accordance with the findings of other studies of income elasticities of demand in Kenya. See for example:
Massel and Heyer, "Household expenditure in Nairobi: a statistical analysis of consumer behaviour". Occasional Paper No. 2. Institute for Development Studies, Nairobi, May 1967.
Kenya Government. Ministry of Finance and Planning, "Estimates of the Income Elasticity of Demand for Various Items in Nairobi, Mombasa and Kisumu", in *Kenya Statistical Digest,* June 1972, vol. X – No. 2. *Hårstad, Jarle,* "Multiplier Effects of Household Incomes in Nyeri and Kisumu, Kenya", Department of Geography, University of Oslo, May 1976.

Table IV.40. *Average savings by sample households.*

	Kombura	Mwogeto	Werugha	Kikoneni
Income	3740	6214	5543	3180
Consumption	2545	3858	4682	3913
Savings	1195	2356	861	−733
Savings ratio (%)	32.0	37.9	15.5	−23.1

Only in Kikoneni do we find a negative savings ratio. And as we saw in the previous chapter, the relatively high consumption in Kikoneni can be partly explained by the relatively low rate of self-sufficiency in food production and the high opportunity cost of growing cash-crops instead of food-crops.

The comparatively poor savings performance in Werugha is due to the relatively high expenditures on various "luxury items", such as sugar (for local gin production) and drinks, but it is also caused by the high price of kerosine for cooking and the large sums of money contributed to various Harambee projects, such as schools, by the households in our sample.

The comparatively good savings performance by the average Kombura household is due to the fact that they spend very little on non-food items other than school fees.

It is usually assumed that rich households have a higher savings ratio than poor households.

This has been tested by the use of a model which explains the savings ratio as a function of income y and family size p.

In summary, we find that there is a strong, positive correlation between savings ratio and income y, i.e., that the rich households have a higher savings ratio than the poor households. In Table IV.41 we see how the savings ratio varies according to income between major income groups. For all the sample areas we see that the savings ratio increases with the size of income. Generally, the low income groups have negative savings while the high income groups save considerable amounts of money with the savings ratio in each sample exceeding 50 per cent for the highest income group. In Mwogeto only the lowest income group (0–999 K.shs. annually) had negative savings, while the group 1000–2999 K.shs. had a small, positive saving. In the other sample areas the income level at which a positive saving was obtained was higher than in Mwogeto. Thus, in Werugha only households with average annual incomes of above 5000 K.shs. annually had a positive savings ratio.

It should be underlined that since expenditures on durables have been calculated as a fixed percentage of all consumption within each sample (in

Table IV.41. *Household consumption per household and saving ratios by size of income in samples.*

	Kombura			Mwogeto			Werugha			Kikoneni		
Income group	Con-sump-tion	Sav-ings ratio	No. of house-holds	Con-sump-tion	Sav-ings ratio	No. of house-holds	Con-sump-tion	Sav-ings ratio	No. of house-holds	Con-sump-tion	Sav-ings ratio	No. of house-holds
0–999	1586	–131.4	15	1142	–47.2	5	2061	–278.7	14	3560	–662.6	37
1000–2999	1770	12.3	60	2036	0.0	27	3509	–72.5	21	4083	–117.3	29
3000–4999	2681	29.8	16	3214	16.6	22	4044	– 6.8	25	3667	5.1	13
5000–6999	5378	1.5	4	3564	39.2	16	5334	12.5	21	3826	32.2	11
7000–9999	3840	51.8	3	3958	50.1	10	5544	67.1	19	5403	32.4	2
10000–	7744	63.2	4	6872	64.3	14	8345	47.5	12	6366	61.2	7

accordance with the results of the 20 per cent subsample surveys undertaken on consumption of durables in each of the four samples), there is a tendency to underestimate the savings of the low income groups, and vice versa to overestimate the savings of the high income groups. Table IV.41 also shows how consumption per household grows with the size of income.

It is interesting to note that even in Kikoneni, which had a negative average savings ratio, we have a large number of households with positive savings. In interpreting these data we should, of course, take into account that income might be over-evaluated, and consumption figures on the other hand might be underestimated. But even allowing, for example, for a 20 per cent bias on the high side for income, and on the low side for consumption, we would still find a relatively high proportion of the households with positive savings ratios.

Some of the savings are used on durable consumer goods, when enough money has been saved, and some of the money is saved as a "reserve" in case of bad harvests, or sickness, or may be set aside as "pension" for old age. But most of the net saving households also accumulate part of their savings as investment in various activities.

A large share of the savings of the rural households are invested in the construction of new houses with iron sheet roofs to replace the traditional houses made of clay and with grass-thatched roofs. However, a number of the households also engage in productive investments.

Investment and Accumulation of Capital

Although considerable proportions of the savings of the rich households of the samples have been used for building new, iron-roof, houses, there is a limit to how much money can be spent for this purpose. In all sample areas we have found that additional savings are being invested in agriculture as well as in non-agricultural business. The most important investment in agriculture is land purchase. We found that a large proportion of the households in the fertile sample areas, where land was in short supply, had been investing in land, either by purchase or by renting more land. As can be seen from Table IV.11 above, as many as 31.3 per cent of the households in Mwogeto and 24.2 per cent of the households in the Werugha sample had invested in more land. On the other hand, only 4.0 per cent of the Kombura sample households had invested in more land, and they all bought land outside the location – in areas where agriculture would yield a better return than in the poor agricultural environment of Kombura Sublocation.

In Kikoneni Sublocation only 7.1 per cent of the households invested in more land. This relatively low figure is due to the fact that land is relatively less scarce in Kikoneni than in the other sample areas (see Table IV.6 on average size of holdings in sample areas). In fact, most of the households in Kikoneni that have been buying land are Kamba families who have settled in the area recently.

But agricultural investment is also taking place in the form of land improvement and – more important – the planting of permanent crops, like coffee and tea in Mwogeto (Table IV.15), coffee in Werugha (Table IV.17), and coconuts, cashew nuts and fruit-trees in Kikoneni (Table IV.19).

In addition, peasant households in Mwogeto and Werugha had started investing in high-yielding dairy cattle, a tendency which has accelerated particularly since the years of high prices for coffee and tea in 1977 and 1978.[10]

On the other hand, very little investment has taken place in farm equipment.

The only agricultural implements owned by the sample households are those which have been used for cultivation for centuries: the traditional hoes and pangas, i.e., long knives. In addition, a few families in the samples owned axes used for clearing bush and for cutting firewood.

Ox-ploughing or tractor-ploughing was only used in Kombura Sublocation, and in a few cases for sugarcane in Kikoneni. But none of the households owned their own tractors, and only a small number of households – all in Kombura Sublocation – had their own ox-ploughs and oxen. They made up only 8.8 per cent of the sample household in Kombura. Tractor-ploughing and investment in mechanized agriculture are now spreading in other areas of Kenya where smallholders have received high incomes, such as in Central Province.

The reason that this development has not taken place in our samples is due to the fact that tractor-ploughing is not possible on the steep slopes of the fertile land in the high potential areas of Mwogeto and Werugha Sublocation.

However, most of the investments of the households in our samples have been undertaken in various non-farm businesses, such as small shops and hotels in the rural market-places, rural industries, transport business or various trades in cattle and agricultural produce. It is quite evident that investment in non-farm businesses has been considered more profitable and less risky than agricultural investment in the past. Investment in non-farm businesses like small shops yielded a relatively good and stable income compared to agriculture, and at the same time made it possible to utilize

[10] The tendency to use the high incomes from coffee and tea to plant more tea and coffee and to buy grade dairy cattle was observed, but not quantified during revisits to the sample areas in 1979. See also Bager, T. *op.cit.*

Table IV.42. *Non-farm investment activities by sample households (No. of investment activities).*

	Shops, hotels	Rural industry	Transport	Other business	Total	% of households
Kombura	2	4	0	6	12	11.8
Mwogeto	7	3	4	12	26	27.1
Werugha	9	6	1	4	20	17.9
Kikoneni	5	7	3	4	19	19.2

family labour economically in seasons where there was little demand for labour in the shambas.

Table IV.42 shows the non-farm investment activities of the households in our samples. Investment in shops and hotels is much more capital-demanding than the other activities, and is therefore mostly undertaken by households which have one or more of the family members in high paid jobs, such as civil servants. Thus, many of the people in our sample who had invested in shops and hotels were employed as school-teachers in the area.

The households in Mwogeto are more active in non-farm investments (as well as in agricultural investment), than the sample households in the other areas. The reason for this is partly that they have higher savings than the households in the other areas, partly that the local demand, and therefore the turnover and profitability in local business, is higher than in the other areas. But also a relatively large proportion of the households in the Werugha sample and in the Kikoneni sample have invested in non-farm businesses.

The high figure for Werugha is partly explained by the relatively high savings of the sample households, but also by the relatively high profits obtained by rural industries in this area (see Chapter V, p. 202).

The relatively high non-farm investment activity by Kikoneni households is undertaken by the few households that have very high incomes from civil servant jobs.

While the sample households in Kombura and Werugha had only invested in one line of business, one of the households in Kikoneni and six of the households in Mwogeto had more than one non-farm business. At the same time these were the households that also receive high salary incomes.

In summary we can conclude that the households which are in a position to save part of their income have invested part of these savings productively in agriculture as well as in non-agricultural activities.

The investment patterns have been determined by profit considerations and by risk considerations, and therefore non-farm business investments

Table IV.43. *Buying and renting of land by income group (percentage of households).*

Income group (K. shs.)	Kombura	Mwogeto	Werugha	Kikoneni
0– 999	0.0	0.0	7.1	10.8
1000–2999	1.7	25.9	14.3	6.9
3000–4999	6.3	31.8	16.0	0.0
5000–6999	0.0	25.0	42.9	0.0
7000–9999	33.3	60.0	26.3	50.0
10000–	25.0	42.9	25.0	0.0

Table IV.44. *Selling or leasing of land by income group (percentage of households).*

Income group (K. shs.)	Kombura	Mwogeto	Werugha	Kikoneni
0– 999	26.7	0.0	0.0	2.7
1000–2999	25.0	7.4	0.0	17.2
3000–4999	37.5	9.1	0.0	15.4
5000–6999	25.0	0.0	0.0	18.2
7000–9999	0.0	0.0	0.0	0.0
10000–	0.0	0.0	0.0	14.3

have been more important than agricultural investment in the past. However, revisits to the high potential areas growing coffee and tea in 1979 revealed a tendency that more of the surplus is likely to be invested in agriculture when prices and profitability go up.

The previous low level of agricultural investment in smallholder agriculture in Kenya should therefore not be seen as the result of the absence of an accumulating class of agricultural producers, but simply as a result of the relatively low profitability of agricultural investment vis-à-vis investment in non-agricultural business. The rural households should not be seen as agricultural producers alone. They are economic entities for which a wide spectrum of agricultural and non-agricultural options are open, and they choose between these options very much like the "economic man" of economic textbooks, optimizing the return to labour and capital, and minimizing risk, but, of course, with the severe constraints facing households at very low income levels.

Capitalist Development, Differentiation and Polarization

Our sample surveys of rural households in four sublocations with different ecological and demographic characteristics support the notion presented in Chapter II that rural development in Kenya has taken place as the result of a process in which a capitalist land market and individual land tenure has been developed, and in which a process of capital accumulation based upon agriculture as well as upon non-agricultural activities has been initiated often with savings from employment in the public sector as the origin of the accumulation process.

This development process, however, has also led to increased inequality in income, wealth and opportunity in the rural areas. The process of differentiation has accelerated.

The differentiation in our samples with regard to buying and selling land, land ownership, cropping patterns, agricultural production, use of hired labour and other inputs has been analysed. Some of the results are shown in the following tables.

The tendency for the high income families to obtain more land by buying or renting, and for poor households to sell or lease out land in order to acquire cash is demonstrated in Tables IV.43 and IV.44. We can see that this process is most developed in Kombura sublocation, but also in Mwogeto and Werugha the richer households are more dominant in buying and renting land than the poor households, while few households here were willing to admit that they had been selling or leasing land.

In Kikoneni a different process seems at work. Here, land is still relatively abundant, and the buyers are predominantly young people who start growing tree-crops, and therefore have low incomes until the trees start yielding, while the sellers are households who have more land than they cultivate.

The differentiation is also demonstrated in the rural labour market. From Table IV.45 we can see that the richer households are much more dominant users of hired labour in agriculture than the poor households, while, on the other hand, Table IV.46 shows that only the poor peasant families work as agricultural labourers for other people in the area.

As a result of the capitalist development process, a process of differentiation has taken place in the sample areas, and has led to increased polarization between rich and poor families. A small group of rich households which are getting high incomes from agriculture, from non-agricultural business, and from civil servant jobs, are buying up land, growing more profitable crops, using hired labour and reinvesting their surpluses in planting more high-yielding crops, and buying high-yielding dairy cattle, but also in non-agricultural activities like small shops, hotels and restaurants in rural market-places and in transport, i.e., small pick-ups and lorries transporting people and agricultural produce, and in small rural industries.

On the other hand, poor families are forced to sell land. They cannot afford to buy seed or seedlings for cultivation of profitable cash crops. They cannot afford to supplement family labour with hired labour when labour

Table IV.45. *Use of hired labour by sample households.*

Income group, K. shs.	Kombura % of house-holds	Kombura shs. per house-hold	Mwogeto % of house-holds	Mwogeto shs. per house-hold	Werugha % of house-holds	Werugha shs. per house-hold	Kikoneni % of house-holds	Kikoneni shs. per house-hold
0– 999	33.3	63.8	40.0	27.5	28.6	135.0	56.8	116.8
1000–2999	33.3	45.2	48.2	35.9	52.4	247.3	75.9	142.6
3000–4999	43.4	71.2	40.9	75.3	52.0	409.8	69.3	135.2
5000–6999	50.0	230.0	68.8	140.3	81.0	357.7	54.6	237.5
7000–9999	33.3	82.0	70.0	215.0	57.9	497.3	50.0	300.0
10000–	75.0	388.3	71.4	347.0	75.0	602.2	71.4	383.6

Table IV.46. *Work by sample household members as agricultural labourers for other holdings (proportion of households working as agricultural labourers by income group (per cent).*

Income group	Kombura	Mwogeto	Werugha	Kikoneni
0– 999	6.7	0.0	1.8	3.1
1000–2999	25.0	14.8	3.6	5.1
3000–4999	12.5	9.1	2.7	2.0
5000–6999	0.0	0.0	0.0	0.0
7000–9999	0.0	0.0	0.0	0.0
10000–	0.0	0.0	0.0	0.0

inputs are the bottleneck in agricultural peak seasons of planting, weeding and harvesting. On the contrary, they have to work for other people in these periods in order to get money to buy food, because their granaries are empty, and to pay school fees. Therefore, their agricultural production is poor, and their harvest is insufficient to provide food for the family, except for a few months. They therefore have to obtain cash in order to buy food, and must therefore seek employment, but since wages are low they might in addition have to sell livestock or even land in order to survive.

In other words, a process has been initiated in which rich households are accumulating capital based upon investment and increased use of hired labour in agriculture and non-agricultural business, while poor households are turned into a landless proletariat which do not own their means of production, and have to sell labour power in order to subsist.

CHAPTER V

The Non-Farm Sector Survey

The historical development of non-farming activities in Kisumu, Kisii, Taita Hills and Kwale District, was discussed in Chapter III and the significance of non-farming activities for employment, incomes and capital accumulation of our sample households in the four selected sublocations was analysed in Chapter IV.

In this chapter, we will present the results of a survey on employment, incomes and productivity that was conducted by interviews with all non-farm rural enterprises that were in operation in the four study areas, i.e., Kombura Sublocation in Kisumu District, Mwogeto Sublocation in Kisii District, Werugha Sublocation in Taita Hills District and Bumbani Sublocation in Kwale District.

Table V.1 shows employment and average income in rural non-farm enterprises in the four sublocations.

Employment and income for self-employed and employed are given by sector for each of the four study areas in Tables V.2, V.3, V.4, and V.5.

The tables show that the share of the adult population employed in non-farm enterprises are somewhat higher in the four study areas than in the country as such. Bumbani, however, is an exception from this general observation. Here, employment in non-farm enterprises is below the overall Kenya average of approx. 4 per cent of the adult population.

The average yearly income from employment in the non-farm sector in the four sublocations was 1,955 K.shs. But in Mwogeto the average yearly

Table V.1. *Population, employment and income in non-farm rural enterprises in the study areas 1975. 1975.*

	Population no.	Employment no.	Employment in per cent of Adult Population	Average Income K. shs./year
Mwogeto	14.000	310	5.49	2.704
Kombura	9.463	262	5.80	1.627
Bumbani	5.780	74	2.39	1.828
Werugha	13.697	215	3.60	1.616

Source: Interviews with all non-farm rural enterprises in four study areas 1975.

Table V.2. *Employment and income in non-farm enterprises by sector in Kombura, 1975.*

	No. of enter-prises	Self-employed No.	Self-employed Average yearly income, K shs.	Employed No.	Employed Average yearly income, K. shs.	Total employ-ment
Maize mills	6	6	7.200	14	1.800	20
Hides and skins	3	3	2.400	1	720	4
Blacksmiths	3	3	600			3
Tailors	14	14	3.680	4	2.700	18
Carpenters	5	5	1.060	5	960	10
Bicycle repair	11	11	2.064	15	1.416	26
Hotels, restaurants	21	21	+	42	720	63
Retail trade	59	59	3.240	59	720	118
Total	122	122	2.647	140	968	262

Note: + not known.

Source: Own interviews 1975.

Table V.3. *Employment and income in non-farm enterprises by sector in Mwogeto, 1975.*

	No. of enter-prises	Self-employed No.	Self-employed Average yearly income K. shs.	Employed No.	Employed Average yearly income K. shs.	Total employ-ment
Maize mills	2	1	7.800	3	1.880	4
Hides and skins	5	5	2.700	5	1.440	10
Blacksmiths	2	2	2.400			2
Tailors	23	19	2.640	21	1.260	40
Carpenters	8	7	3.140	12	1.420	19
Bicycle repair	2	2	2.100	1	600	3
Shoemakers	6	6	1.750	1	480	7
Hotels, restaurants	25	25	+	50	720	75
Retail trade	75	75	5.000	75	720	150
Total	148	142	4.170	168	878	310

Note: + not known.

Source: Own interviews 1975.

Table V.4. *Employment and income in non-farm enterprises by sector in Werugha, 1975.*

	No. of enter-prises	Self-employed		Employed		Total employ-ment
		No.	Average yearly income K. shs.	No.	Average early income K. shs.	
Maize mills	2	1	5.000	3	840	4
Brickmaking	2	1	2.000	4	840	6
Tailors	9	9	3,600	9	720	18
Carpenters	11	11	6.000	33	1.080	44
Bicycle repair	1	1	2.400			1
Shoemakers	1	1	2.500	1	480	2
Hotels, restaurants	13	+	+	26	600	26
Retail trade	57	57	2.400	57	600	114
Total	96	82	3.038	133	739	215

Note: + not known.

Source: Own interviews 1975.

Table V.5. *Employment and income in non-farm enterprises by sector in Bumbani 1975.*

	No. of enter-prises	Self-employed		Employed		Total employ-ment
		No.	Average yearly income K. shs.	No.	Average yearly income K. shs.	
Maize mills	2	2	4.000	2	1.200	4
Blacksmiths	5	5	1.800			5
Tailors	11	11	2.400	11	1.500	22
Carpenters	5	5	1.400	3	600	8
Bicycle repair	2	2	2.400	2	600	4
Wooden utensils	3	3	600			3
Hotels, restaurants	4	4	9.000	4	600	8
Retail trade	10	10	1.200	10	600	20
Total	42	42	2.500	32	947	74

Source: Own interviews 1975.

Table V.6. *Average yearly incomes in non-farm rural manufacturing enterprises by profession and skill 1975 (K. shs.)*

Selected professions	Skilled	Unskilled	Apprentices
Blacksmiths	4.032	1.908	600
Carpenters	2.328	1.788	420
Tailors	2.040	1.104	48
Weighted average of all professions+	3,096	2,052	636

Note: + exclusive of retail trade and services.

Source: Own data from interviews conducted in 1975.

Table V.7. *Employment in manufacturing enterprises in the four study areas by profession and skill 1975 (per cent).*

	Skilled	Unskilled	Apprentice	Not Known	Total
Blacksmiths	76	12	11	1	100
Carpenters	34	24	26	26	100
Tailors	55	7	23	9	100
Bicycle repair	34	0	55	10	100
Shoemakers	50	6	13	31	100
All	53	16	18	13	100

Source: Own data from interviews conducted in 1975.

income in the non-farm sector was considerably higher than in the other three sublocations.

It should be noted also that the self-employed in the non-farm enterprises have a considerably higher average income than their workers as they receive both a "salary" and a profit. The average income of the self-employed in the sector was 3,089 K.shs. against an average worker's income of K.shs. 883.

It can be seen from Table V.6 that skilled workers in non-farm manufacturing enterprises on average had incomes comparable to those of the self-employed in the whole sector, i.e., including trade and services. But unskilled workers and apprentices had much lower levels of average incomes.

The distribution of employment by profession and skill in the four study areas is shown in Table V.7.

Blacksmith in Kisumu Industrial Area. (Jesper Kirknæs)

More than half of the workers in manufacturing enterprises in the four study areas have relatively high incomes. The low average incomes for people employed in non-farm enterprises in general are mostly due to the great number of low paid workers in shops, hotels and restaurants in the rural market places.

For comparative purposes the average incomes for people employed in the "modern" sector are shown in Table V.8. Wage incomes in non-farm enterprises in rural areas are far below the income levels that are obtained in the modern urban sector. However, it is important to note that skilled workers in small-scale manufacturing rural enterprises can obtain higher incomes than agricultural labourers working in the large farm sector in Kenya. One should also note that 21 per cent of the people employed in the urban sector had lower average incomes (below 1,800 K.shs. yearly) than the average income of all self-employed and wage-employed working in non-farm rural enterprises, and that more than one-third of the people employed in the modern sector had lower average incomes than skilled workers in rural small-scale industries (3,000 K.shs. yearly).

Apprentices making chairs in a carpenter's workshop as they can be seen at market-places all over rural Kenya. (Jesper Kirknæs)

In the remaining part of this chapter we will discuss the capacity of the rural non-farm sector to provide productive jobs, its ability to accumulate capital and its competitiveness vis-à-vis the modern large industries in the urban areas.

Table V.8. *Average income per year for people employed in the modern sector 1975 (K. shs).*

Private Sector	Average income
Agriculture	2,312
Mining	8,026
Manufacturing	9,796
Construction	8.220
Commerce	11.500
Transport	12.382
Banks, etc.	19.250
Other Services	5.460
Public Sector	9.158
Total	7.626

Source: Republic of Kenya, Economic Survey 1977, Table 5.10.

The development perspective of small scale rural industries in Kenya

Development assistance to the rural non-farm sector in Kenya has been concentrated on supporting *small-scale industries* within the organizational framework of the Rural Industrial Development Programme.[1] This has probably been based on the assumption that the small-scale industries had specific features and potentials for increasing employment and income opportunities in the rural areas.

This point-of-view has been supported by various studies that have indicated that rural small-scale industries are profitable from an economic as well as a social point of view. From a study of 87 small-scale industries sampled among the enterprises which had received assistance from the four Rural Industrial Development Centres, Frank C. Child concludes: "We have found that the intermediate sector in Kenya offers a favourable return on scarce capital, generates productive jobs at low investment per job, utilises savings not otherwise available, develops new skills at low cost to society – a combination hard to beat. It might even slow the rate of urbanisation. A developing economy can hardly ask for more".[2]

[1] For a discussion of this programme which previously received Danish assistance see H. Kristensen, "En vurdering af støtten til småindustrien i Kenya", i *Den Ny Verden,* vol. 9, no. 3 and I. Livingstone, *Kenya's Rural Industrial Development Programme: An Evaluation of Experience and Proposals for Action,* Working Paper No. 210 IDS, University of Nairobi 1975 and P. Kongstad, *Rural Industrial Development Programme, Kenya – R.I.D.P. and Danish Assistance 1975–77,* C.D.R. Paper A.77.3. Copenhagen 1977.

[2] F.C. Child *op.cit.* p. 72.

Table V.9. *The sample enterprises by branch.*

No. of enterprises	Per cent	
Blacksmiths	64	27.5
Carpenters	52	22.3
Tailors	48	20.6
Bicycle repair	23	9.9
Shoemakers	18	7.7
Maize mills	8	3.4
Construction	6	2.6
Hide & skins	4	1.7
Other	10	4.3
Total	233	100.0

Source: own data.

Table V.10. *The sample enterprises by location.*

	No. of enterprises	Per cent
1. Kisumu District		
urban	23	9.9
rural	78	33.5
2. Kisii District		
urban	23	9.9
rural	49	21.0
3. Taita Hills	13	5.6
4. Kwale District	11	4.7
5. Nairobi	29	10.3
6. Dagoretti (Central Province)	3	3.4
7. Mombasa	4	1.7
Total	233	100.0

Source: own data.

Another study based upon 62 enterprises in commerce and services which received advice and assistance from a private American consultancy organization reached similar conclusions.[3]

On the other hand, Per Kongstad concludes that the assistance to the small-scale industries in Kenya has been very costly and that the capital cost in generating new jobs through extension programmes has been very high.[4]

Thus there seems to be good reason to study rural small-scale industries and their development potential in greater detail. We have tried to do this

[3] W. Loehr and P.J. Powelson *op.cit.* p. 1.

[4] P. Kongstad *op.cit.*

Table V.11. *Sample enterprises by size of labour force.*

No. of people employed	No. of enterprises		Employment		
	No.	%	Self-employed	Workers	Total
0	74	31.6	74	0	74
1	62	26.6	62	62	124
2	41	17.6	41	82	123
3	18	7.7	18	54	72
4	19	8.2	19	76	95
5	4	1.7	4	20	24
6	15	6.4	15	115	130
Total	233	99.8	233	409	642

Source: own data.

by collecting information through interviews of a total of 233 small manufacturing enterprises in various branches and regions in Kenya. The distribution by branch and region of the 233 enterprises is shown in Tables V.9 and V.10.

For Kisumu and Kisii District all manufacturing enterprises were included, in Taita Hills and Kwale District all manufacturing enterprises of the two selected sublocations, Werugha and Kikoneni, were included, whereas enterprises from other areas were randomly selected.

In this chapter we will analyse the capacity of the rural small-scale industries as far as their ability to earn a profit and accumulate capital is concerned and we will further analyse the ability of the rural small-scale industries to survive in competition with the large industries in the urban areas of Kenya.

Table V.11 gives the sample enterprises by size according to employment. The average number of people working as self employed and workers in the small-scale industries in our sample is 2.75 per enterprise. For the enterprises included in the study undertaken by F.C. Child this figure was as high as 7.4 people per enterprise which shows that selection from the group of entrepreneurs assisted by the Rural Industrial Development Centres gives a bias towards larger enterprises. More than 50 per cent of the enterprises in our sample have no workers employed, or only one (see Table V.11).

Do the small scale industries accumulate capital?

We shall now turn to the crucial question of capital accumulation in the small-scale industries. As pointed out previously, F.C. Child found that the

Table V.12. *Small-scale industries net profit per month by branch and region (K. shs.).*

	Kisumu urban	District rural	Kisii urban	District rural	Taita Hills District	Kwale District	Nairobi	Dago-retti	Mombasa	Total	No. of enter-prises
Blacksmiths	893	94	103	–59		–148	1531	1179		579	64
Carpenters	374	268	356	191	600	47	1630	827	888	525	49
Tailors	127	93	2786	179	2006	27			460	48	
Bicycle repair	90	146	–60	17	445	1330	680			546	23
Shoemakers	–50	59	157	8	213		3372			264	17
Maize mills		5969		632	313					2553	8
Construction		–85								–85	5
Hide & Skins		1022								132	4
Other	249	567	502	165	12931					1682	10
Total (weighted average)	513	365	593	141	1895	358	1607	1047	888	587	
Number of enterprises	23	77	23	49	13	11	21	8	3		228

Source: own interviews.

Note: Net profit is calculated as average monthly sales, less monthly production costs, including depreciation and salary to owners who work in the enterprise. Depreciation has been calculated as 10 per cent of the initial investment per year. Salary to owners who work in the enterprise has been calculated as the average salary of skilled workers of the same profession among the enterprises in our sample.

small-scale industries in his sample showed a very high return to the invested capital.

Table V.12 shows the average profit per month for the 228 enterprises in our sample for which net earnings could be calculated. As can be seen, our findings differ drastically from those of F.C. Child. The difference is most probably due to the various methods used in selecting the two samples as also apparent by the difference in the average size of enterprises in the two samples.

We find that the average net profit per month is only 587 K.shs, or equivalent to an average annual profit per enterprise of K.shs 7.044. For comparison the average yearly profit by enterprise in the Child sample was as high as K.shs 38.890.

Table V.12 shows very large differences in the monthly profit by branch as well as by region. Some branches have considerably higher net profits than other branches. Thus, maize mills with average monthly profits of K.shs 2.553 and the group "Other" consisting of boat builders, automobile repair and bakeries with an average monthly profit of K.shs 1.682 seem to belong to a category of very profitable small-scale enterprises (like those in the Child sample).

Another category consisting of blacksmiths, carpenters, tailors and bicycle repair shows similar levels of monthly profits of approx. K.shs 500, whereas shoemakers, hide and skin processors and construction enterprises (masons) show very low or even negative monthly profits.

We can also see from Table V.12 that urban small-scale industries generally show higher average profits than small-scale rural industries. But besides these very general observations, it should be noted that the variations in net profit between enterprises are so large that average figures for many of the subgroups become more or less meaningless.

Tables V.13 and V.14 show the small-scale enterprises of our sample by size of profit/month and by region and branch. As can be seen from these tables, a very high proportion of the enterprises is working at a negative net profit as defined in the footnote of Table V.12.

As many as 43 per cent of the enterprises in our sample operated at a loss and only 29 per cent of the enterprises had monthly profits of more than K.shs. 400.

From Table V.13 it appears that the small *rural* enterprises dominate among the enterprises with negative or very low levels of profit, whereas the small-scale urban industries are predominant among the high profit enterprises. The *urban* industries of our sample which are located in Nairobi, Kisumu and Kisii account for 29 per cent of the enterprises with more than K.shs 1000 in monthly profit. It is noticeable that a relatively high proportion

Table V.13. *Sample enterprises by size of monthly profit and by region.*

Monthly profit (K. shs.)	Kisumu urban	Kisumu rural	Kisii urban	Kisii rural	Taita Hills	Kwale	Nairobi	Dagoretti	Mombasa	Total
Negative (loss)	11	40	7	24	3	7	2	3	1	98
0–99	3	7	4	7	1	0	1	0	0	23
100–199	0	7	2	1	1	2	3	0	0	16
200–399	0	10	5	6	3	1	0	1	0	26
400–599	2	4	0	6	1	0	0	1	0	14
600–799	1	2	0	1	0	0	3	0	1	8
800–999	1	1	1	1	0	0	2	0	0	6
1000–	5	6	4	3	4	1	10	3	1	37

Source: own data.

Table V.14. *Sample enterprises by size of monthly profit and by branch.*

	Blacksmiths	Carpenters	Tailors	Bicycle repair	Shoemakers	Maize mills	Construction (masons)	Hide & Skin	Other	Total
Negative (loss)	33	15	23	10	5	1	4	3	4	98
0–99	2	3	7	4	4	1	1	0	1	23
100–199	5	5	2	1	3	0	0	0	0	16
200–399	4	4	7	3	4	3	0	0	1	26
400–599	1	7	2	3	0	1	0	0	0	14
600–799	3	3	1	1	0	0	0	0	0	8
800–999	1	2	1	0	0	0	0	0	2	6
1000–	15	10	5	1	1	2	0	1	2	37
Total	64	49	48	23	17	8	5	4	10	228

Source: own data.

of the small-scale enterprises in Taita Hills are making relatively good profits. This can be explained by the natural protection given to the rural industries in Taita Hills due to the difficulties in communications and high cost of transporting goods to the mountain areas.

The distribution of enterprises by the level of profit and by branch follows a more complicated pattern. Thus, for example more than 52 per cent of the blacksmiths in our sample are operating at a loss and at the same time this branch accounts for a relatively high proportion of the "high profit" enterprises.

The shoemakers seem to be a more homogeneous group. Only 29 per cent are working at a loss. On the other hand, only 6 per cent receive a net profit of more than K.shs 400 a month.

Carpenters are doing better than the average small enterprise in our sample, whereas tailors and blacksmiths are generally doing worse.

For comparative reasons it should be mentioned that only 14 per cent of the enterprises in the Child sample operated at a loss.[5]

In summary, our analysis cannot support the findings of the study undertaken by F.C. Child that the small-scale industries are *generally* a dynamic sector, which yields a high return to invested capital and provide productive jobs. We believe that this conclusion is only valid for a small fraction of the small-scale industries operating in the rural areas and that the majority of the rural enterprises are stagnant, low productivity enterprises which are hardly able to produce a surplus and are incapable of getting involved in a continuous process of long-term capital accumulation.

In other words, our findings support the notion suggested by Chris Gerry that small-scale rural industries should not be analysed as capitalist entrepreneurs but rather as a very diversified group of such different characteristics as ranging from "wage earners in disguise", petty commodity producers, and artisans, to small capitalist entrepreneurs.[6]

According to our findings, the small-scale rural industries are better described and analysed within the framework and using the categories and the characteristics of the different categories as presented in Figure V.1.

Figure V.1. *Framework for analysis of capital accumulation and productive employment in small-scale rural industries.*

	Category of producer			
Important characteristics of producer	(1) Wage earner in disguise	(2) Petty commodity producer	(3) Artisan	(4) Capitalist entrepreneur
1. Ownership of means of production	–	+	+	+
2. Produces for stock (not only on orders)	–	–	±	+
3. Employs non-family labour	–	–	+	+
4. Uses machines	–	–	–	±
5. Accumulates capital	–	–	–	+

[5] F.C. Child *op.cit.* p. 39.

[6] See Chris Gerry, *Petty Production and Capitalist Production in Dakar: The crises of "self-employed"*, in Britha Mikkelsen (ed.) forthcoming.

The small-scale rural industry sector can be divided into four broad categories of enterprises according to a set of characteristic features such as ownership of means of production, whether production is undertaken only on order from the customers or also for stocks, the employment of non-family labour, the utilization of machines and finally the accumulation of capital.

The figure should not be interpreted too rigidly as it would be very difficult to place unambiguously the individual enterprises in one of these boxes. The purpose of this figure should be understood only as an analytical tool.

When applied to our sample of 228 enterprises from different urban and rural areas of Kenya we find that only a small group (less than 1/3) of the enterprises can be categorized as belonging to group 4 of small capitalist entrepreneurs, which based upon the exploitation of wage labour and machines obtains a positive net profit which is reinvested productively in the business.

By far the majority of the enterprises in our sample would have to be categorized as group 2 enterprises characterized by small self-employed petty commodity producers, who work in this sector as a defensive device against hunger because they have no alternative job or income opportunity. They therefore accept a remuneration on their capital and on their own labour which is below the ordinary salary of people of their profession and therefore less than the income they would get if there were any vacant jobs.

These petty commodity producers do not accumulate capital and therefore contribute very little to the long-term growth of the rural economy. On the other hand, the very small amounts of savings on which their business is founded would hardly have found profitable investment opportunities elsewhere.

The social benefit of this category, however, is undeniable. It provides income opportunities and cheap consumer goods to the needy poor populations of the rural as well as the urban areas of Kenya. Finally, it should be emphasized that income opportunities for the people involved in small-scale industries are often better than they are in most agricultural activities and that these activities more often support each other than compete.

The competitiveness of small-scale rural industries in Kenya

The competition among small-scale industries resembles in many ways the situation described as perfect competition in economic text books. A large number of producers manufacture homogeneous products by using similar techniques (often only hand tools). The necessary investment to start a new business is very small – often only a few hundred shillings – and is therefore no serious hindrance to the entrance of new producers. Moreover, the many small producers are often located side by side in the market-places so that the customers are able to compare quality and prices.

It is this situation of perfect competition which explains why profits are generally low in the small-scale industries and why the small-scale industries are in general incapable of accumulating capital.

The mutual competition among small-scale producers is fierce but in addition they increasingly find themselves competing with large urban industries expanding their market by penetrating into the rural areas as the purchasing power of the rural population increases.

This is a matter of great significance for the evaluation of the long-term development potential of small-scale rural industries in Kenya. In this chapter we will discuss the competitiveness of the small-scale rural industries vis-à-vis the large urban manufacturing enterprises.

A number of factors influence the relative competitiveness of small-scale rural industries. Some of these factors will be considered here. They are; the productivity of labour and capital, the cost of labour and capital, the cost of raw materials and the relative cost of transporting raw materials and the finished product, respectively.

We mentioned previously that a number of recent studies have found that besides being more labour intensive than large-scale industries, small-scale industries utilize capital as well as labour in a more efficient way. According to these studies, then, the development of small-scale industries results simultaneously in increased employment and faster economic growth.

A few of these studies compare the small-scale industry sector as a group with modern industry as a group.[7] This, however, is not very illuminating. As the two groups of industries produce very different products, such a comparison will be affected by the obvious fact that some products are produced with a more labour intensive technique than other products. We are interested in the impact of scale on the choice of technique and the efficiency in utilization of capital and labour for the manufacturing of products which satisfy the same needs of the consumers. We are therefore comparing small-scale and large-scale industries by branch, i.e., small and large producers of comparable products.

We have applied this method for three branches of industry, namely, maize mills, tailors and furniture makers. It has not been possible to get hold of applicable comparable data for other products produced in small-scale rural industries.

[7] See, for instance, F.C. Child *op.cit.*

The data concerning the small-scale industries in the following analysis has been collected by interviews in the four study areas in 1975 as mentioned previously. All enterprises in the various branches in the four sublocations are thus included in the study. The data on large-scale industries are from the survey of industrial production in 1971, which includes all manufacturing enterprises of more than 50 employees.[8] The fact that the data on large-scale industry originated in 1971 while those on small-scale industry were collected in 1975 means that the efficiency of large-scale industry will be somewhat underestimated.

The problem of measuring productivity is a difficult one which has not yet found an acceptable theoretical solution. One can of course measure the productivity of labour by the number of items produced per labour hour and the productivity of capital by the number of items produced per machine hour in the single production process. But the efficiency of labour depends on individual skill (human capital) and the efficiency of one machine hour depends on scale of production and embodied technical progress. Moreover, the efficiency of labour depends upon the efficiency of the capital equipment being used and vice versa. Therefore, theoretically one ought to measure productivity as the relation between output and an index for labour and capital, but this cannot be done without somehow weighing physical labour and physical capital by the use of market values, opportunity cost or shadow prices. With our method we do not get a "pure" measurement of efficiency but rather of competitiveness, which depends upon the prices of labour and capital.

Since labour cost differs greatly between small-scale and large-scale industries the question of the relative efficiency of small-scale industries depends upon whether the productivity of labour is measured as output per man or as output in relation to labour cost.

In Table V.15 the productivity of labour has been measured as value added divided by the number of people employed. This measurement of productivity of labour is influenced by differences in the skill of labour, hours worked and the speed of work. We can see from the table that there are big differences in the productivity of labour between rural areas, between rural industries and urban industries and between different branches of industry. The big differences in labour productivity between rural industries in the four study areas are mostly due to differences in number of hours worked "at full capacity". It can thus be used as an indication of disguised unemployment. The table shows that the productivity of labour is smaller in rural industries than in urban industries.

[8] See *Republic of Kenya,* Survey of Industrial Production, 1971.

Table V.15. *Productivity of labour in small-scale rural industries and in large-scale industries in Kenya (value added/employment) K. shs.*

	Small rural industries				Large industries
	Mwogeto (Kisii)	Kombura (Kisumu)	Bumbani (Kwale)	Werugha (Taita H.)	
1. Maize mills	7.392	4.990	13.860	3.465	18.053
2. Clothing	3.926	7.137	7.804	9.354	9.354
3. Furniture	2.735	1.010	2.525	3.690	10.689
1 + 2 + 3 (weighted average)	3.801	3.856	6.843	4.887	11.925

Source: own data, 1975 and *Kenya, Survey of Industries,* 1971.

Table V.16. *Productivity of labour in small-scale rural industries and in large-scale industries in Kenya (value added/labour cost) K. shs.*

	Small rural industries				Large industries
	Mwogeto (Kisii)	Kombura (Kisumu)	Bumbani (Kwale)	Werugha (Taita H.)	
1. Maize mills	3.9	2.8	5.5	2.9	2.6
2. Clothing	2.3	1.6	3.6	3.7	2.0
3. Furniture	1.3	1.1	2.3	3.4	1.9

Source: see Table V.15.

If, however, one takes into account that labour in urban industries might be better educated and trained and therefore – assuming that wage differentials reflect differences in skill – weighs employment by wages paid to labour we get an entirely different picture. This is done in Table V.16 which shows that measured in this way the productivity of labour is generally higher in rural industries than in urban large-scale industries.

It should, however, be noted that the wage differences between urban and rural industries appear to be much greater than differences in the levels of skills. The labour productivity figures in Table V.16 are therefore strongly influenced by the fact that the cost of labour is much lower in the rural than in the urban areas of Kenya.

Table V.17. *Productivity of capital in small-scale rural industries and in large-scale industries in Kenya (value added/capital cost) K. shs.*

	Small rural industries				Large industries
	Mwogeto (Kisii)	Kombura (Kisumu)	Bumbani (Kwale)	Werugha (Taita H.)	
1. Maize mills	4.8	4.8	4.8	4.8	5.3
2. Clothing	8.6	5.6	5.6	5.6	3.6
3. Furniture	13.0	13.0	13.0	13.0	8.6

Source: see Table V.15.

It has been even more difficult to obtain a satisfactory measurement for the efficiency of capital because of difficulties involved in the measurement of capital.

For the rural industries the capital cost has been calculated as the replacement cost of capital equipment multiplied by the opportunity cost of financial capital (the interest rate offered to savers in the rural financial institutions). For the urban large-scale industries, however, we do not have figures for the value of capital stock sectorwise. As an approximation of the yearly capital cost we have therefore used depreciation figures from the survey of industrial production, 1971. We realize that this is not a good measurement of capital cost but it is the only measurement available.

The productivity of capital measured as value added divided by capital cost for small and large industries, respectively, is given in Table V.17. It appears that small-scale clothing- and furniture industries are more efficient in their utilization of capital than large-scale industries are. On the other hand, large-scale grain mills utilize their capital more efficiently than small mills.

An overall view of the efficiency of small-scale rural industries is obtained by comparing the efficiency in the utilization of capital and labour. As expected, the result depends on how the efficiency of labour is measured.

When value added per man is used as a measurement of the efficiency of labour we get the following results by comparing Table V.15 and Table V.17.

1. Small-scale maize mills are less efficient than the large mills since they use more labour as well as more capital for the production of a given output.

2. We cannot prove from these data whether small-scale or large-scale producers of cloth etc. and of furniture are the more efficient. The small producers are the more labour intensive but they are at the same time more efficient in their utilization of capital.

When, on the other hand, the efficiency of labour is measured by value added in relation to labour cost we get the following results:

Table V.18. *Competitiveness of small and large industries in Kenya (value added/cost of labour plus cost of capital) K. shs.*

	Small rural industries				Large industries
	Mwogeto (Kisii)	Kombura (Kisumu)	Bumbani (Kwale)	Werugha (Taita H.)	
1. Maize mills	2.2	1.8	2.6	1.8	1.7
2. Clothing	1.8	1.2	2.1	2.2	1.8
3. Furniture	1.2	1.0	2.0	2.7	1.6
1 + 2 + 3 (weighted average)	1.7	1.6	2.2	2.4	1.7

Source: see Table V.15.

1. The small tailors in three of the four sublocations (Mwogeto, Bumbani and Werugha) plus the small furniture producers in two of the four sublocations (Bumbani and Werugha) are more efficient than their large-scale competitors, since they utilize both labour and capital more efficiently.

2. We cannot from these data draw conclusions on the relative efficiency of other small-scale industries since they are either more capital intensive and less labour intensive or more labour intensive and less capital intensive than their large-scale competitors.

In order to know whether these small enterprises are more or less efficient than large-scale industries we need a single measurement for the combined efficiency of capital and labour. Such a measurement is given in Table V.18 where output per unit of capital is combined with output per unit of labour by using the unit cost of capital and the unit cost of labour as weights. Unfortunately, we do not obtain a very precise picture of the relative efficiency of small-scale industry by using these measurements, since the relative cost of capital and labour hardly reflects the relative scarcity of these two factors of production.

The figures in Table V.18 reflect the ability of small- and large-scale producers to compete rather than their ability to utilize scarce resources efficiently. However, these measurements of the competitiveness are quite useful for our purpose of discussing the long-term development possibilities of small-scale rural industries.

Based upon Table V.18 we can draw the general conclusion that the small-scale rural industries in the four sublocations selected for our study are quite competitive vis-à-vis their large-scale urban competitors, mainly due to the fact that small rural industries are paying their labour much lower wages than the large-scale industries.

Analysed by branch we have the following situation:

The small-scale maize mills in the rural areas have a competitive advantage over large-scale grain mills in spite of the fact that they are less efficient in their utilization of both capital and labour. The explanation is that they are paying much lower wages than the large mills in Kenya. Consequently we found no rural households in our four study areas that were buying maize flour milled in the large-scale factories. The employment and income possibilities in the small-scale maize mills depend therefore, for the time being, only upon the consumption of rural households.

The small rural producers of clothing and furniture are competitive partly because they are quite efficient in their utilization of capital and partly because they benefit from low labour cost. However, the clothing industry in Kombura Sublocation in Kisumu District and the furniture producers in Kombura and Mwogeto Sublocations in Kisii District are exceptions from this general observation. As far as the small producers of clothing and furniture in Kombura Sublocation are concerned the relative weak competitive position is caused by the generally low levels of income and the lack of local demand which results in low utilization of productive capacity and disguised unemployment due to the lack of alternative employment opportunities.

The relatively weak competitive position of small furniture producers in Mwogeto Sublocation in Kisii District has a very different explanation. They have to pay relatively high wages in order to attract labour due to the very good alternative income opportunities in agriculture in the high potential agricultural area of Kisii.

In summary, we have seen that on the one hand the small-scale rural industries are quite efficient and quite competitive because of their low labour cost. On the other hand the mutual competition among small rural industries is so keen that only a few are in a position to obtain a large profit and to accumulate capital with a view to the expansion of production. Generally, therefore, the small-scale rural industries are not able to increase their market share of the internal Kenya market.[9] Also other factors work against the development of small-scale industries. The fact that small-scale industries generally produce "low quality" products and that rural consumers change their consumer patterns in favour of products produced in large-scale industries when income rises, makes it a difficult task for small-scale rural industries to expand their market.

[9] See the interesting case of small bakeries in Kenya which, in spite of their superiority in choice of technique and in efficiency, are unable to expand in the market. R. Kaplinsky, *op.cit.*

The development perspective of the rural non-farm sector

In order to determine the factors which are decisive in the long-term development perspective for the various types of non-farm activities we have attempted to "explain" the historical development of non-farm activities. This historical analysis was given in Chapter III.

In addition to this historical analysis we have attempted to "explain" the present differences in the significance of rural non-farm activities for the employment and income situation in the four sublocations we had selected for our study.

The following explanatory variables were included in the analysis:

1. The value of agricultural production
2. The disposible income of rural households
3. The distribution of income among the rural households
4. The competitiveness of small rural industries

The distribution of income is included as an explanatory variable in our analysis because it has been argued that the distribution of income influences the pattern of demand and that low incomes have a higher propensity to consume locally produced goods than high incomes which prefer products from large-scale industry or imported. It follows from this that, *ceteris paribus,* equality in the distribution of income in an area is positively correlated to incomebased non-farm productive activities and negatively correlated to employment and earnings in trade with "imported" products.

The hypothesis that low incomes have a higher propensity to consumer products that are locally produced was tested by the use of the model

$$C_{ij} = \alpha_i + \beta_i \cdot Y_j + \gamma_i \cdot P_j$$

where C_{ij} is the yearly consumption of item i in household j; Y_j is the disposable income of household j; P_j is the size of household j (the number of adults) and α_i, β_i and γ_i are the parameters that we have to estimate. Thus β is the income elasticity and γ the household size elasticity of demand.

The double log function

$$\log (C_{ij}) = \alpha_i + \beta_i \cdot \log (Yj) + \gamma_i \cdot \log (P_j)$$

was used for estimating α, β and γ because of its simplicity.

The data collected by interviews with the sample households in Mwogeto in Kisii District and Kombura in Kisumu District were used for the test of the hypotheses. The consumption of each household was divided into groups according to place of production (rural industry, urban industry or imported from outside Kenya).

Table V.19. *Income elasticities of demand for locally produced goods and goods "imported" into the area. 1975.*

	Mwogeto Sublocation		Kombura Sublocation	
	locally produced	'imported'	locally produced	'imported'
	income elasticities			
Drinks	0.38	0.94	0.24	
Housing	0.51	1.13		
Furniture	0.68	0.33	0.43	0.60
Mattresses		1.22		0.56
Blankets		0.67		0.51
Kitchen utensils	0.46	0.48	0.19	0.39
Agricultural implements		0.44	0.36	0.07
Radios, clocks, watches		0.73		1.25
Lamps	0.00	0.84	−0.01	0.21
Bags, suitcases, etc	0.54	0.45	0.05	0.58
Shoes	0.59	0.50	−0.04	0.41

Source: Consumer survey of sample households in Mwogeto and Kombura Sublocation. Own data. 1975.

The best way of testing the hypothesis about the relationship between income distribution and demand for locally and non-locally produced goods would have been to subdivide our samples from each of the areas into income groups. Then the income elasticities of demand for locally produced goods and "imported" goods could have been estimated for each of the income groups in the different areas.

However, subdividing the samples in more income groups would not have given a sufficient number of observations in each subgroup to justify the use of regression analysis for estimating the parameters.

We have therefore used the second best solution in order to test our hypothesis. For each of the sample areas, income elasticities have been estimated for goods produced locally, for goods produced in urban large-scale industries and for imported goods.

If the income elasticities of demand, estimated in this way, are lower for locally produced goods fulfilling the same "needs" of the consumer, than income elasticities of demand for goods produced in urban industries or imported, it means that low incomes consume relatively more and high incomes relatively less of locally produced goods. The findings of this analysis is shown in Table V.19.

As can be seen from this table, the income elasticity of demand is generally lower for locally produced goods than for goods imported into the sublocation. But there are some important exceptions to this general observation, such as furniture, bags etc. and shoes in Mwogeto Sublocation and agricultural implements in Kombura Sublocation. It should also be emphasized that for some commodity groups the differences in the income elasticities of locally and imported products are so small that they are not statistically significant.

By comparing the explanatory variables listed above, with the level of activity in the various categories of non-farm activities, we are able to determine the importance of each of the variables. As mentioned previously, the analysis has been undertaken both over time (the historical analysis) and by comparing the situation in the four different sublocations. The main findings are listed below:

(1) There seems to be a strong positive correlation between the development of regular full-time output based non-farming activities in the rural areas and the level of agricultural production.

(2) There seems to be a strong negative correlation between occasional part-time non-farming resource based activities as well as output based activities and (a) the level of agricultural production and (b) the level of disposable income.

(3) There seems to be a strong positive correlation between the level of income-based non-farming activities and the level of disposable incomes.

(4) There seems to be a positive correlation between the ratio of manufacturing to trading activities and (a) the equality in the distribution of incomes as well as (b) the relative efficiency of rural industries, i.e., a more equal income distribution and a better competitive situation of the local small rural industries will increase the proportion of locally produced items in the consumption of the rural households at the cost of sales and employment in the local shops.

Summary and conclusion

In this and the preceding chapter we have shown that rural non-farm activities are of great significance for the rural households in Kenya. This is particularly the case as far as the poor peasant families and the low potential agricultural areas are concerned. For these groups of rural households non-farm income makes up the greater part of the total family income and is thus of greater importance than agriculture.

But it is in the high potential agricultural areas that non-farm activities are most developed. Here the level of non-farm income is highest and the number of *productive* non-farm jobs are of importance.

It is very important to make this distinction between on the one hand non-farm activities which have a subsistence character, i.e., occupations with low income opportunities that are taken up in periods of low income from other sources in order to survive, and on the other hand, *productive* jobs in the non-farm sector which yield relatively high income opportunities.

The possibilities to obtain this kind of productive, relatively well-paid employment in the rural non-farm sector in Kenya do not at present, look very bright. There is already a large number of petty commodity producers in the rural areas who compete in a very limited market with the result that only a few are able to earn a profit which can form the basis for capital accumulation and an expansion of their economic activity.

In the long run, the development of the sector will depend upon the growth in agricultural production and the increase in the incomes of the rural population. How large a share of the increasing market for consumer goods in the rural areas of Kenya that will be covered by production from small local workshops and rural industries will partly depend upon the development in labour cost facing the small producers but also the development in the distribution of rural incomes will be a decisive factor.

The conclusions which can be drawn from this study of non-farm activity in the rural areas of Kenya in relation to development assistance might seem rather pessimistic.

First, our analysis suggests that development programmes aimed at supporting individual "entrepreneurs" will be a waste from a socio-economic point-of-view. The long-term development perspective of the sector as such is not determined or limited by lack of entrepreneurial skill. Such individual oriented programmes will most likely only have the effect of promoting some producers at the cost of others. Studies undertaken to evaluate these programmes support our conclusions that they are of little value and extremely costly.[10]

Secondly, our analysis shows that the development perspective of the small enterprises is first and foremost determined and depends upon the development of agricultural production. The income elasticity of demand for the products produced by rural enterprises might be lower than for the products produced by large-scale urban industries, but it is still positive and for many products it is close to 0.5. An increase in the income of poor peasant

[10] It has been calculated that extension service consultancy to small-scale industry in Kenya had an average cost of K.shs 150–200 per hour. See P. Kongstad *op.cit.* Ian Livingstone mentions that in 1973, 61 employees at Rural Industrial Development Centres in Kenya assisted 205 small-scale industries at an average cost of K.shs 8000 per client annually, or in other words a much higher sum of money than a whole year's profit of the small rural industries in our sample. See Ian Livingstone *op.cit.*

families will therefore be an efficient indirect support for small rural enterprises.

But it should be emphasized that it is important and possible to support existing small-scale industries where they suffer from unfair legislation or unfair competition. The viability and profits of small rural producers can be increased considerably through bulk purchase programmes for raw materials which make raw materials available to the small producers at the same price as paid by large-scale industries. Small enterprises often pay very high prices for raw materials because of lack of working capital to buy in bulk or simply because raw materials are in short supply in the rural areas.

Also the abolition of legislation which discriminates against small-scale enterprises such as for instance the payment of trading and business licences, will have a positive impact upon the ability of small-scale industries to accumulate capital.

However, in order to become a dynamic factor in the economic development of the rural areas of Kenya, the small-scale rural industries would necessarily have to expand at a faster rate than the agricultural production. But this is only possible if small rural industries can produce high quality products to be sold in the urban areas and even in the export markets. These are properties which made small-scale industry a dynamic factor in the development of, for instance, Japan, but such a development has not yet started in Kenya and is unlikely to do so for many years to come.

CHAPTER VI

Summary and Conclusions

In this book we have analysed the process of economic and social transformation in rural Kenya in a historical perspective. Various sources of information have been used. We have used historical information from archives and from secondary sources and we have used more recent official data published by the Kenyan Bureau of Statistics. Finally, we have based our analysis on data that was collected through interviews of households and non-agricultural enterprises in four different rural areas of Kenya during 1974–75.

The Kenyan development experience since Independence in the beginning of the sixties is an interesting case. In the generally depressive picture of development experiences among the low income group of developing countries, Kenya stands out as one of the more successful exceptions. The annual economic growth in Kenya between 1960–1977 has been very impressive taking into account that the country has had no oil or other natural resources which could be exploited for an easy export-oriented growth process.

Agriculture is the basis of the Kenya economy and it has been agriculture and more specifically the expansion of smallholder agricultural production that has been the dynamic element in the Kenyan growth process since the mid-fifties.

The agricultural reforms that were introduced in 1954 as part of the Swynnerton Plan removed some of the elements of the colonial agricultural policy, which had been a hindrance to development in the African rural areas, such as the prohibitions against the growing of profitable cash crops like coffee and tea and the restrictions on keeping grade cattle. The consolidation of land fragments into single holdings and the issuing of registered freehold titles to individuals made it possible for the wealthy farmers, that had accumulated wealth in their positions as civil servants during colonial rule or from their participation in local trade, to plant coffee and tea and to buy grade cattle. Later, vegetables and hybrid maize contributed to the expansion of smallholder agricultural production.

The expansion in smallholder production was discussed in Chapter II. We concluded that the growth process was associated with the creation of great inequalities between high and low potential areas of Kenya and between rich and poor peasants within each area.

The high potential areas with high and reliable rainfall and the right temperature for coffee, tea and pyrethrum have benefitted most from these agricultural reforms. But they have had very little to offer for the drier low potential areas, such as Kisumu District.

The growth of agricultural production has also led to increased inequality between rich and poor households within the different areas because the planting of permanent crops is associated with investment in land preparation and in seedlings and involves a relatively long waiting period before the first crop can be harvested. Therefore, only peasant households with stable and reliable sources of income have been able to plant *larger* areas with coffee and tea. Access to non-agricultural incomes rather than land ownership on its own has been the original basis for the process of rural capital accumulation in Kenya, that we have seen accelerating in Kenya since the mid-fifties.

Over the years more and more small peasant holdings in the high potential areas have adopted the "new" cash crops. Small areas have been planted with coffee, tea and pyrethrum and lately also with hybrid maize and vegetables.

So, even smallholdings have been able to obtain rising incomes from agricultural production. Particularly the planting of coffee and tea by small producers in Central Province, but lately also in, for example Kisii District, have improved the situation for small peasant holdings.

During the adoption process of new crops like tea, the incomes from this crop will gradually spread to more producers and thus introduce an element of equality in the income distribution between rural households in the area.

Based upon the observation of this process in parts of Central Province, some scholars have drawn the conclusion that the expansion in smallholder production in the sixties was associated with the formation of a non-accumulating class of middle peasants. They argued that the rapid growth in agricultural production did not contribute to local capital accumulation, that the benefits from agricultural growth have been reaped by "international finance capital", and that consequently the development of a Kenyan national bourgeoisie on which a future capitalist development process could be based, has been blocked.[1]

As we have noted, it is quite correct that the incomes from certain crops become more equitably distributed between the growers over the time period in which the crop is adopted by more and more producers. This is so because the rich peasants are the first who can afford the investment and the risk involved. However, this is not the case with most other sources of

[1] See Cowen, M. and Kinyanjui, K, *op.cit.*

income. The process of capital acccumulation and differentiation must be analysed in its totality and the whole spectrum of rural activities – agricultural as well as non-agricultural – in which rural households are involved, has to be taken into consideration as elements in a dynamic process.

In this study we find no evidence that the growth in smallholder production has led to the formation of a non-accumulating class of "middle-peasants". On the contrary, the data from the Integrated Rural Survey 1974/75 and the data collected through our own sample surveys of rural households in Kombura, Mwogeto, Werugha and Kikoneni Sublocation show that the upper income groups of the rural households save and invest a large proportion of their incomes.

Previously, most of that part of the agricultural surplus which was left with the peasants, was invested in non-agricultural activities. But only the very rich rural households could save enough money for this sort of investment. The relatively high returns that they received from their investments have accentuated income inequality in the rural areas. Thus, we find that incomes are much more unequally distributed when non-agricultural incomes are also taken into consideration.

Since 1975 the prices paid for most agricultural products have increased and the terms of trade for agricultural producers have been improved. More of the investible surpluses of the peasant households have been invested in agricultural production and a more diversified pattern of capital accumulation has emerged in the rural areas.

The fact that agricultural investment has been low in smallholder agriculture in Kenya in the past, does not prove, as often argued, that peasants are a non-accumulating class. The reason for the low investment in smallholder agriculture has simply been the relatively low profitability of agricultural investment vis-à-vis investment in non-agricultural business.

Any analysis of rural development and peasant household production must take into account that rural households are not merely agricultural producers. They are economic entities to whom a wide spectrum of agricultural and non-agricultural options are open. An interesting study by Diana Hunt shows that the peasant households choose between these various options very much like the "economic man" of economic textbooks.[2] They allocate their labour and little capital between various activities in order to maximise returns, while taking into consideration elements of risk and uncertainty. At very low levels of income the risk considerations are a severe constraint on peasant households, but for rural households with

[2] See Hunt, D., *op.cit.*

incomes well above subsistence level a number of quite profitable investment opportunities are open.

Our sample surveys of rural households in four sublocations with different ecological and demographic characteristics support the notion that rural development in Kenya has taken place as the result of a process in which a capitalist land market and individual land tenure has been developed, and in which a process of capital accumulation based upon agriculture as well as non-agricultural activities has been initiated often with the savings from employment in the public sector as the origin of the accumulation process.

As a result of this capitalist development process, a process of differentiation has taken place, and has led to increased polarization in the rural areas between rich and poor families. A small group of rich households which are getting high incomes from agriculture, from non-agricultural businesses and from civil servant jobs, are buying up land, growing more profitable crops, using hired labour and reinvesting their surpluses in planting more high-yielding crops, in buying grade dairy cattle, but also in non-agricultural activities like small shops, hotels and restaurants in rural market places and in transport, i.e., small pick-ups and lorries transporting people and agricultural produce. They even invest in small rural industries like maize mills.

On the other hand, poor families are forced to sell land, they cannot afford to buy seed or seedlings for cultivation of profitable cash crops, they cannot afford to supplement family labour with hired labour when labour inputs are the bottleneck in agricultural production during the peak seasons of land preparation, planting, weeding and harvesting. On the contrary, they have to work for the rich families in these periods in order to get more money to buy food, because their granaries are empty, and to pay school fees for their children. Therefore, their agricultural production is poor, and the harvest is sufficient to provide food for the family only for a few months. They there fore have to obtain cash in order to buy food, and must continue to look for employment. However, since wages are low they might in addition have to sell some of their livestock or even part of their land in order to survive.

In other words, a process has been initiated in which rich households are accumulating capital based upon investment and increased use of hired labour in agriculture and in non-agricultural business, while poor households are turned into a landless proletariat, which do not own their means of production, and have to sell their labour power in order to subsist.

The speed of this process is being accelerated by the very high population growth rate in Kenya. On the basis of the latest available information, it has been estimated that population in Kenya is growing at the very high rate of 3.9 per cent per annum. This rate for Kenya is one of the highest in the world.

The high growth rate of the population aggrevates the already severe problem of land shortage in the high potential areas of the country and means that holdings inherited and parted between the sons after the death of their father become too small to feed a family.

But can this process continue indefinitely? What are the dynamic elements and what are the contradictions involved? Is this process of capital accumulation and differentiation self-perpetuating, or will it come to an end when the easy options of capitalist development that became possible with the removal of the restrictive colonial agricultural policy have come to an end?

One might disagree on the question of whether it will be possible for Kenya to continue its rapid economic growth in the future. But one thing is certain. Agriculture will continue to be the key sector. If agricultural expansion continues the country will prosper, but without agricultural growth the development of other sectors will also be halted.

We have seen that income from non-farming activities like civil servant jobs and trade have played a crucial role in the initial phase of capitalist accumulation in the rural areas of Kenya and that part of the surplus from the agricultural sector has been invested here. The linkages between agriculture and non-agricultural activities have been quite important.

But agriculture has been the leading sector in the economic growth process since the 1950's and will continue to be so. Income and employment in the rural small-scale industries will continue to be important, but as we have seen, their development depends upon agricultural production and rural household incomes. But in the long run, the rural small-scale industries will lose some of their markets to urban large-scale industries, because high income consumers in the rural areas prefer "high quality" products.

On the other hand, there are no signs that large-scale industries will be a leading sector in the development of Kenya for many years to come. Very few Kenyan industries are competitive in a world market sense. Most of them are import substitution industries producing for the local market, many are also processing agricultural or other local raw materials, but at production cost that a higher than world-market prices. Very few industries are exporting. Thus, even the large-scale industries in Kenya depend on agricultural production not only for raw materials but also as a market for their products. Kenya is now making a major effort to expand its industrial export particularly to the booming markets in oil exporting Arabian countries. But competion is fierce and the Kenyan labour cost per unit produced is still very much higher than in competing countries like India, Pakistan, Hong Kong, Singapore and South Korea.

Agriculture will no doubt continue to be the leading sector for many years to come. But will it be possible to expand agricultural production at the same rate as we have seen in the last 15 years? Or is it true that the easy options have been exploited, so that agricultural production will be much slower and much more capital-demanding in the future than in the past?

There are certainly severe limitations to the expansion of agricultural production but we believe that there is still an enormous potential for agricultural development in Kenya.

The constraints are both on the production side and on the marketing side.

The scarcity of high potential land is probably the most severe constraint on agricultural production. In the past it has been possible to expand agricultural production by cultivating more land without intensifying production. In relative terms very little irrigation is used, very few chemical inputs are used and almost no mechanization has taken place in Kenyan agriculture. The expansion of production in the past has taken place with very little additional investment in inputs, comparatively speaking.

But to increase production further, more inputs will have to be used on existing land and huge investments in irrigation will be necessary to irrigate the drier areas in Kenya in order to expand the area cultivated.

Huge and very expensive irrigation schemes are now being constructed in Kenya by the National Irrigation Board. The construction costs are very high and it is questionable whether these projects are economically feasible even in the long run. No doubt, the political pressure to make land available to the increasing number of landless families has been at least as important a motive behind these irrigation schemes as have economic considerations.

We believe that large areas of land could be irrigated by much more inexpensive means as self-help projects in most parts of Kenya. Very poor use is made of the rain, which – even in the low potential areas – falls heavily during the rainy season. Usually, the water just runs into small streams or rivers and finally ends in the Indian Ocean or in one of the big lakes in Kenya. Very little is done in order to preserve the rainwater by, for example, building dams and water reservoirs which could be used for irrigation. But in the few places in which it has been done – on private initiative – the results in terms of increased fertility of the soils and therefore increased production have been very impressive. And the cost of such rainwater preservation schemes need not be very high. Most work on dams and water reservoirs can be done by the local population as self-help projects and very little capital will be needed.

However, the easy options of Kenyan agricultural development have still not been fully utilized. High-yielding varieties of maize, millet and sorghum have still only been adopted by a minority of the peasants. Much more could be done to increase production if drought resistent high-yielding varieties could be developed. More research in this area is needed.

Also the potential of high-yielding dairy cattle has not yet been fully exploited. But the present methods of tick control in use in Kenya, dipping in large cattledips, are very expensive.[3] Alternative, less expensive methods of tick control should be developed.

The potential of mixed farming has hardly been realized in Kenya outside Central Province. Cattle are mostly kept on grazing land and animal husbandry is seldom integrated into crop production. No fodder crops are grown and often the manure from the cattle is not even used on the fields. We believe the integration of animal production and crop production has a very high potential and could lead to a new phase of rapid agricultural growth.

Lately, the Maize and Produce Board in Kenya have had problems of storage capacity. Therefore, they have not been able to buy all the produce that farmers wanted to sell. The storage capacity problem is now being solved as the Board's storage capacity has been increased. The Board has planned to export some 100.000 tons of maize during the first half of 1979 and if these sales are made it would be possible to buy more maize from the farmers than would otherwise have been possible. However, the low prices available in export markets might mean that the Board will have to sell at a loss.

Thus, Kenya has been facing marketing problems for its increased agricultural production, and the low maize prices paid in 1978 might have discouraged farmers to plant this crop in 1979.

Also, the major export crops, coffee and tea, are exposed to big price fluctions due to fluctuations in supply from other producers. However, the biggest marketing problem does not seem to be that of demand, or that Kenyan producers are not efficient, as is the case for industrial exports. The biggest problem seems to be the capacity of the State bureaucracy to manage the collection, storage and final export of agricultural produce in an efficient manner. Otherwise, there will be no money to pay the producers and as a result the peasants will stop producing for the official marketing system.

The biggest problem related to future rural development in Kenya is not one of increased production. Peasants will invest and improve their farming methods provided the terms of trade do not move against agricultural production.

The biggest problem is a social one; that of the increased polarization of

[3] See Raikes, *op.cit.* pp. 16–23.

small peasants into a landless proletariat. This group will not be able to find sufficient employment in the rural areas – neither in agriculture, nor in productive non-agricultural jobs. They will be forced to exist on casual jobs on big farms and in the urban economy in combination with various subsistence low productivity types of non-agricultural activities in the so-called "intermediate" sector.

The increasing proportion of the Kenyan population which will belong to this group of landless proletarians is the most serious economic, social and political problem in Kenya today. It will only be possible to continue the past successful growth performance in Kenya over a longer period if serious efforts are undertaken to make productive use of this huge reserve of underutilized human resources.

References

Adelman, I and Morris, T.C. — "An anatomy of patterns of Income Distribution in Developing Countries", USAID Development Digest, Oct. 1971.

Alpers, A.E. — "The Nineteenth Century: Prelude to Colonialism" in Ogot, B.A. and Kieran, J.A. *op.cit.* p. 247.

Amin, S. — "Accumulation on a World Scale", *Monthly Review Press*, New York 1974.

Anderson, J.E. — *Organization and financing of self-help education in Kenya*, Unesco, Paris 1973.

Atwood, R.H. — *Cotton-growing in Central Nyanza Province, Kenya 1901–39: An Appraisal of African Reactions to Imposed Government Policy.*, Ph.D. dissertation, Michigan State University, 1975.

Barclay, A. — *The Mumias Sugar Project: A study of rural development in Western Kenya*, Ph.D. thesis, Columbia University 1977.

Barnes, C. — *An Experiment with African Coffee Growing in Kenya: The Gusii, 1933–1950.* Ph.D. dissertation, Department of History, Michigan State University, U.S.A. 1976 (unpublished).

Brett, E.A. — *Colonialism and Underdevelopment Africa, The Politics of Economic Change 1919–1939*, Heinemann, Nairobi 1973.

Carlsen, J. and Moody, T. — "Population Pressure and Rural Employment in Kenya", *CDR Project Papers*, A 76, 13. Copenhagen, December 1976, and Carlsen, John, "Population Pressure and Non-Farming Activities in Rural Areas in Kenya – A Historical Review and Analysis of Prevailing Development Trends", *CDR Project Papers*, D. 76, 2, Copenhagen 1976.

Chenery, H. et al. — *Redistribution with Growth:* IBRD and Oxford U.P., Oxford 1974., and I.L.O., *op.cit.*

Child, F.C. — "An Empirical Study of Small-scale Rural Industry in Kenya", University of Nairobi, *I.D.S. working paper 127*, 1973.

Child, F.C. — *Employment, Technology and Growth – the Role of the Intermediate Sector in Kenya*, Occasional Paper No. 19, IDS, University of Nairobi. 1976.

Clayton, A. and Savage, D.C. — *Government and Labour in Kenya 1895–1963*, London 1974, p. 9.

Cowen, M. — *Differentiation in a Kenyan Location*, East African Universities Social Science Council, 8th Annual Conference, Nairobi 1972.

Cowen, M. and Kinyanjui, K. — *Some Problems of Income Distribution in Kenya*, Institute for Development Studies, University of Nairobi, March 1977.

Fearn, H. — *An African Economy – A Study of the Economic Development of Nyanza Province of Kenya, 1903–1953.* London, 1961, p. 31.

Frank, A.G. — "Capitalism and Underdevelopment in Latin America", *Monthly Review Press*, New York, 1969.

Garst, R.D. — *The Spatial Diffusion of Agricultural Innovations in Kisii District*, Kenya. Ph.D. dissertation. Michigan State University, Department of Geography, U.S.A., 1972 (unpublished) pp. 124–140.

Gerry, C. — *Petty Production and Capitalist Production in Dakar: The crises of "self-employed"*, in Britha Mikkelsen (ed.) forthcoming.

Gilette, C. — *A Test of the Concept of Backwardness: A Case Study of Digo Society in Kenya.* Ph.D. thesis, Cornell University, U.S.A., 1978, p. 157, table 8.

Godfred, M. and Langdon, S. "Partners in Underdevelopment? The Transnational Thesis in a Kenyan Context", in *Journal of Commonwealth and Comparative Politics,* Vol 14, No. 17, March 1976.

Government of Kenya, Central Bureau of Statistics, *Social Perspectives* Vol. 2, No. 2, June 1977, p. 2.

Gray, R. and Birmingham, D. (eds.) *Pre-colonial African Trade – Essays on Trade in Central and Eastern Africa before 1900.* Nairobi 1970.

Heyer, J., Maitha, J.K. and Senga, M.M. (eds.) Agricultural Development in Kenya, An Economic Assesment, Nairobi, 1976.

Heyer, J. "The origins of inequalities in smallholder agriculture in Kenya, 1920–73" in *Eastern African Journal of Rural Development,* Vol. 8, Nos. 1 and 2 (1975) pp. 142–181.

Hodd, M. Income Distribution in Kenya (1963–72), *In Journal of Development Studies,* Vol. 12, No. 3 April 1976.

Hubert, K. et al. *Agricultural Production in Kisii District, Kenya and Proposals for its Development,* Technische Universität, Berlin 1972.

Hunt, D. *An Examination of the Distribution of Economic Status and Opportunity in Mbere, Eastern Kenya,* Occasional Paper, No. 11, 1975. Institute for Development Studies, University of Nairobi.

Hunt, D. *Growth versus Equity – an examination of the distribution of economic status and opportunity in Mbere, Eastern Kenya.* Occasional Paper No. 11, IDS, Nairobi 1975.

Hunt, D. Resource Use in a Medium Potential Area: The Mbere Rural Economy, Working Paper No. 180, I.D.S., University of Nairobi, August 1974.

Hårstad, J. "Multiplier Effects of Household Incomes in Nyeri and Kisumu, Kenya", Department of Geography, University of Oslo, May 1976.

Inukai, I. and Okelo, J.A. *Rural Enterprise Survey in Nyeri District, Kenya.* A report of the consultants to DANIDA, Nairobi 1972.

I.L.O. *Employment, Growth and Basic Needs,* Geneva 1976.

I.L.O. *Employment, incomes and equality – a strategy for increasing productive employment in Kenya,* Geneva, 1972.

Jansen, E.G. *The development of the Lake Victoria Fisheries and the Possibilities for Norwegian Participation,* DERAP PAPERS No. 75, The Chr. Michelsen Institute, Norway, September 1976.

Kaplinsky, R. "Appropriate Technology and Political Economy: A Case Study of the Bread Industry in Kenya" in Westley, S.B. (ed.) *"The Informal Sector in Kenya",* Occasional Paper No. 25, I.D.S., University of Nairobi, January, 1978.

Kay, G. *Development and Underdevelopment. A Marxist Analysis,* London 1975.

Kenya Government. Ministry of Finance and Planning, "Estimates of the Income Elasticity of Demand for various items in Nairobi, Mombasa and Kisumu", in *Kenya Statistical Digest,* June 1972, Vol. X–No. 2. *Kisumu District Development Plan,* August 1974.

Kmietowicz, T. and Webley, P. "Statistical Analysis of Income Distribution on the Central Province of Kenya". in *Eastern African Economic Review.* Vol. 7, No. 2. December 1975.

Kongstad, P. *Rural Industrial Development Programme, Kenya – R.I.D.P. and Danish Assistance 1975–77,* C.D.R. Paper A.77.3. Copenhagen 1977.

Kongstad, P. and Mönsted, M. — *Family, Labour and Trade in Western Kenya,* Publications from the Centre for Development Research, Copenhagen, No. 3. Uppsala 1980.

Lamb G. — *Peasant Politics – conflict and development in Muranga.,* London 1974.

Lamphear, J. — The Kamba and the Northern Mrima Coast, in Gray, R. and Birmingham, D. (eds.), *op.cit.* p. 85.

Leonard, K.D. — *Bureaucracy, Class and Inequality in Kenya and Tanzania.* Paper presented at Conference on Inequality in Africa, Mt. Kisco, New York 1976. (mimeo)

Leys, C. — "Capital Accumulation, Class Formation and Dependency – The Significance of the Kenyan Case" in *Socialist Register* 1978.

Leys, C. — Development strategy in Kenya since 1971, in *Canadian Journal of African Studies,* Vol. 13, Nos. 1–2, 1979.

Leys, C. — *Underdevelopment in Kenya,* London, Heinemann 1975.

Liedholm, C. — *Research on Employment in the Rural Non-Farm Sector in Africa,* African Rural Employment Paper No. 5, Department of Agricultural Economics, Michigan State University, April 1973.

Liedholm, C. and Chuta, E. — *"The Economics of Rural and Urban Small-Scale Industries in Sierra Leone,* African Rural Economy Paper No. 14, Department of Agricultural Economics, Michigan State University, U.S.A. 1976.

Lijoodi J.L. and Ruthenberg, H. — "Income Distribution in Kenya's Agriculture" in *Zeitschrift für Ausländische Landwirtschaft,* Jahrgang 17, Heft 2, April–June 1978, pp. 115–128.

Livingstone, I. — *Kenya's Rural Industrial Development Programme: An Evaluation of Experience and Proposals for Action,* Working Paper No. 218 IDS, University of Nairobi 1975.

Loehr, W., Powelsen, J.P. — *A Financial Study of Rural Business in Western Kenya,* Discussion Paper No. 122, Department of Economics, University of Coba.

Marris, P. and Somerset, A. — *African Businessmen – a Study of Entrepreneurship and Development in Kenya,* London 1971.

David, M. — "Marketing of foodcrops and purchase of industrial commodities by Nyanza smallholders, 1970–71". Working Paper No. 247, Institute for Development Studies, University of Nairobi. December 1975.

Massel, B.F. and Heyer, J. — "Household expenditure in Nairobi: a statistical analysis of consumer behaviour". Occasional Paper No. 2. Institute for Development Studies, Nairobi, May 1967.

Mature and Kreya — Kisii Iron Industry before the Coming of the Europeans. Bishop Otunga High School. *African Historical and Culture Quarterly Report,* April 1970.

Maxon, R. — *British Rule in Gusiiland 1907–1963,* unpublished thesis, Syracuse, 1972.

Mbithi, P.M. — "Non-Farm Occupation and Farm Innovations in Marginal, Medium and High Potential Regions of Eastern Kenya and Buganda". I.D.S. Working Paper No. 114, University of Nairobi 1971.

Mbithi, P.M. and Chege, F.E. — "Linkages between Agriculture and Rural Small-scale Enterprises" in Child and Kempe (ed.), *"Small-scale Enterprise",* Occasional Paper No. 6, IDS University of Nairobi, 1973.

McIntosh, B.G. — *The Eastern Bantu Peoples,* in Ogot, B.A. and Kieran, J.A. (eds.) *op.cit.* pp. 198–215.

Merrit, E. H. — *A History of the Taita of Kenya to 1900.* Ph.D. thesis, Department of History, Indiana University, August 1975.

Mokamba, D. et al. — "The Kisii-Kipsigis Wars of the Late 19th Century", in *Kenya Historical Review,* Vol. 2, No. 2, 1974. pp. 221–234.

Moody, T. — "Peasant Agriculture, Commercial Production and Employment in Kenya", in *Africa Development,* Vol 1, No. 2 1976, p. 66.

Murray, R. — "The Chandarias: The development of a Kenya Multinational" in Kaplinsky, R., Readings on the Multinational Corporation in Kenya. Oxford University Press, 1978, pp. 284–308.

Njonjo, A.L. — *The Africanisation of the White Highlands: A Study in Agrarian Class Struggles in Kenya 1950–1974.,* Ph.D. dissertation, Princetown University, 1977

.Nellis, R. J. — "Who pays tax in Kenya", in *The African Revue* Vol. 2, No. 2, 1972.

Ogot, B.A. and Kieran, J.A. (eds.), — Zamani – *A Survey of East African* History, Nairobi 1968.

Okelo, J.A — *Rural Enterprise Survey in Kakamega District, Kenya.* Report of the consultant to DANIDA. Nairobi 1973.

Ogendo, R.B. — *Industrial Geography of Kenya,* Nairobi, 1972, table 2a p. 239.

Palmer, G.B. — *The Shimba Hills Settlement Scheme: The administration of large-scale innovation in Kenya,* Ph.D. thesis, University of Minnesota, April 1971.

Paukert, F. — "Income Distribution at Different Levels of Development: a survey of evidence", *International Labour Review,* 108 Nos. 2–3, Aug.–Sept. 1973.

Raikes, P. — "The development of a middle-peasantry in Kenya. Discussion of some hypotheses and examples from the dairy and horticulture sectors", *CDR project papers A.78.3.,* Centre for Development Research, Copenhagen 1978.

Republic of Kenya — *Economic Survey,* 1964.

Republic of Kenya — Economic Survey 1978.

Republic of Kenya — *Integrated Rural Survey, 1974–75. Basic Report.* March 1977.

Republic of Kenya — *Statistical Abstract 1970 and 1977.*

Republic of Kenya — Survey of Industrial Production, 1971.

Shinnie, P.L. (ed.) — *The African Iron Age,* Clarendon Press Oxford, 1971, pp. 140–183.

Singer, H.W. and Reynolds, S.D. — "Aspects of the Distribution of Income and Wealth in Kenya", *IDS Discussion Paper* No. 41, February 1974, University of Sussex, England.

Smith, L.D — "An Overview of Agricultural Development Policy", in Heyer, J. et al., *Agricultural Development in Kenya – An Economic Assessment,* Oxford University Press, 1976.

Spencer, D.S.C. May-Parker, I.I. and Rose, F.S. — *Employment, Efficiency and Income in the Rice Processing Industry* of Sierra Leone, in African Rural Economy Paper No. 15, Department of Agricultural Economics, Michigan State University, U.S.A. 1976.

Swainson, N. — "The Rise of a National Bourgeoisie in Kenya", in *Review of African Political Economy,* No. 8, January–April 1977.

Swainson, N. — "Company formation in Kenya before 1945 with particular reference to the role of foreign capital" in Kaplinsky, R., (ed.), *Readings on the Multination Corporation in Kenya,* Oxford University Press, 1978, pp. 22–95.

Swynnerton, R.J.M. — *A Plan to Intensify the Development of African Agriculture in Kenya.*, Nairobi, 1954, Report of the Committee on African Wages, Nairobi, 1955.

Le Vine, R.A. — "Wealth and Power in Gusii-Land" in Bohannan, P. and Dalton, G. (eds.), *Markets in Africa,* Evanston, 1962, pp. 524–525.

Warren, B. — "Imperialism and Capitalist Industrialization", in *New Left Review,* No. 27, Sept.–Oct. 1973.

Were, P.O. — *The Origin and Growth of the Iron Industry and Trade in Samla (Kenya),* Dissertation, University of Nairobi, Dept. of History, Nairobi 1972.

World Bank/Annual Report 1978. — Washington, 30 June, 1978, p. 32.

World Bank. — *World Development Report, 1978.* Washington, D.C., August 1978.

World Bank. — *Rural Enterprise and Non-farm Employment.* A World Bank Paper, Washington, Jan., 1978.

Zarwan, J.I. — *Indian Businessmen in Kenya during the Twentieth Century: A case study.* Ph.D. dissertation, Yale University, 1977.

Zwanenberg, R. Van — "Aspects of Kenya's Industrial History", in *Kenya Historical Review,* No. 1 Vol. 1. 1973.

Zwanenberg, R. Van — "Neocolonialism and the origin of the National Bourgeoisie in Kenya between 1940 and 1973", in *Journal of Eastern African Research and Development,* Vol. 4, No. 2, 1974.

Zwanenberg, R. Van — *Primitive Colonial Accumulation in Kenya, 1919–1939,* Ph.D. dissertation, Sussex, 1971.

Zwanenberg, R. Van — "The Development of Peasant Commodity Production in Kenya, 1920–40", in *The Economic History Review,* 2nd Series, XXVII, No. 3, August 1974.

Öström, I.S. and Öström, K. — *Rural Industrial Development Centers in the Kisii District and the Siaya District, Nyanza* Province, Kenya. March 1974.